Praise for MONEY AND CLASS IN AMERICA

"*Money and Class in America* is an angry book; it is also frequently right."
—*The Washington Post*

"Acerbic in tone . . . Amusing and provoc
—*The New York Times Book Review*

"Roams over the glitzy terrain of contem~~p~~ ~~orary~~ ~~consumerism~~ . . . Lapham effectively ridicules the widespread notion that money is omnipotent and can make everything all right."
—*Time*

"Lapham is a wonderful writer, a connoisseur of the perfect world. Stimulating ideas are expertly interlarded with amusing anecdotes, and the catholic assortment of quotations is marvelous."
—*Businessweek*

"A Brillo pad chafing the social psyches of this Teflon crowd . . . Lapham peppers his observations with priceless anecdotes of the absurdities of the rich and the only-wishing-to-be-so. Some of Lapham's gems are side-splitting, culled from a lifetime amid the ivied walls and red-leather wingbacks of the nation's clubby capitals . . . The author offers a sobering look at where we are headed if we do not see that we have sold our very humanness for the sake of the dollar bill."
—*Chicago Tribune*

"*Money and Class in America* is an intelligent, well-written and witty book, and replete with insights and deflating anecdotes and observations about the fatuities of the rich and powerful—and their retainers."
—*The Boston Sunday Globe*

"Lewis Lapham's trenchant and stinging indictment of obsessive wealth in America is refreshingly direct. The issue itself is one many people would prefer not to have discussed—to the detriment, unfortunately, of a nation."
—Barry Lopez

"A master satirist, [Lapham] has written a needed and important book . . . We should be indebted to Lapham for taking up the cudgels so trenchantly in the name of a more cultivated use of America's wealth."
—*The Philadelphia Inquirer*

"Contains as many hilarious, embarrassing truths about our society as a John Waters movie. Lapham writes with tongue firmly in cheek, celebrating the cheapness and vulgarity of mass consumption even as he pokes fun at it . . . His witty commentary takes in all of contemporary America . . . An irresistably funny work of social commentary masquerading as satire, with enough one-line gems of wisdom to stock several quote notebooks."

—*The Cleveland Plain Dealer*

"A scathing indictment of American attitudes toward money and class. It is a witty, often disturbing diatribe against what he calls the 'equestrian class.'"

—*The Houston Post*

"Lewis Lapham is blessedly cantankerous, stylish, elegant, erudite, unpredictable, cosmopolitan, cranky. What Mr. Lapham tells us about America's love affair with money would make for awfully sad reading, were he not so witty, wickedly observant of the precincts of wealth through which, detached, he moves, and ultimately, wonderfully wise. Edith Wharton would have saluted him."

—Barbara Grizutti Harrison

"Wonderfully witty . . . This book chronicling Americans' obsession with money, status, consumption and other vices is satirical humor at its best . . . it's Henny Youngman firing off Swiftian one-liners. Don't try to read it all at once. Bite off half a chapter an evening—and laugh yourself into oblivion . . . It's simply delightful social satire."

—*The San Diego Union*

"This is a rich book . . . Lapham shows how the government, its people, and the business worlds have come to worship money and how that worship diminishes us all and leads us toward that ruin . . . Lapham the source is as important as the message. He's no huckster. He's not crying sour grapes. His work is credible and crafted keenly."

—*Topeka Capital-Journal*

"In *Money and Class in America* Lewis Lapham incisively separates the reality of the contemporary United States from the layers of spurious cliché with which generations of false moralizing and special pleading have surrounded her . . . An angry masterpiece of insight. More than any work I know, it captures the essence of America in this second Gilded Age. Mr. Lapham's book will endure in the literature of social observation."

—Robert Stone

MONEY AND CLASS IN AMERICA

Also by Lewis H. Lapham

Fortune's Child
Imperial Masquerade
The Wish for Kings
Hotel America
Waiting for the Barbarians
Lapham's Rules of Influence
The Agony of Mammon
Lights, Camera, Democracy!
Theater of War
30 Satires
Gag Rule
With The Beatles
Pretensions to Empire
Age of Folly

MONEY AND CLASS IN AMERICA

LEWIS H. LAPHAM

WITH A NEW INTRODUCTION BY
THE AUTHOR AND A FOREWORD BY

THOMAS FRANK

OR Books
New York · London

Foreword © 2018 Thomas Frank

Published by OR Books, New York and London

All rights information: rights@orbooks.com
Visit our website at www.orbooks.com

Money and Class in America: Notes and Observations on Our Civil Religion
was fi rst published by Weidenfeld & Nicolson, New York, in 1988.

Cataloging-in-Publication data is available from the Library of Congress. A
catalog record for this book is available from the British Library.

ISBN 978-1-944869-89-2 paperback
ISBN 978-1-944869-90-8 e-book

This book is set in the typeface Pobla Book.
Typeset by Aarkmany Media, Chennai, India.

For Andrew, Delphina and Winston

CONTENTS

FOREWORD
Thomas Frank

This following catalogue of the tastes and delusions of America's "equestrian class" comes to us from 1988, but you will be excused if, as you turn its pages, you feel you are reading an unusually articulate anthropologist's description of a tribe that goes about its loutish rituals in the present day. Nearly everything in *Money and Class in America* still applies: The insane CEO paydays that Lewis Lapham noted still go on; so do the aristocrats' dreams of godhead and their acts of extraordinary pettiness to one another, all of which he scrutinizes in fascinating detail.

We were living through "our own gilded age" Lapham wrote in 1988, and like many of the descriptions he invented, that historical comparison has today become a truism, repeated constantly by pundits and presidential candidates alike. What the phrase meant, for Lapham, was the triumph of capital over labor and the emergence of a billionaire class—a phenomenon that modern scholars like to imagine they have only recently discovered and to which they have given the pseudo-technical name of "inequality." In truth, however, a considerable literature on the subject was already under production by the late 1980s, and Lapham's observations on it sit on the shelf beside a number of contemporary analogues, including Kevin Phillips's *The Politics of Rich and Poor*, the movie *Wall Street*, or the initial run of *Spy* magazine. All addressed the extraordinary fortunes then being assembled, the showy pretentiousness of the new aristocracy, the bull market that seemed to recreate the bubble of the 1920s—and what it all meant for a republic like ours.

Money and Class in America was written during the first decade of what Lapham called the "Republican Risorgimento," a time of tax cuts for the rich and deregulation for business. These developments were still fairly new in 1988, and people like me found reason to expect that all of it was but a passing phase—that a chastened nation would soon grow wise to Reaganism and its pasteboard plutocracy in favor of the more democratic habits that had been America's default position since World War II.

It never happened. The tumbrels never arrived for the Marie Antoinettes of the 1980s. Today Lapham's Risorgimento is nearly forty years old and fully bipartisan; instead of slowing, it grows ever more extreme, the manners and displays of its beneficiaries ever more grotesque. Indeed, even as I write this, the presidential throne is occupied by Donald Trump, a leading vulgarian of the 1980s whose taste in décor approximates that of Louis XVI. Trump is the real estate developer responsible for the work of luxury porn that Lapham quotes in Chapter 6 of the book that follows; President Trump's cabinet is the wealthiest this country has ever seen; Trump's capital is the richest city in the nation; Trump's one big achievement in his dazzlingly awful first year on the job was to secure yet another tax cut for business.

Money and Class is not a political book, however. Lapham doesn't try to imagine a federal solution to the problem he describes; he doesn't even acknowledge that it's a problem, really. It simply is, and his object is to study it, to give us his almost clinical observations on the thoughts and habits and prejudices of his equestrian subjects: their high ambitions, their petty vindictiveness, their lurid fantasies, their fancy and pointless educations, their "dreams of avarice," their quasi-criminal business ventures.

Lapham points out that the ways and means of the rich have fascinated American writers since the beginning of our republic;

in particular they have been a favorite subject of two groups: the "booster press," who approach the topic with drooling lasciviousness; and Jeffersonian democrats (together with those further to the left), who regard it all as a moral obscenity.

Lapham, however, comes to us from a different direction. He writes as an insider, "born into the ranks of the equestrian class" and thus granted a first-hand view of "the pathologies of wealth." As a child, he tells us, "I came to imagine that I was born to ride in triumph and that others, apparently less fortunate and more numerous, were born to stand smiling in the streets and wave their hats." As an adult, he attends the dinner parties of the "golden horde" and participates in their banal conversations. Troubled aristocrats bare their souls to him; he watches others rejoice in the suffering of their friends. He shows us top-shelf butchers who deal in the flesh of rare species, executives who use the company jet to go shopping, apartment dwellers who require a dedicated refrigerator to chill their perfume.

It is not really correct to describe Lapham's approach as cynical; it is more that he shuns illusions that might obstruct him from setting down what he sees so clearly. All of it goes: The myth of the corporation's efficiency, the myth of the government's beneficence, the many myths of money. His tactic instead is to describe things with a kind of sharpness unavailable to those who peer through the dark lens of idealism. His larger strategy is constantly to confront this nation of democrats with the outrageous but overwhelming evidence that we don't practice what we believe—that this country where all are supposedly created equal is in fact a land of aristocratic privilege on the scale of pre-revolutionary France. Nearly everything we hold dear in our public lives is a fraud. Politicians spend their time fundraising. Experts are judged not by their expertise but by how much they charge. Not the crucifix, but the dollar sign, is the symbol of our faith.

If this is cynicism, it is of a peculiarly bracing and refreshing kind. It is, on every page, a pleasure to read. Lapham was the champion

American essayist during the period described in this book—he still is, for my money—and his sentences simply radiate elegance. They are arranged as carefully as the foyers and dining rooms he describes. Always does he choose the precise phrase: "drink the wine of orgy"; "an atmosphere of intimate sadism." Always does he find the perfect example: the carnation petals decorating the water in the toilet bowl, for example, or the idealistic beachfront hostess rushing forth with a pair of hedge trimmers to liberate fish from a fisherman's net.

I was an enthusiastic reader of Lapham's columns in *Harper's Magazine* during the period covered by this book. I found not only the quality of his prose invigorating, but the man's refusal to participate in one of the schools of ready-made thought for which almost every other American columnist had signed up. You will not find here any of the hackneyed ideas ("year of maximum danger") or tendentious moralizing or pseudo-solemn meditations on the august institutions of Washington that cluttered the writing of his contemporaries. He was, I thought, just about the only commentator worth reading. Compared to Lewis Lapham, I believed back then, nearly everyone else was a phony. When I turn the pages that follow, I believe it still.

June 2018

AUTHOR'S INTRODUCTION
TO THE NEW EDITION

> A frivolous society can acquire dramatic significance
> only through what its frivolity destroys. Its tragic
> implications lie in its power of debasing people and
> ideals.
>
> —EDITH WHARTON

> The populace may hiss me, but when I go home and
> think of my money, I applaud myself.
>
> —HORACE

AT THE HIGHER ELEVATIONS OF INFORMED AMERICAN OPINION in the spring of 2018 the voices of reason stand united in their fear and loathing of Donald J. Trump, real estate mogul, reality TV star, forty-fifth president of the United States. Their viewing with alarm is bipartisan and heartfelt, but the dumbfounded question, "How can such things be?" is well behind the times. Trump is undoubtedly a menace, but he isn't a surprise. His smug and self-satisfied face is the face of the way things are and have been in Washington and Wall Street for the last quarter of a century.

Trump staked his claim to the White House on the proposition that he was "really rich," embodiment of the divine right of money and therefore free to say and do whatever it takes to make America great again. A *deus ex machina* descending an escalator into the atrium of his eponymous tower on Manhattan's Fifth Avenue in June 2015, Trump was there to say, and say it plainly, that money is power, and power, ladies and gentlemen, is not self-sacrificing or democratic. The big money cares for nothing other than itself, always has and always will. Name of the game, nature of the beast.

Not the exact words in Trump's loud and thoughtless mouth, but the gist of the message that over the next seventeen months he shouted to fairground crowd and camera in states red, white and blue. A fair enough share of his fellow citizens screamed, stamped and voted in agreement because what he was saying they knew to be true, knew it not as precept borrowed from the collected works of V.I. Lenin or Ralph Lauren but from their own downwardly mobile experience on the losing side of a class war waged over the past forty years by America's increasingly frightened and selfish rich against its increasingly angry and debt-bound poor.

Trump didn't need briefing papers to refine the message. He presented it live and in person, an unscripted and overweight canary flown from its gilded cage, telling it like it is when seen from the perch of the haves looking down on the birdseed of the have-nots. Had he time or patience for looking into books instead of mirrors, he could have sourced his wisdom to Supreme Court Justice Louis Brandeis, who in 1933 presented the case for Franklin D. Roosevelt's New Deal: "We must make our choice. We may have democracy, or we may have wealth concentrated in the hands of a few, but we can't have both."

Not that it would have occurred to Trump to want both, but he might have been glad to know the Supreme Court had excused him from further study under the heading of politics. In the world according to Trump—as it was in the worlds according to Ronald Reagan, George Bush *pere et fils*, Bill Clinton and Barack Obama—the concentration of wealth is the good, the true and the beautiful. Democracy is for losers.

Ronald Reagan was elected President in 1980 with an attitude and agenda similar to Trump's—to restore America to its rightful place where "someone can always get rich." His administration arrived in Washington firm in its resolve to uproot the democratic style of feeling and thought that underwrote FDR's New Deal. What was billed as the Reagan Revolution and the dawn of a New Morning in America recruited various parties of the dissatisfied right (conservative, neoconservative, libertarian, reactionary and evangelical) under one flag of abiding and transcendent truth—money ennobles rich people, making them healthy, wealthy and wise; money corrupts poor people, making them ignorant, lazy and sick.

Re-branded as neoliberalism in the 1990s the doctrine of enlightened selfishness has served as the wisdom in political and cultural office ever since Reagan stepped onto the White House stage promising a happy return to an imaginary American past—to the home on the range made safe from Apaches by John Wayne, an America once again cowboy-hatted and standing tall, risen from the ashes of defeat in Vietnam, cleansed of its Watergate impurities, outspending the Russians on weapons of mass destruction, releasing the free market from the prison of government regulation, going long on the private good, selling short the public good.

For forty years under administrations Republican and Democrat, the concentrations of wealth and power have systematically shuffled public land and light and air into a private purse, extended the reach of corporate monopoly, shifted the bulk of the nation's income to its top-tier fatted calves, let fall into disrepair nearly all the infrastructure—roads, water systems, schools, bridges, hospitals and power plants—that provides a democratic commonwealth with the means of production for its mutual enterprise. The subdivision of America the Beautiful into a nation of the rich and a nation of the poor has outfitted a tenth of the population with three-quarters of the nation's wealth. The work in progress has been accompanied by the construction of a national security and surveillance state backed by the guarantee of never-ending foreign war and equipped with increasingly repressive police powers to quiet the voices of domestic discontent. In the 1950s the word *public* indicated a common good (public health, public school, public service, public spirit); *private* was a synonym for selfishness and greed (plutocrats in top hats, pigs at troughs). The connotations traded places in the 1980s; private to be associated with all things bright and beautiful (private trainer, private school, private plane), public a synonym for all things ugly, incompetent and unclean (public housing, public welfare, public toilet).

Reagan left office in 1989, the same year Donald J. Trump emerged as poster child for what the news media were touting as the second coming of an American Gilded Age more gloriously frivolous than the one known to Commodore Vanderbilt and Big Jim Fisk. Money was the hero with a thousand faces, greed the creative frenzy from which all blessings conspicuously flow. *Time* magazine in 1989 posed Trump on its cover fondling the ace of diamonds; Trump's photograph was decorating college dormitory walls once reserved for posters of Dylan and Che; Trump's 1987 book, *The Art of the Deal*, was up there in lights with Oliver Stone's *Wall Street* and Tom Wolfe's *Bonfire of the Vanities*.

When *Money and Class in America* was published in 1988, Trump showed up for the welcoming dinner party given by Ann Getty, billionaire patron of the arts and proud new owner of Weidenfeld & Nicolson, the book's publisher. She didn't expect Trump to read the book; his simple acknowledgement of its existence could be construed in 1988 as baptism in the temple of Mammon. Although the joke was unintended, his presence in Getty's Fifth Avenue apartment seconded the motion of the book, which was to draw a satirical portrait of a society captivated by the story of Midas, mighty king in Greek and Roman legend, who wished that everything he touched be turned to gold. So too in 1988 the consummation devoutly wished in all quarters of the American body politic, on every tabloid forehead, breast and buttock angling to become commodity or brand, minted into the immortal coin of divine celebrity.

Midas's wish was granted by Dionysus, god of wine and ecstasy, and for one bright new morning in antiquity the king rejoiced in changing sticks and stones and sunflowers into precious heavy metal. But then so did his food and drink turn to gold when he touched it with his wonder-working hands, and he would have died of thirst before he died of hunger had not Dionysus released him from the prison of his golden wish.

The ancient king at least had the wit to know something had gone wrong with the IPO. Unable to lift or taste *les poissons d'or* he begged the god of wine and ecstasy for deliverance, and in 1988 I expected America's propertied classes to experience a similar awakening. To mark the Midas touch to market—not a glad tiding of comfort and joy, the kiss of peace and death bestowed by the mobster god in the machine of creatively destructive capitalism. The writing of *Money and Class in America* followed from the assumption that the country's befuddled overlords would soon regain their wits. At Ann Getty's dinner table listening to Trump talk—lovingly about himself, loudly about stray topics running around loose in his Rush Limbaugh ditto-head—I took solace in the thought that any trend or spirit of the times shaped in the image of his willful ignorance and grotesque vanity was on final approach to its sell-by date.

I was mistaken. Thirty years later Trump is president of the United States, and what in 1988 was a weakened but still operational democracy has become a dysfunctional, stupefied plutocracy. No matter who occupies the White House, or what the issue immediately to hand in Congress (environment or debt, military spending, immigration, health care, education, the wars on poverty, drugs and terror), the concentrations of wealth and power impose more laws restraining the liberty of persons, fewer laws restricting the license of property; open an ever-widening spread of income inequality, reserve an ever-larger share of the nation's wealth to an ever-smaller fraction of its people.

The nation's political discourse meanwhile has dwindled into the staging of election campaigns with candidates prized for the gift of saying nothing. Forbidden the use of words apt to disturb a Gallup poll or offend a bagman, they stand and serve as product placements for concentrated wealth, their quality to be inferred from the cost of their manufacture. Machine-made tools so well-contrived they can be played for jokes and presented as game show contestants until on election night they come to judgment before the throne of cameras by which and for which they are produced.

THE DREAM OF RICHES HAS BEEN THE HALLMARK of the American experience ever since the first settlements in the seventeenth century wilderness were set up as joint ventures backed by Divine Providence and British gold. Among the gentlemen adventurers offloading Dutch cannon and Geneva bibles on the shores of Massachusetts Bay, there were those who had come in search of El Dorado, betting their lives and fortunes if not their sacred honor on rumors of precious metal and grade-A beaver pelt. Others arriving with blueprints for a new Jerusalem were content to lay up stores of virtue awaiting heavenly reward after the long, New England winter in the grave. No congregation was at a loss for a sermon, a real estate deal, or a discussion about the nature of their newfound wealth—wages of sin or sign of grace, proof of the good Lord's infinite wisdom or the result of a sharp bargain with a drunken Pequot Indian.

The framers of the Constitution, prosperous and well-educated gentlemen assembled in Philadelphia in the summer of 1787, shared with John Adams the suspicion that "democracy will infallibly destroy all civilization," agreed with James Madison that the turbulent passions of the common man lead to "reckless agitation" for the abolition of debts and "other wicked projects." With Plato the framers shared the assumption that the best government incorporates the means by which a privileged few arrange the distribution of property and law for the less fortunate many. They envisioned an enlightened oligarchy to which they gave the name of a republic. Adams thought "the great functions of state" should be reserved for "the rich, the well-born, and the able," the new republic to be managed by men to whom Madison attributed "most wisdom to discern and most virtue to pursue the common good of the society."

The words for their enterprise the framers borrowed from the British philosopher John Locke, who had declared his seventeenth century willingness "to join in society with others who are already united or have a mind to unite, for the mutual preservation of their lives, liberties, and estates, which I call by the general name *property*." Locke could not conceive of freedom established on anything other than property. Neither could the eighteenth century framers of America's Constitution. By the word *liberty*, they meant liberty for property, not liberty for persons.

But unlike our present-day makers of money and law, the founders were not stupefied plutocrats. They knew how to read and write (in Latin or French if not also in Greek) and they weren't preoccupied with the love and fear of money. From their reading of history they understood that oligarchy was well-advised to furnish democracy with some measure of political power because the failure to do so was apt to lead to their being roasted on pitchforks. Accepting of the fact that whereas democracy puts a premium on equality, a capitalist economy does not, the founders looked to balance the divergent ways and means, to accommodate both motions of the heart and the movement of a market. They conceived the Constitution as both organism and mechanism and offered as warranty for its worth the character of men presumably relieved of the necessity to cheat and steal and lie.

The presumption in 1787 could be taken at fair and face value. The framers were endowed with the intellectual energy of the eighteenth century Enlightenment, armed with the moral force of the Christian religion. Their idea of law they held to be sacred, a marriage of faith and reason. But good intentions are a perishable commodity, and even the best of oligarchies bear comparison to cheese. Sooner or later they turn rancid in the sun. Wealth accumulates, men decay; a band of brothers that once aspired to form a wise and just government acquires the character of what Aristotle likened to that of "the prosperous fool," a class of men insatiable in their appetite for more—more banquets, more laurel wreaths and naval victories, more temples, dancing girls and portrait busts—so intoxicated by the love of money "they therefore imagine there is nothing it cannot buy."

Aristotle derived his understanding of politics from his study of Greek history in the fourth and fifth centuries B.C., which encompassed the rise and fall of the Periclean aristocracy, the democratic experiments (most of them failures) spawned by the catastrophe of the Peloponnesian War, and the petty tyrannies that preceded the conquest of Greece by the barbarians descending from the mountains of Macedon. In every instance an oligarchy, its lifespan dependent on the character of the men charged with the management of its economic, political and moral enterprise. Recurrent outbreaks of the appetite for more—a sickness the Greeks diagnosed as *pleonexia*—divided Athens into a city of the poor and a city of the rich, the one at war with the other and neither of them inclined to temper its bitterness in the interest of a common good. Aristotle mentions a faction of especially reactionary oligarchs who swore an oath of noble purpose: "I will be an adversary of the people, and in the council I will do it all the evil that I can." So also the 272 members of America's 112th Congress, all but three of them Republican, who in 1986 signed a solemn pledge to oppose any and all efforts to increase marginal income tax rates for individuals and businesses, resist net reduction or elimination of deductions and credits unless matched dollar for dollar by further reducing tax rates. The pledge was still in force in 2001 when its author, the anti-tax zealot Grover Norquist, explained he didn't want to abolish government, he simply wanted to reduce it to a size "where I can drag it into the bathroom and drown it in a bathtub."

THE MAKING AND RE-MAKING OF AMERICA'S POLITICS over the last 231 years can be said to consist of the attempt to ward off, or at least postpone, the feasting of prosperous fools. Some historians note that what the framers of the Constitution hoped to establish in 1787 didn't survive the War of 1812; others suggest the republic was gutted by the spoils system introduced by President Andrew Jackson in the 1830s. None of the informed sources doubt that it perished during the prolonged heyday of the late nineteenth century Gilded Age. Mark Twain coined the phrase to represent his further observation that a society consisting of the sum of its vanity and greed is not a society at all but a state of war. In the event that anybody missed Twain's meaning, President Grover Cleveland in 1887 set forth the rules of engagement with his veto of a bill passed by Congress offering financial aid to the poor—"the lesson should be constantly enforced that, though the people support the government, the government should not support the people." Twenty-one years later, Arthur T. Hadley, the president of Yale, certified the policy as morally sound and politically correct: "The fundamental division of powers in the Constitution of the United States is between voters on the one hand and property owners on the other. The forces of democracy on the one side . . . and the forces of property on the other side."

At no moment in its history has the country not been nailed to a cross of gold. Mark Hanna, the Ohio coal merchant managing William McKinley's presidential campaign against William Jennings Bryan in 1896, reduced the proposition to an axiom: "There are two things that are important in politics. The first is money, and I can't remember what the second one is." The Supreme Court's *Citizens United* ruling in 2010 deregulated the market in political office and ratified the opinion of John Jay (coauthor of the *Federalist Papers*, appointed chief justice of the Supreme Court in 1789) that "those who own the country ought to govern it."

The Constitution doesn't contemplate the sharing of the commons inherent in a bountiful wilderness. Drafted by men of property setting up a government hospitable to the acquisition of more property, the Constitution provides the means of making manifest an unequal division of the spoils. Thomas Jefferson didn't confuse the theory ("All men are created equal") with the practice ("Money, and not morality, is the principle of commerce and commercial nations").

The divisions of race and class were present at the American creation. The planting of colonies in seventeenth century America conformed to medieval Europe's feudal arrangements of privilege and subordination. The aristocratic promoters of the project received land as a gift from the English king; the improvement of the property required immigrants (God-fearing or fortune-seeking) skilled as fishermen, farmers, saltmakers and mechanics. Their numbers were unequal to the tasks at hand, and in both the plantation south and merchant north the developers imported African slaves as well as what were known as "waste people" dredged from the slums of Jacobean England—vagrants, convicts, thieves, bankrupts, strumpets, vagabonds, lunatics and bawds obliged to pay their passage across the Atlantic with terms of indentured labor on its western shore. The prosperous gentry already settled on that shore regarded the shipments of "human filth" as night soil drained from Old World sewers to fertilize New World fields and forests. By the time the colonies declared their independence from the British crown, the newborn American body politic had been sectioned, like the carcass of a butchered cow, into pounds and pence of prime and sub-prime flesh.

All men were maybe equal in the eye of God, but not in the pews in Boston's Old North Church, in the streets of Benjamin Franklin's Philadelphia, in the fields at Jefferson's Monticello. The Calvinist doctrine of predestination divided the Massachusetts flock of Christian sheep into damned and saved; Cotton Mather in 1696 reminded the servants in his midst, "You are the animate, separate passive instruments of other men . . . your tongues, your hands, your feet, are your masters's and they should move according to the will of your masters." Franklin, enlightened businessman and founder of libraries, looked upon the Philadelphia rabble as coarse material that maybe could be brushed and combed into an acceptable grade of bourgeois broadcloth. His *Poor Richard's Almanac* offered a program for turning sow's ears if not into silk purses, then into useful tradesmen furnished with a "happy mediocrity." For poor white children in Virginia, Jefferson proposed a scheme he described as "raking from the rubbish" the scraps of intellect and talent worth the trouble of further cultivation. A few young illiterates who showed promise as students were allowed to proceed beyond the elementary grades; the majority were released into a wilderness of ignorance and poverty, dispersed over time into the westward moving breeds of an American underclass variously denominated as "mudsill," "hillbilly," "cracker," "Okie," "redneck," Hillary Clinton's "basket of deplorables."

Nor at any moment in its history has America declared a lasting peace between the haves and have-nots. Temporary cessations of hostilities, but no permanent closing of the moral and social frontier between debtor and creditor. The notion of a classless society derives its credibility from the relatively few periods in the life of the nation during which circumstances encouraged social readjustment and experiment—in the 1830s, 1840s, and 1850s, again in the 1940s, 1950s and 1960s—but for the most part the record will show the game securely rigged in favor of the rich, no matter how selfish or stupid, at the expense of the poor, no matter how innovative or entrepreneurial. During the last thirty years of the nineteenth century and the first thirty years of the twentieth, class conflict furnished the newspaper mills with their best-selling headlines—railroad company thugs quelling labor unrest in the industrial East, the Ku Klux Klan lynching Negroes in the rural South, the U.S. army exterminating Sioux Indians on the Western plains.

Around the turn of the twentieth century the forces of democracy pushed forward an era of progressive reform sponsored by both the Republican president, Theodore Roosevelt, and the Democratic president, Woodrow Wilson. During the middle years of the twentieth century America at times showed some semblance of the republic envisioned by its eighteenth century founders—Franklin D. Roosevelt's New Deal, a citizen army fighting World War II, the

Great Depression replaced with a fully employed economy in which all present shared in the profits.

The civil rights and anti-Vietnam war protests in the 1960s were expressions of democratic objection and dissent intended to reform the country's political thought and practice, not to overthrow its government. Nobody was threatening to reset the game clock in the Rose Bowl, tear down Grand Central Terminal or remove the Lincoln Memorial. The men, women and children confronting racist tyranny in the South—sitting at a lunch counter in Alabama, riding a bus into Mississippi, going to school in Arkansas—risked their lives and sacred honor on behalf of a principle, not a lifestyle; for a government of laws, not men. The unarmed rebellion led to the enactment in the mid-1960s of the Economic Opportunity Act, the Voting Rights Act, the Medicare and Medicaid programs, eventually to the shutting down of the Vietnam War.

Faith in democracy survived the assassination of President John F. Kennedy in 1963; it didn't survive the assassinations of Robert Kennedy and Martin Luther King in 1968. The 1960s and 1970s gave rise to a sequence of ferocious and destabilizing change—social, cultural, technological, sexual, economic and demographic—that tore up the roots of family, community and church from which a democratic society draws meaning and strength. The news media promoted the multiple wounds to the body politic (the murders of King and Kennedy, big-city race riots, the killing of college students at Kent State and Jackson State, crime in the streets of Los Angeles, Chicago and Newark) as revolution along the line of Robespierre's reign of terror. The fantasy of armed revolt sold papers, boosted ratings, stimulated the demand for heavy surveillance and repressive law enforcement that over the last fifty years has blossomed into the richest and most innovative of the nation's growth industries.

By the end of the 1970s democracy had come to be seen as a means of government gone soft in the head and weak in the knees, no match for unscrupulous Russians, incapable of securing domestic law and order, unable to disperse the barbarians (foreign and native born) at the gates of the gated real estate in Beverly Hills, Westchester County and Palm Beach. The various liberation movements still in progress no longer sought to right the wrongs of government. The political was personal, the personal political. Seized by the appetite for more—more entitlements, privileges and portrait busts—plaintiffs for both the haves and the have-nots agitated for a lifestyle, not a principle. The only constitutional value still on the table was the one constituting freedom as property, property as freedom. A fearful bourgeois society adrift in a sea of troubles was clinging to its love of money as if to the last lifeboat rowing away from the *Titanic* when Ronald Reagan in 1980 stepped onto the stage of the self-pitying national melodrama with the promise of an America to become great again in a future made of gold.

IN 2018, THE FEW OPTIMISTIC VOICES at the higher elevations of informed American opinion regard the advent of Trump as a blessing in disguise, one that places the society in sufficiently dire straits to prompt the finding of a phoenix in the ashes, the best chance in two generations to resurrect America's democratic life force. I like to think the same thought, but I rate the odds of rescue at 6-1 against.

Trump is product of the junk entertainment industry but also product of what Marshall McLuhan recognized nearly half a century ago as an "acoustic world" in which there is "no continuity, no homogeneity, no connections, no stasis . . . an information environment of which humanity has never had any experience whatever." McLuhan's *Understanding Media* appeared in 1964 with the proposition that new means of communication give rise to new structures of feeling and thought. "We shape our tools and thereafter our tools shape us." We become what we behold, and "the medium is the message." Shift the means of communication from printed page to electronic screen, and they establish new rules for what counts as knowledge. The visual order of print sustains a sequence of cause and effect, tells a story with a beginning, middle and end. The speed of light spreads stories that run around in circles, eliminate the dimensions of space and time, construct a world in which nothing follows from anything else. Sequence becomes additive instead of causative, "Graphic Man" replaces "Typographic Man," and the images of government become a government of images.

Infotainment is made with, by, and for machines. The sound bites come and go on a reassuringly familiar loop, the same footage, the same spokespeople, the same commentaries. What was said last week is certain to be said this week, next week and then again six weeks from now. The ritual returns as surely as the sun, demanding of the constant viewer little else except devout observance. Pattern recognition becomes applied knowledge; the making of as many as 12,000 connections in the course of a day's googling and shopping (Miller beer is wet, Nike is a sneaker or a cap, Rolex is not a golf ball), adds to the sum of wisdom, and the assurance of being in the know. The images of wealth and power signify nothing other than their own transient magnificence. Like the moon acting upon the movement of the tides, the idols of divine celebrity (Ronald Reagan and Madonna, Lady Gaga and Donald Trump) call forth collective surges of emotion that rise and fall with as little inherent meaning as the surf breaking on the beach at Malibu.

Among people who worship the objects of their own invention, money chief among them, technology is the knack of so arranging the world that one need not experience it. Better to consume it, best of all to buy it, and to the degree that information can be commodified (as corporate logo, Facebook page, designer dress or politician), the amassment of wealth and the acquisition of power follows from the naming of things rather than from the making of them. The future is a product to be sold, not a story to be told.

McLuhan regarded the medium of television as better suited to the sale of a product than to the expression of a thought. The constant viewer's participation in the ever-present promise of paradise regained underwrites what McLuhan described as "the huge educational enterprise we call advertising." Not the teaching of man's humanity to man; the processing of exploitable social data by

"Madison Avenue's frogmen of the mind" intent upon retrieving the sunken subconscious treasure of human credulity and desire, ignorance and fear. Madison Avenue's frogmen have morphed over the past thirty years into Silicon Valley data-mining dwarves equipped with more efficient tools to dig for gold.

Advertising is the voice of money talking to money, a dialect characterized by Toni Morrison in her 1993 Nobel Prize speech as "language that drinks blood . . . dumb, predatory, and sentimental," prioritized to "sanction ignorance and preserve privilege." Which is the language in which we do our shopping and our politics. Typographic Man wrote the Constitution and the Gettysburg Address; Graphic Man elects the president of the United States. The media on the campaign trail with Donald Trump weren't following a train of thought. Like flies to death and honey, they were drawn to the splendor and flash of money, to the romance of crime and the sweet decaying smell of over-ripe celebrity.

The camera sees but doesn't think, makes no distinction between a bubble bath in Las Vegas staffed by pretty girls and a bloodbath in Palmyra staffed by headless corpses. The return on investment from both photo-ops is the flow of bankable emotion drawn from the dark pools of human wish and dream in unlimited and anonymous amounts. It didn't matter what Trump said or didn't say, whether he was cute and pink or headless. He was maybe short on sense and sensibility, but he was long on market share. The prosperous fool sold newspapers, boosted television ratings, campaigned as sales promotion for concentrated wealth.

The camera doesn't do democracy. Democracy is the holding of one's fellow citizens in respectful regard not because they are rich, or beautiful, or famous but because they are one's fellow citizens and therefore worth knowing what they say and do. The camera isn't interested in cheap shoes on common ground; it prefers polished boots on horseback. Always a sight for sore eyes, the boots on horseback. The media pitched Trump's campaign on the story-line the movie-going American electorate loves beyond all others—knight errant up against the system and the odds, rough justice in the trail-weary saddle riding into town to gun down the corrupt sheriff and rescue the God-fearing settlers, set the crooked straight, distribute a fair share of the loot to the shepherd, the schoolteacher and the storekeep. The casting of Trump as underdog outlaw hoisted him to the top of the leaderboard with robber barons Vanderbilt and Rockefeller, gunslingers Eastwood and Stallone, Mafia dons Corleone and Soprano. The comic book hero won the comic book election.

WHEN *MONEY AND CLASS IN AMERICA* WAS FIRST PUBLISHED IN 1988 the reviews in the *Wall Street Journal* and the *New York Times* denied the existence of its subject and misread the intention of its author. The critics were at pains to point out that in America there is no such thing as class consciousness. Americans are egalitarian born and bred, and those among them who acquire riches do so unaided by anything other than their own industry and merit. Which is why Americans are the happiest, freest and most exceptional people ever to walk the earth. To suggest otherwise is blasphemy.

The judgment was backed by the supposition on the part of the judges that I was an aggrieved liberal intellectual, envying the fame and fortune of his social and financial betters, a "wacko" according to David Brooks in the *Journal,* throwing sticks and stones at the sanctity of money in hope of the sticks and stones being changed into gold if the book sold enough copies to bestow the Midas touch on an apostate sour grape.

In point of fact I was attempting to clear my head of the stupidity and fear that is the consequence of assigning to money powers it doesn't possess. Born in 1935 into an American propertied class, I couldn't pretend it didn't exist. Brought up under the protection of money on San Francisco's Pacific Heights in the 1940s (son, grandson and great-grandson in a family owning oil and shipping companies), I was welcomed at an early age into the hospitality tent of giftwrapped humbug that shelters bourgeois privilege from the rain that raineth every day. The humbug divided, like Caesar's Gaul, into three parts:

Money ennobles rich people, corrupts poor people.

Money in sufficient quantity entitles its possessor to the reverence and respect owed to the statue of George Washington.

Money is the elephant always in the room, never to be addressed or seen but whose will is done on earth as it is in heaven.

The message didn't come as handwritten note on a silver tray; it was to be inferred by the weight of the silver tray. Whether in polite company or home alone with the children, my parents never mentioned the presence of money. The subject was in poor taste, a mystery best left unmolested and unknown, what Plato would have spotted as "the noble falsehood" that is a society's self-preserving myth. *The Republic* calls upon Socrates to inform a young aristocrat that the children of the city must be told that the god who made all of them mixed some of them with gold, entitling the Grade A beaver pelts to rule "because they are the most valuable." Whether the intel is true or false matters less than the children of the city not forgetting their duty to remember it, to know what their rulers would have them know in order to maintain the health and well-being of the body politic.

At the age of four I had no reason to ask whether the intel was true or false. The house was well supplied with silver trays, the picture windows afforded handsome views of the bay, the servants knew their place. But before coming to write *Money and Class in America* in 1988 I had been playing hide-and-seek with the elephant for half a century (at prep school and college in Ivy League Connecticut in the 1950s, as journalist and editor resident in Manhattan in the 1960s through the 1980s), and I'd become good enough at the game to catch frequent sight of the elephant unattended by publicists. The doing so—various of the encounters duly noted in the pages of this book—pegged the power of money to the proverbial emperor minus clothes. Overrated and overpriced; mindless and unwitting agent of it knows not who or what, happy to tune Mozart's piano, glad to lend a hand with the brickwork at Auschwitz.

Money acquires meaning from the uses to which it is put. Contrary to the ruling handed down with the cucumber sandwiches on the silver tray, money corrupts the rich people (most of them, not all of them) who grant it power of attorney over the human assets of heart and mind. The German philosopher Arthur Schopenhauer reduced the consequence to an apothegm; "Money is human happiness *in abstracto*; consequently he who is no longer capable of happiness *in concreto* sets his whole heart on money."

Employed as energy made by mortal men for the use of mortal men, money bankrolls the Marshall Plan in Europe at the end of World War II, arranges the Medici bank's funding of the arts and letters in fifteenth century Florence, underwrites the making of a world fit for human beings. Worship money as immortal idol of one's preferably immortal self, and the substitution of the price of a thing for the worth of a thing makes the world safe for machines. Downsize any and all values that do not pay, and the freedom to think and build becomes the license to exploit. Sooner or later it comes to pass that instead of the people holding the money, the money holds the people, flash-frozen and freeze-dried in the states of petrified dysfunction that currently decorate the halls of government in Washington.

The last chapter of *Money and Class in America* reaches for the thought that the American masters of the universe were, in 1988, on the verge of discovering the design flaw in the Midas touch. I expected some sort of soon forthcoming calamity, man-made or heaven-sent, to break them out of the prison of their golden wish. Neither the loss of the Manhattan trade towers in 2001, nor the Great Recession of 2007–09, prompted the peers of the realm of America's consumer paradise to give up on the notion that there is nothing money cannot buy.

My mistake was with the arithmetic. I overestimated the supply of democratic energy still available to the American body politic, and underestimated the number of enthusiastic converts to the belief that money owns and rules the world. The holding of that belief is the defining characteristic of what in America constitutes a ruling class—all ye know or need to know to possess the most wisdom to discern and the most virtue to pursue the common good of society. Class consciousness in the United States isn't a matter of ancestral bloodline or a veneer of gentrified deportment. It's the assignment to money of the last and final word on what is done or not done—on earth as it is on television—by the few hundred thousand people who control the bulk of the nation's wealth. They wield its instruments of power, run the government, the corporations, and the banks, guide the universities, the think tanks and philanthropic foundations, staff the law courts and the Congress, own and operate the media. Absent recommendation from Mammon on the résumé (customarily phrased as "strong leadership qualities") the candidate for a berth on the A-deck of America's corporate ship of state doesn't qualify for an interview with the search or steering committee.

The immense prosperity accruing to the account of the United States in the aftermath of World War II produced a spectacular abundance of new money. What in 1940 had been a relatively small propertied class resting on the laurels of its inheritance became by 1988 a large crowd of eager speculators booming the consumer market for colossal bourgeois humbug, reveling in the glories of compound self-interest. In 1982, for the first time in the country's history, the share of the national income gleaned from capital (rents, dividends, commissions, fees) exceeded the share of income produced by labor. The percentage of Americans who were self-employed had dropped from roughly 90 percent in the first decade of the twentieth century to 4 percent in the ninth.

Corporations scaled to the size and splendor of medieval dukedoms or Roman galley fleets—60,000 wearing the badge of J.P. Morgan Chase, 600,000 pulling at the oars of General Motors—configure the American laboring classes (blue collar, white collar, temporary and tenured, lower, middle, upper-middle, adjunct and retired) to fit the job description devised by Cotton Mather for indentured servants in seventeenth century Boston—" . . . your tongues, your hands, your feet . . . should move according to the wish of your masters." The upwardly networking careerist depends on the favor of a feudal overlord (executive producer, director of sales, managing editor, divisional vice-president) for the terms and conditions of his or her existence—for wages, healthcare, expense account, pension and parking privileges, but also for the definitions of self, for elevation from the anonymity of human resource to the visibility of human being.

The dancing for coins drains the American body politic of its democratic vitality and deprives it of the political virtue that James Fenimore Cooper named as most necessary to the republic's survival—the capacity of its citizens to speak and think without cant. "By candor," says Cooper in 1838 in *The American Democrat,*

> We are not to understand trifling and uncalled for expositions of truth; but a sentiment that proves the conviction of the necessity of speaking truth, when speaking at all; a contempt for all designing evasions of our real opinions.
>
> In all the general concerns, the public has a right to be treated with candor. Without this manly and truly republican quality . . . the institutions are converted into a stupendous fraud.

The television camera is the world's leading manufacturer of designed evasions. Under its protection and jurisdiction, democratic self-government becomes representative in the theatrical, not the constitutional, sense of the word. The business at hand is show business, and no performance in recent memory better than the one that elected Ronald Reagan to the White House in 1980. For eight years he was near perfect in his lines, sure of hitting his marks on Omaha and Malibu Beach, snapping a sunny salute to a Girl Scout cookie or a nuclear submarine. Facts didn't matter because, as he was apt to say, "facts are stupid things." What mattered was the Gipper's golden album of red, white and blue sentiment instilling consumer confidence in the virtuous virtual reality of an America that wasn't there. The cameras loved him; so did the voters.

The cameras also loved Bill Clinton, who conducted his presidency as television talk show starring himself as both big-hearted celebrity host and shamefaced celebrity guest. He was admired not only for the ease with which he told smiling and welcome lies but also for his capacity to bear insult and humiliation with the imperturbable calm of a piñata spilling forth presidential largesse as corporate subsidy and tabloid scandal. For Clinton as for Reagan the difference between what is and what is not was simply a matter of what was in or out of the camera shot. They were elected, as were the presidents George Bush and Barack Obama, to hearten and amuse the country, not to govern it. To show that Justice Brandeis had it wrong, that the true meaning of American exceptionalism is the not having to choose between democracy and concentrated wealth.

THE MOTIVE FOR WRITING *MONEY AND CLASS IN AMERICA* IN 1988 was personal. As indicated in the original subtitle (*Notes and Observations on the Civil Religion*), my quarrel was with the humbug I was heir to, not with a form of government but with a system of belief characterized by Upton Sinclair in 1918 as the "pecuniary standards of culture which estimate the excellence of a man by the amount of other people's happiness he can possess and destroy."

Sinclair was a muckraking journalist in America's early twentieth century era of progressive political reform, famous for his 1906 book, *The Jungle*, describing the working conditions in Chicago's meat-packing industry. In 1918 he was talking about the consequences of World War I, attributing the collapse of a civilization and the deaths of roughly 40 million soldiers and civilians to the fear and stupidity of a European *haute bourgeoisie* paralyzed by the belief that money is the father of all things human and divine.

Sinclair thought the pecuniary standards of culture certain to destroy mankind unless held in check by democracy lived and practiced (as it was by Abraham Lincoln and Martin Luther King), as the motion of the heart. Sinclair over the course of his lifetime published 100 books (poetry, fiction and polemic), and in 1934, campaigning on a Socialist ticket, was nearly elected governor of California. Ten years later my grandfather was still referring to him as a dangerous lunatic.

The motive for republishing *Money and Class in America* in 2018 is political. I share Sinclair's mistrust of the pecuniary standards of culture, and in 2018 they are more heavily armed with the powers to destroy mankind than they were in 1918 or 1988. Consider the estimates of excellence that currently bring the cups of wine and ecstasy to the feasting of prosperous fools:

The estimate of *excellence* in the holdings in the nation's banks, $13 trillion of other people's happiness imprisoned in the golden bowls of lifelong consumer debt.

The estimate of *excellence* in the government's security and surveillance apparatus, $47 billion a year to protect the American people from having thoughts of their own. The keepers of the nation's plutocratic conscience declare the practice of democracy to be uncivil and unsafe. Entirely too many people in the room or the parking lot who don't do what they're told, and who must be carefully and constantly watched.

The estimate of *excellence* in Facebook's market capitalization of over $400 billion accrued from the sale and resale of other people's lives and liberties—their voices, fears and sorrows included in the bargain price for their likes and hopes and happiness. The oracles in residence at Google announce the dawn of a new day in which the human species breaks the shackles of its genetic legacy, soars to inconceivable heights of machine-made intelligence, and achieves evolutionary union with things.

The excellence of Mark Zuckerberg is the excellence of Donald Trump, product placements of concentrated wealth but also embodiments of the spirit of an age convinced that technology is the salvation of the human race. Citizens of a world in which, increasingly over the last thirty years, it is the thing that thinks and the human being downgraded to the thing. We have machines to scan the flesh and track the heart, cue the GPS and the ATM, tell us where to go and what to do, how to point a cruise missile or a toe shoe. The optimists in our midst look to machines to revive and resurrect America's democracy. They won't.

What can be said about the big money can also be said about technology: it cares for nothing other than itself, collects and stores the dots but connects them only to other dots. Like money, technology neither knows nor cares to know who or what or where is the human race, why or if it is something to be deleted, sodomized, or saved. Siri, Watson and Alexa can access the Library of Congress, but they don't read the books. Not knowing what the words mean, the bots can't hack into the vast store of human consciousness (history, art, literature, religion, philosophy, poetry, myth) that is the making of ourselves as once and future human beings.

It isn't with machines that mankind makes its immortality. We do so with what we've learned on our travels across the frontiers of the millennia, salvaging from the sack of cities and the wreck of empires what we've found to be useful, beautiful, or true. The historical record is mankind's most precious inheritance, telling us that the story painted on the old walls and printed in the old books is also our own.

America's democracy is founded on the meaning and value of words. So is the structure of what goes by the name of civilization. Silicon Valley's data-mining engineers have no use for the meaning and value of words; they come to bury civilization, not to praise it. Bury it in the avalanche of an instantly dissolving present that carries away all thought of what happened yesterday, last week, 200 or 2,000 years ago. The losing track of our own stories (where we've been, who we are, where we might be going), is the destruction not only of the past but also the future. The consequence of the twentieth century information revolution is the same one the poet William Wordsworth ascribed in 1807 to the nineteenth century industrial revolution.

> The world is too much with us; late and soon,
> Getting and spending, we lay waste our powers;
> Little we see in nature that is ours;
> We have given our hearts away, a sordid boon!

For the past fifty years it has been apparent to the lookouts on the watchtowers of western civilization that the finite resources of our planet cannot accommodate the promise of unlimited economic growth and greatness, a.k.a the wish and touch of Midas. Too many people coming into the world, and no miracle of loaves and fishes to feed the multitude. The collateral damage—climate change, environmental degradation, unredeemable debt, extinction of species, pandemic disease, nuclear proliferation, never-ending war—suggests that if left to its own devices, the Dionysian god in the machine of creatively annihilating capitalism must devour and destroy the earth. Not with malice aforethought, but because it is a machine, and like all machines knows not what else to do.

The internet is blessed with miraculous applications, but language is not yet one of them. The strength of language doesn't consist in its capacity to pin things down or sort things out. "Word work," Toni Morrison said in Stockholm in 1993, "is sublime because it is generative," its felicity in its reach toward the ineffable. "We die," she said. "That may be the meaning of life. But we do language. That may be the measure of our lives." Shakespeare shaped the same thought as a sonnet, comparing his beloved to a summer's day, offering his rhymes as surety on the bond of immortality—"So long as men can breathe or eyes can see,/So long lives this and this gives life to thee."

Our technologies produce wonder-working weapons and information systems, but they don't know at whom or at what they point the digital enhancements. Unless we find words with which to place machines in the protective custody of languages that hold a common store of human energy and hope, we surely will succeed in murdering ourselves with our shiny new windup toys.

June 2018

MONEY AND CLASS IN AMERICA

Note: All monetary values here are in 1988 dollars, less than half of the amount adjusted for inflation in 2018.

Passions are like the trout in a pond; one devours the others until only one fat old trout is left.

OTTO VON BISMARCK

Chastise your passions that they may not chastise you.

EPICTETUS

PREAMBLE

WITHIN THE FREE-FIRE ZONES OF THE AMERICAN LANGUAGE the uses of the words "money" and "class" shift with the social terrain, the tone of voice and the angle of the sales pitch. Few words come armed with as many contradictions or as much ambivalence. On more than one occasion I have passed half the night in earnest argument with a number of otherwise intelligent people who, although they thought they were talking about money and class, were talking about something else. Only at the end, when the wine was gone and the host was no longer speaking to most of the guests, did it occur to the company still in the room that one of us had been talking about freedom, another about his lost youth, still another about God.

The profusion of meanings is peculiarly American. Among the Europeans the two words refer to phenomena more or less concrete—to a store of wealth or an accident of birth. With Americans it isn't so simple. We like to assign spiritual meanings to the texts of money, and it is this transfer of value that forms the subject of this book. What interests me is not so much our vanity and greed (vanity and greed being as common among Balts or Kurds as among Texans), but the place of money in the American imagination. What do we expect of it, and what do we think it means? How does it come to pass that we can transform a stock market trade into a symbol of salvation or a grocer's bill into "the romance, the poetry of our age"?

Because the book is more speculative essay than social history, it makes no attempt at a formal portrait of the American rich, who, whether dressed in the raiment of the old or the new money, decorate the pages of the nation's fashion press. Such people appear from time to time in the narrative, but they do so as exemplary figures in a cautionary tale, as comic variations on a theme as old as Aristophanes, Juvenal or Molière.

Nor can the book be read, at least not with any hope of advancing anybody's social ambition, as an instruction manual. I don't know where to meet "the right people," and I never can remember what wine to order with which fish. Nor can I offer any advice about the supervision and manufacture of money. I admire people who can change $100 into $100 million, but I've never learned to imitate their profitable example. Most of my investments have gone as far south as the Brazilian loans made by the Chase Manhattan Bank.

My curiosity veers off in less practical directions. I begin by asking myself why, after all these years in the Puritan wilderness, do we still find it so hard to decide whether money is a virtue or a sin? A testimony to God's infinite wisdom and grace or a short-term contract with the Devil? The alpha and omega of human existence, or, as Lucius Beebe was fond of saying, "a stuff best suited to throwing off the back of moving trains"?

Why so many questions, and why does a comparable ambivalence inform our attitudes toward social rank? Our political rhetoric relies on the promise that nobody is better than anybody else, that all men are made of the same egalitarian clay. The more expensive rhetoric of our commercial advertising mocks the promise as a sop for fools and promotes the antipodal truth that anybody with enough cash in hand can become, by noon tomorrow, better than everybody else. No nation gives so much of its wealth to charity; no nation invests so much of its earned income in the desperate buying and selling of status.

This double-mindedness is as American as baseball. We have a genius for holding in our minds innumerable sets of passionately opposed beliefs—about the land, religion, scientific invention and the law—and it is the energy generated by these opposites that, like the positive and negative charges of electrical current, drives the juggernaut of the American enterprise. America is most itself when most at odds with itself, when nearly equal forces—expressed as dreams or catcalls or bribes—balance one another in a unified field of mutual suspicion. The dialectic assumes conflict not only as the normal but also as the necessary condition of existence and defines itself as a continuous process of change. The structure of the idea resembles a suspension bridge rather than an Egyptian tomb. Its strength rests on the transient nature of its forms. The idea collapses unless the stresses oppose one another with more or less equal weight and intensity—unless enough people have enough courage to sustain the argument between government and governed, city and town, capital and labor, men and women, matter and spirit.

None of our traditional disputes better exemplify the American dialectic than the ones about money and class. The first American fortunes, blessed by the prayers of Calvinist divines, derived from the slave trade and the traffic in bootleg rum. Well before American colonists declared their independence from Britain, they declared themselves of two minds about the purposes of their New Jerusalem. One faction thought that money was merely a commodity (as drab as wood, or straw or cloth) and that the American experiment was about the discovery of a moral commonwealth. Another faction, equally idealistic but not as pious, thought money was a sacrament and America was about the miracle of self-enrichment. The congenital enmity between these two temperaments gives rise to the argument, as confused in Philadelphia in 1787 as it is in New York in 1987, that runs like a theme for trumpet and drums through the whole music of our history, literature and politics.

The argument rises and falls in a cyclical but irregular rhythm. At different moments, one or the other of the two factions embodies the wisdom in office. With the advent of the Reagan administration in 1981 the majority clearly favored the party of self-enrichment and the singing of hymns to Mammon. The antiphonal voices didn't fall silent, but they were harder to hear.

The passions of the moment and attentions of the media center upon shows of opulence. No topic of conversation, no labor of love or work of the imagination, can diminish the wonder of money. The best-selling authors of the most welcome truths do their best to clothe the god of the world's leading religion in the milk-white robes of a Christian conscience or the glittering uniforms of a military band.

The history books report equivalent passions abroad in the land in the 1830s, when President Andrew Jackson's friends invented the spoils system, in the 1870s amid the gaudy corruptions of the Grant administration, again in the 1920s under the dispensations of jazz music and bathtub gin. Whether the spirit of the times was different then—whether Boss Tweed was less venal than Mayor Edward Koch, or Andrew Mellon more rapacious than Donald Trump—I cannot say. I do know that all the numbers have been raised to the power of ten and that our own gilded age finds more people with more money in their hands.

The immense prosperity accruing to the accounts of the United States after the victories of the Second World War produced a correspondingly immense crowd of newly enriched citizens. What was once a relatively small plutocracy, almost homespun in its pretensions and amounting to no more than a few thousand semiliterate millionaires, has evolved into a large spawn of affluent mandarins— in government, the corporations, the professions and the media. If these people were counted as a simple percentage of the population they might be construed as a negligible minority, but the reach of their influence far exceeds both their numbers and their grasp. Whether new rich or old rich, Protestant or Jew, celebrity or anonym, they constitute the American equestrian classes that own the bulk of the nation's wealth, wield the instruments of power, write the newspapers and arrange the television schedules. They perform the feats of higher shopping and personify the tenor of the age.

My acquaintance with this equestrian class reflects my long employment in the media trades as well as my long sojourn in "the holy city of New York." They happen to be people I know well enough to write about with some degree of verisimilitude. I don't think these limitations are as provincial as they might have been in the 1880s. Attitudes once specific to Ward McAllister's "Four Hundred" dining at Delmonico's in New York have become general among like-minded plutocracies in Washington, Los Angeles, Dallas and Chicago.

The temporary ascension of the party of self-enrichment has not been achieved without cost and ill effect. To the extent that the delight in money becomes a transcendent faith, converts to "the world's leading religion" imagine that money stands as surrogate for all other denominations of human currency—for love, work, art, play and thought. Believing they can buy the future and make time stand still, the faithful fall victim to a nameless and stupefying dread. They possess all the goods and services a rich society can afford, but because they expect from money more than it can supply they feel themselves deprived. They rent the Philadelphia Orchestra and complain that the musicians don't know how to play the music of the spheres. No matter how much they spend on shows of their magnificence, they have trouble proving to themselves the theory of their own existence. Their avarice testifies not to the fullness of their appetite but to the failure of their imagination. They worry about the provenance of their shoes and the politics of their dinner invitations, about unknown microbes loose in the rose garden and the humiliation of having to live at a minor street address. Drifting through their afternoons in increasingly somnambulistic states of mind, they discover themselves herded into a gilded cage from which they find it increasingly harder to escape.

Unhappily for all concerned, the pathologies of wealth afflict the whole society, inhibiting the conduct of government as well as expressions of art and literature. The rituals of worship produce deformations of character in institutions as well as individuals, in the making of third marriages as well as in the making of laws and Broadway musicals. It isn't money itself that causes trouble, but the use of money as votive offering and pagan ornament.

The methodology of the book assumes an analogy between public and private confessions of faith in money. Because the faith is ecumenical, embracing most of the texts of American experience, the book borrows from a plurality of sources—from newspapers and economic tracts as well as from scenes observed and conversations overheard. The reader shouldn't infer from my criticism of the presiding theology that I bear a grudge against money. I take as much pleasure in it as the circumstances allow, and like anybody else old enough to fear the IRS and pay entirely too many pipers, I'm always glad to know that it's coming in the mail. To the best of my knowledge I have never professed—not even in California in the early 1960s—the faintest allegiance to Marxist heresy. Nor can I muster the scolding tone of voice sometimes deemed obligatory in any discussion of money and class. Possibly this is because the fear and resentment of the impoverished rich moves me to sadness rather than anger.

What interests me is the cramped melancholy habitual among a citizenry that proclaims itself the happiest and freest ever to have bestrode the earth. Never in the history of the world have so many people been so rich. Never in the history of the world have so many of those same people felt themselves so poor. It is an odd paradox, and one that seems deserving of a few notes and observations, if not a theory or sermon.

1. THE GILDED CAGE

Money is human happiness in abstracto; *consequently he who is*
no longer capable of happiness in concreto *sets his whole heart on*
money.

—ARTHUR SCHOPENHAUER

What I want to see above all is that this remains a country where
someone can always get rich.

—RONALD REAGAN

AT YALE UNIVERSITY IN THE MIDDLE 1950S THE MAN whom I prefer
to call George Amory I knew chiefly by virtue of his reputation for
wrecking automobiles. He was heir to what was said to be a large
Long Island fortune, and I remember him as a blond and handsome
tennis player embodying the ideal of insouciant elegance seen in a
tailor's window. During the whole of our senior year I doubt I spoke
to Amory more than once or twice; we would likely have seen one
another in a crowd, probably at a fraternity beer party, and I assume
we exchanged what we thought were witty observations about the
differences between the girls from Vassar and Smith. At random
intervals during the 1960s and 1970s I heard rumors of Amory's
exploits in the stock market and the south of France, but I hadn't seen
him for almost thirty years when, shortly after President Reagan's

second inaugural in the winter of 1985, I ran across him in the bar of the Plaza Hotel. He seemed somehow smaller than I remembered, not as blond or as careless. Ordinarily we would have nodded at one another without a word of recognition, and I remember being alarmed when Amory carried his drink to my table and abruptly began to recite what he apparently regarded as the epic poem of his economic defeat. Presumably he chose me as his confessor because we scarcely knew each other, much less belonged to the same social circles. I wasn't apt to repeat what I heard to anybody whom he thought important enough to matter.

"I'm nothing," he said. "You understand that, nothing. I earn $250,000 a year, but it's nothing, and I'm nobody."

Amory at Yale had assumed that the world would entertain him as its guest. He had little reason to think otherwise. Together with his grandmother's collection of impressionist paintings and the houses in Southampton and Maine, he looked forward to inheriting a substantial income. Certainly it never had occurred to him that he might be obliged to suffer the indignity of balancing his checkbook or looking at a bill.

Things hadn't turned out the way he had expected, and in the bar of the Plaza he looked at me with a dazed expression, as if he couldn't believe that he had lost the match. He had three children, but his wife was without substantial means of her own, and somehow he failed to generate enough money to carry him from one week to the next. He explained that most of the paintings had been sold, that he had been forced to rent the house in Southampton for $40,000 during the season, and that the property in Maine had been stolen from him by his sister. He had been busy in the bar making lists of those expenses he deemed inescapable. Handing me a sheet of legal foolscap, he said:

You figure it out. I can't afford to go to a museum, much less to the theater. I'm lucky if I can take Stephanie to dinner once every six months.

His list of disbursements appears as he gave it to me, the numbers figured on an annual basis in 1985 dollars and annotated to reflect the narrowness of the margin on which Amory was trying to keep up a decent appearance:

Maintenance of a cooperative apartment on Park Avenue: $20,400[1]

Maintenance of the house in Southampton: $10,000

Private school tuitions (one college, one prep school, one grammar school): $30,000

Groceries: $12,000[2]

Interest on a $200,000 loan adjusted to the prime rate: $30,000

Telephone, household repairs and electricity: $12,000

A full-time maid and a part-time laundress: $25,000

Insurance (on art objects, the apartment and his life): $8,000

Lawyers and accountants: $5,000

Club dues and bills: $5,000[3]

Pharmacy (cosmetics, medicine, notions): $5,000

Doctors (primarily for the children): $4,000

Charitable donations: $6,000[4]

1. Given the expense of New York real estate, Amory could count himself lucky to be paying so low a price. He had inherited the apartment, ten rooms at East Seventy-sixth Street, from his mother. By 1985 comparable apartments cost at least $1 million to buy and between $2,000 and $3,000 a month to maintain.

2. An extremely modest sum, implying the absence of a cook, an inability to give dinner parties and a reliance on canned goods.

3. Again, a pittance. At his clubs in town Amory could have afforded to do little more than pay his dues and stand his friends to a quarterly round of drinks. At the beach club on Long Island his children would have had to be careful about signing food chits and losing golf balls.

4. $1,000 to each of his children's schools, the minimum donation acceptable under the rules of what Thorstein Veblen, in *The Theory of the Leisure Class*, defined as "pecuniary decency": $1,000 to Yale University and $2,000 meted out in small denominations to miscellaneous charities dear to Stephanie Amory's friends.

Clothes for his wife: $5,000[5]

Clothes for his children: $7,000

Cash expenditures (taxis, newspapers, coffee shops, balloons, etc.): $8,000

Maintenance of children's expectations (stereo sets, computers, allowances, dancing school, books, winter vacations): $30,000

Maintenance of his own expectations: $3,000

Taxes (city, state, federal): $75,000

Total: $300,400

It was no use trying to play the part of a niggling accountant or to suggest it might be possible to lead a presentable life on less than $250,000 a year. Amory was too desperate to fix his attention on small sums. When I remarked that he might cut back on his children's expectations he said these were necessary to allow his children to compete with their peers, to give them a sense of their proper place in the world. In answer to a question about club bills and charitable donations, Amory pointed out that he allocated nothing for luxury or pleasure, no money for dinner parties, paintings, furniture, for a mistress, psychiatrists, even for a week in Europe.[6]

"As it is," he said, "I live like an animal. I eat tuna fish out of cans and hope that when the phone rings it isn't somebody dunning me for a bill."

Not knowing what else to do, Amory had resolved to leave New York, maybe for Old Westbury or Westport, "someplace unimportant," he said, where he could afford "to stay in the game." He couldn't do for his children what his parents had done for him, and his feeling of

5. Most of the women in Stephanie Amory's set could draw on an annual clothes allowance of $30,000. Evening dresses designed by Givenchy or Bill Blass cost between $3,000 and $5,000.

6. In May 1987 the fashion tabloid W fixed the price of keeping a young mistress in New York City at $5,000 per month; the sum included rent, clothes, maid and exercise trainer, but not jewels, furs or weekends in Mexico.

failure showed in his eyes. He had the look of a man who was being followed by the police.

Seen from a safe distance, Amory's despair seems comic or grotesque, the stuff of dreaming idiocy that Neil Simon could turn into a commercial farce or *The New York Times* editorial page into an occasion for moral outrage. If the average American family of four earns an annual income of $18,000, by what ludicrous arithmetic could a man of Amory's means have the effrontery to feel deprived?

It is a question that on a number of occasions in my life I could as easily have asked myself. Like Amory, I was born into the ranks of the equestrian class and educated to the protocols of wealth at prep school and college.[7] Given the circumstances of my childhood in San Francisco, I don't know how I could have avoided an early acquaintance with the pathologies of wealth. The Lapham family enjoyed the advantages of social eminence in a city that cared about little else, and most of its members consoled themselves with the telling and retelling of tales about the mythical riches of my great-grandfather. He died the year I was born, by all accounts a very severe but subtle gentleman who had been one of the partners in the founding of the Texas Oil Company. It was said that he translated poetry from the ancient Greek, played both organ and cello, collected shipping companies and oriental jade, and at one point in his life considered the possibility of buying the Monterey Peninsula. That he didn't do so—deciding to acquire instead a less dramatic but more convenient estate in Connecticut—was a source of vast disappointment to his descendants. As a child I occasionally accompanied my elders around the golf courses at Pebble Beach and Cypress Point, and by

7. None of the phrases commonly used to describe the holders of American wealth strike me as being sufficiently precise. The United States never has managed to put together an "establishment" in the British sense of the word; "upper class" implies a veneer of manners that doesn't exist. Borrowed from the Roman usage, equestrian class comprises all those who can afford to ride rather than walk and who can buy any or all of the baubles that constitute the proofs of social status. As with the ancient Romans, the rank is for sale.

listening to their conversation gathered that I had been swindled out of a proprietary view of the Pacific Ocean.

In 1942, during the first autumn of the Second World War, my grandfather was elected mayor of San Francisco. I often rode in municipal limousines, either to Kezar Stadium for the New Year's Day football game or to the Presidio for military ceremonies among returning generals. Somewhere on the journey through streets I remember as always crowded, I confused pretensions of family with imperatives of public interest. I came to imagine that I was born to ride in triumph and that others, apparently less fortunate and more numerous, were born to stand smiling in the streets and wave their hats.

My self-preoccupation was consistent with the ethos of a city given to believing its own press notices. The citizens of San Francisco dote on a romantic image of themselves, and their provincial narcissism would be difficult to exaggerate. The circumference of the civic interest extends no more than a hundred miles in three directions, as far as Sonoma County on the north, to Monterey on the south and to Yosemite in the east. In a westerly direction the zone of significance doesn't reach beyond the Golden Gate Bridge. We lived in a fashionable quarter of the city, surrounded by spacious houses belonging to people in similar circumstances, and I attended a private school that nurtured social rather than intellectual ambitions. Everybody went to the same dancing classes, and none of us had any sense of other voices in other parts of town.

The accident of being born into the American equestrian class has obvious advantages, but it also has disadvantages not so obvious. Children encouraged to believe themselves either beautiful or rich assume that nothing further will be required of them, and they revert to the condition of aquatic plants drifting in the shallows. The lack of oxygen makes them giddy with ruinous fantasy.[8] Together with my classmates and peers, I was given to understand that it was sufficient

8. William K. Vanderbilt made the point in a newspaper interview in 1905. "Inherited wealth," he said, "is a big handicap to happiness. It is as certain death to ambition as cocaine is to morality."

accomplishment merely to have been born. Not that anybody ever said precisely that in so many words, but the assumption was plain enough, and I could confirm it by observing the mechanics of the local society. A man might become a drunkard, a concert pianist or an owner of companies, but none of these occupations would have an important bearing on his social rank. If he could pay the club dues, if he could present himself at dinner dressed in the correct clothes for whatever the season of the year, if he could retain the minimum good sense necessary to stay out of jail, then he could command the homage of headwaiters. Headwaiters represented the world's opinion, and their smiling respect confirmed a man in his definition of himself. That definition would be accepted at par value by everyone whom one knew or would be likely to know. A man's morals or achievements would be admired as if they were lawn decorations, with the same cries of mindless approbation that society women bestow on poets and dogs. The gentleman's inadequacies, whether a tendency toward confused sadism or a habit of cheating customers on the stock exchange, could be excused as unfortunate lapses of judgment or taste. What was important was the appearance of things, and if these could be decently maintained, a man could look forward to a sequence of pleasant invitations. He would be entitled to a view from the box seats.

From the box seats, the world arranges itself into a decorous entertainment conveniently staged for the benefit of the people who can afford the price of admission. The point of view assumes that Australians will play tennis, that Italians will sing or kill one another in Brooklyn, that blacks will dance or riot (always at a seemly distance), and that holders of a season subscription will live happily ever after, or, if they are very rich, forever.

The comfortable assurance of this point of view implies a corollary refusal to see anything that doesn't appear on the program. Nobody could imagine that they might be dislodged by social upheaval, of no matter what force and velocity, and it was taken for granted that the embarrassments of sex and death would be transformed into the lyrics of a Cole Porter song. The Oedipal drama took place only on stage, in roadshow companies sent out from the darkness of New York, or possibly in certain poor neighborhoods in the Mission District. All manifestations of intelligence remained suspect, as if they were contraband for which a man could be arrested if they were found in his possession. Later in life, if he discovered that he needed the commodity for the conduct of his business, he could hire a Jew.

Similar attitudes of invulnerable privilege were characteristic not only of the students at the Hotchkiss School and Yale University but also of most of the people whom I later came to know in the expensive American professions. Within the labyrinths of the big-time media, in the corridors of Washington law firms and Wall Street brokerage houses, within the honeycombs of most institutions large enough and rich enough to afford their own hermetic models of reality (e.g., the State Department, the Mobil Oil Corporation, Time Inc.), I found myself in the familiar atmospheres of reverie and dream.

Neither at Hotchkiss nor at Yale did I come across many people who placed their trust in anything other than the authority of wealth. The members of the faculty at both institutions often made fine-sounding speeches about the wonders of the liberal arts—as if they (the liberal arts, not the members of the faculty) were a suite of virgins set upon by Philistine dogs—but the systems of value that governed the workings of the schools were plainly those that prevailed in the better neighborhoods of San Francisco.[9]

Hotchkiss received the majority of its students from the affluent middle class residents in New York City, Connecticut and Long

9. The attitude doesn't appear to have changed much over the last thirty years; if anything, the emphasis on money has become more pronounced. Tuition at an Ivy League college is now $17,000 a year, and the students apparently worry about preserving the assumptions of ease so expensively maintained by their parents.

In *Campus Life*, a study of undergraduate attitudes published in 1987, Helen Lefkowitz Horowitz remarks on the virulent preoccupation with wealth now afflicting students everywhere in the country. She quotes a senior at Duke University. "It seems like all we talk about is money. I try to say that it's not that important. But it's really important to be comfortable, and you can't be comfortable without money."

Island. Given the plausible expectations of inheritance among these young men, it was hardly surprising that few of them felt obliged to learn much more than the elementary geography of the civilization in which they would happen to be spending the income. They assumed, as did the faculty, that the mere fact of being present ratified their admission to the ranks of "the best people." A prep school education in the autumn of 1948 was something that one couldn't afford to do without (like dancing school or swimming lessons), but it was not something that deserved much thought or attention. It was a necessary ornament, perhaps, but not the equal of a good shotgun or a trust fund yielding $300,000 a year. Ambition, like leather jackets, was best left to the poor. Everybody who mattered already had arrived at all the places that mattered, and anybody who seemed to be in too much of a hurry to get somewhere else (presumably somewhere he or she didn't belong) must be considered a person of doubtful character or criminal intent. Why would anybody want to strive for anything if all the really important prizes had been handed out in the maternity ward at New York Hospital?[10] Scholarship students might be forgiven the wish to become secretary of state or chief justice of the United States, but the heirs of affluence didn't need to think beyond the horizon of their amusements. What was necessary would be given to them; for what they desired over and above those necessities they would pay, grudgingly, the going price.[11]

10. A variation of this attitude accounted for the more refined Republican opposition to John F. Kennedy's seeking of the presidency in 1960. Politics was an expensive form of social climbing, and the Kennedys conceivably could be forgiven their vulgarity on the ground that they had no other way of being admitted to the Bath and Tennis Club at Palm Beach.

11. From the point of view of the *jeunesse dorée* matriculating at the Hotchkiss School in the early 1950s the "bare necessities" would have included property equivalent in value to an apartment on Park Avenue, a house in Southampton or Newport, a seat on the New York Stock Exchange, substantial trust funds (both for oneself and one's eventual wife), memberships in the Racquet, Brook and Piping Rock clubs, miscellaneous paintings and art objects falling due on the deaths of various relatives. Luxuries (i.e., those diversions that had to be ordered à la carte) included such items as a divorce, racing stable, third house, political office and art collection.

The faculty did its best to apply a veneer of cultural polish, to impart a sense that somehow it was important to learn at least a few polite phrases of Latin or Greek. Nobody stated the operative principles more succinctly than an English master whom I accompanied on a walk through the countryside in the autumn of my sophomore year. The walk was compulsory, the result of an offense against the rules. The few of us who followed the master across stubbled fields listened with a degree of attentiveness appropriate to the magnitude of our transgressions. I must have been in fairly bad trouble at the time because I can remember the master's reflections on education with unusual clarity. He was a large and untidy man, notable for his constant puffing on a pipe and the holes in the elbows of his tweed jacket. He spoke slowly and obscurely, the words sometimes garbled by the pipe. His thought revealed itself in cryptic episodes, apparently taking him by surprise. He would interrupt himself just as abruptly, subsiding for no discernible reason into a diffident silence that continued for another two or three miles. As follows:

> What we are trying to do here, gentlemen, is to give you an idea of the whole man . . . character, you see, character is what we are interested in. The rest is not very important. Politics and business, I suppose, must get done somehow, and I don't mean to say anything against commerce, of course, but none of it has anything to do with character, you see, with the idea of a gentleman.

Or again, some miles down the road at the edge of a stream in which the first skein of ice had formed:

> You are heirs to a great tradition, the magnificent edifice of Western civilization. It's a rich heritage, gentlemen, and we are trying to teach you to find your way around its corridors, its labyrinthine corridors, I might say.

Or lastly, two hours later, while walking up the hill to the gymnasium, with hearty and reassuring laughter:

Never read so much that you wear yourselves out in study. Remember the whole man. No poem can take the place of a tramp through the woods in winter. Know the difference between different orders of things. Most of you have been given a great deal and will be given a great deal more. I think you should learn to respond with informed gratitude.

The guarantee of privilege extended to everybody at Hotchkiss, even to the molelike grinds who hoped only to serve the system that temporarily made fun of their accents and their shoes. Nobody seriously questioned the legitimacy of the regime; nor could anybody conceive of an alternative hierarchy of ideas. A small and dissident minority counted among its members several of the most intelligent boys in school, but they were content to make common cause with the social majority in the elaboration of the manner defined as "casual." The motives of the two factions didn't quite coincide—there is a difference between the ennui of people who own things and the ennui of people who fear the owners—but they shared an equivalent egoism. To be casual at prep school was everything—a manner that implied fluidity, grace, ease, absence of commitment, urbanity, lack of sentiment, indifference to the rules and courage under circumstances always ironic. The style discouraged enthusiasm on the ground that it exposed a person to the risk of failure. Anybody investing time or effort in anything took the appalling risk that the market in his enterprise (i.e., himself) might collapse. Jazz musicians defined the attitude as "cool," and variations of the style later appeared in the 1960s under the rubric of the counterculture. But just as I never met a hippie whom I could have described as a revolutionary, so also I never met a social critic—especially the more eminent among them—whose complaint had more to do with substance than with gesture.

At Yale University in the 1950s the expression of "informed gratitude" meant having the good manners to learn the difference between a Beethoven sonata and a logarithm table. Whitney

Griswold, then president of the university, welcomed the members of the freshman class to Woolsey Hall and reminded us in his introductory remarks of the many feats performed on our behalf by the venerable sages whose busts could be seen resting on pedestals along the walls. Griswold's discussion of "the well-rounded man" reiterated the word of advice offered by the Hotchkiss English master. Western civilization had apparently been acquired at some cost, and the class of 1956 had an obligation to maintain it in a decent state of repair.

As an intellectual proposition Yale proved to be a matter of filling out forms. Over a term of four years the representative celebrities of the human soul (Plato, Montaigne, Goethe et al.) put in guest appearances on the academic talk show, and the audience was expected to welcome them with rounds of appreciative applause. Like producers holding up cue cards, the faculty identified those truths deserving of the adjective "great." The students who received the best marks were those who could think of the most flattering explanations for the greatness of the great figures and the great truths.

A few professors made a self-conscious point of taking testimony on all sides of an argument, earnestly considering (pipe thoughtfully in mouth, head inclined diffidently forward and to the left) even the most preposterous hypothesis and keeping an always-open mind to the chance of "meaningful dialogue." At the end of the hour or semester, of course, the questions had to be answered in the manner recommended at the beginning. Failure to conform to presiding truths resulted in second-rate grades and a reputation for being either arrogant or odd.

Before the winter of freshman year the students understood that the politics of a Yale education would have little to do with the university's statements of ennobling purpose. A Yale education was a means of acquiring a cash value. Whatever the faculty said or didn't say, what was important was the diploma, the ticket of admission to Wall Street, the professions, the safe havens of big money. As an undergraduate I thought this discovery profound; it had a cynical glint to it, in keeping with the novels of Albert Camus and the plays of Bertolt Brecht then in vogue among the apprentice intellectuals who frequented the United Restaurant on Chapel Street. The diner stayed open all night, and one morning at about 3 a.m. I remember telling the cognoscenti about an English professor who had marked one of my papers with an F because I had proposed an unauthorized view of a seventeenth-century poet. In the margin of the paper the professor had written: "I don't care what you think, I'm only interested in knowing that you know what I think." The message pretty much defined the thesis of a Yale education at the time, and the professor was, of course, right. Schools serve the social order and, quite properly, promote the habits of mind necessary to the maintenance of that order.

The education offered at Yale (as at Harvard, Princeton or the University of Michigan) bears comparison to the commercial procedure for stunting caterpillars prior to their moment of transformation into butterflies. Silkworms can be made useful, but butterflies blow around in the wind and do nothing to add to the profits of the corporation or the power of the state. Brilliance of mind is all well and good if it leads to some visible improvement (preferably technological) or if it can be translated into a redeeming sum of cash. Otherwise, like the Soviet embassy, it is to be placed under surveillance.[12]

At Yale I was introduced to the perennial American debate that might well be entitled, "What are the humanities, and why do

12.   Much later in life I became a trustee of schools and universities, and I was sorry to see my earlier impressions so resoundingly confirmed. University presidents devoted their principal time and effort to the labor of raising money. Even if they had entered office with a fondness for literature or scholarship (as did A. Bartlett Giamatti at Yale in the late 1970s) they had no choice but to suppress their enthusiasms when flattering the alumni. Giamatti used to say that he couldn't afford to speak plain English. He was obliged to translate his thought into the empty abstraction of a language that he called "the higher institutional."

they mean anything to us here in the last decades of the twentieth century?" The debate has been going on for at least thirty years, becoming more agitated and abstract as it steadily loses meaning. Nobody wants to say, at least not for publication, that we live in a society that cares as much about the humanities as it does about the color of rain in Tashkent. The study of the liberal arts is one of those appearances that must be kept up, like a belief in the rule of law and a devout observance offered to the doctrines of free enterprise and equal opportunity. By advocating the tepid ideals of "the graceful amateur" and "the well-rounded man," the universities make of humanism a pious and wax-faced thing. Works of art and literature become ornaments preserved, like bank notes or trust funds, in the vaults of an intellectual museum. The society doesn't expect its "best people" (i.e., the Hotchkiss students who grow up to become investment bankers and corporation presidents) to have read William Shakespeare or Dante. Nor does anyone imagine that the secretary of state will know much more history than the rudiments of chronology expounded in a sixth-grade synopsis. If it becomes necessary to display the finery of learning, the corporation can hire a speechwriter or send its chairman to the intellectual haberdashers at the Aspen Institute. Education is a commodity, like Pepsi-Cola or alligator shoes, and freedom is a privilege fully available only to those who can afford it.[13]

The lessons learned at school were confirmed by my experience at different elevations in the choir lofts of the media. After leaving Yale I first found work as a reporter for the *San Francisco Examiner*,

13. The humor implicit in the phrase "the best people" is plain enough even to the editors of journals recommending conservative lines of opinion. Apropos the Reagan administration's practice of the arts of chicane, Thomas Fleming, editor of *Chronicles*, observed, in the winter of 1987, "Except in a few rare and fortunate cases, the powers that be, in this and any land, are a remarkably uniform set of real-estate swindlers, market manipulators and well-oiled office seekers." The observation would not have surprised Tom Paine, Ambrose Bierce or Dorothy Parker.

a Hearst newspaper known for the artful sensationalism of its headlines. From the *Examiner* I went to the *New York Herald-Tribune* in 1960 and then to various magazines, among them *Life, The Saturday Evening Post* and *Harper's*.

Before I was twenty I thought the pathologies of wealth were confined to relatively small numbers of people preserved in the aspic of a specific social class. By the time I was thirty I understood that much of what could be said about the children of the rich could also be said about the nation as a whole and about a society that comforts itself with dreams of power, innocence and grace.

The United States came so suddenly into its inheritance that the fortune bears more of a resemblance to a family estate than to the wealth of a nation accumulated over centuries. It is no more than eighty-nine years from the closing of the frontier to the walk on the moon—the same span of time that measures the building of Chartres Cathedral and the period between John D. Rockefeller's entry into business and his death amid incalculable riches.

During the first half of the twentieth century the European powers twice attempted suicide, and at the end of the Second World War what was left of Western Civilization passed into the American account. The war prompted the country to invent a miraculous economic machine that seemed to grant as many wishes as were asked of it. The continental United States escaped the scourge of battle, and it was easy enough for Americans to imagine that they had been singularly favored by God. In 1945, as in the seventeenth century when the founders of the Puritan enterprises accepted into their hands the blessings of a bountiful wilderness, the United States once again seemed to have received the mandate of Heaven. No wonder Americans believed themselves heirs apparent—not only of the classical and Christian past but also of the earth and all of its creation. As the inheritors became increasingly profligate (witness over the last forty years the steadily rising levels of inflation, consumption and debt), so also the presumptions of entitlement were extended throughout the whole of the society. Habits of extravagance once plausible only among the happy few became as commonplace among the sons of immigrant peddlers as among the daughters of the *haute bourgeoisie*. At the same time and for the same prices the rich and the not-so-rich collected speedboats, amphetamines, second houses or mortgages, and assurances (from professors of creative writing) that they could write novels no less great than those of Melville and James.

The feeling of amplitude was sustained by the miracle of reawakened consumer markets, and as larger numbers of people acquired the emblems of wealth, so also they acquired the attitudes of mind appropriate to the worship and defense of that wealth.[14]

Why else had the war been won if not for the enjoyment of the heirs? Why else had the immigrant fathers made so many sacrifices (during the Depression as well as at Anzio and Guadalcanal) if their sons and daughters couldn't become whatever they wished to become—poets and statesmen as well as talk-show personalities and owners of subsidiary rights? What else does it mean to be an heir or heiress if he or she cannot have anything that it occurs to them to want?

In 1905 Edith Wharton published *The House of Mirth*, a novel in which the heroine, a young and beautiful woman named Lily Bart, drifts like a precious ornament on the bright surface of the frivolous, albeit brutal, society summoned into existence by the riches of Twain's Gilded Age. Wharton intended a bitter satire on the self-preoccupation of an ignorant plutocracy. Her heroine declines to sell herself as a commodity, and the novel shows her being inexorably forced out of the soft, well-lighted atmospheres of luxury, "the only climate in which she could breathe," into the deserts of poverty. She cannot live in a world without carriages, engraved

---

14. It goes without saying that the attitudes of entitlement enjoy the fond endorsement of the federal government, which currently donates $400 billion a year (in Social Security, Medicare, military and civil service pensions) to the comfort of the middle and upper classes.

invitations, new clothes and the round of frivolous amusements to which she had become accustomed; unable to eat from broken china in a squalid part of town, she prefers to die rather than suffer the "humiliation of dinginess."

The House of Mirth addresses itself to what in 1905 was an irrelevantly small circle of people entranced by their reflections in a tradesman's mirror. In the seventy-odd years since Wharton published the novel the small circle has become considerably larger, and the corollary deformations of character show up in all ranks of American society, among all kinds of people caught up in the perpetual buying of their self-esteem.

The pathologies of wealth usually afflict the inheritors, not the founders, of fortunes, but by 1982 the United States supported a *rentier* class of sizable dimensions. In that year, for the first time in the nation's history, the money that the American people earned from capital (i.e., from rents, dividends and interest) equaled the amount earned in wages. In 1859 the country boasted the presence of only three millionaires—John Jacob Astor, William Vanderbilt and Augustus Belmont. In 1982, it entertained (by the estimate of *M Magazine*) at least 1.3 million millionaires, not counting the innumerable peers of the same financial realm who fail to pay taxes adjusted to their incomes or who derive their wealth from the criminal trades. The demographers at *M* further assume that 70,000 citizens possess assets worth upwards of $10 million and that another 20,000 citizens (the happiest few) hold assets worth upwards of $20 million. The real estate agents on Manhattan's Upper East Side define a millionaire not as an individual who owns assets worth $1 million but as one who earns $1 million a year. To the extent that the United States as a whole has adopted the persona of the rich kid, the widespread presumptions of divine grace and eternal credit have become as characteristic of American democracy playing with the toys of art and government as of the spendthrift and still prodigal sons squandering the available patrimony.

Some weeks after Amory had gone not to Westport but to New Rochelle, I listened to a variation on his lament from a television producer's wife who no longer could go confidently into department stores. Her husband granted her an allowance of $75,000 a year for clothes and jewelry, but the money wasn't enough, not nearly enough, to maintain her sense of well-being. Unlike Amory, she had been born poor, in a middle-class suburb of Philadelphia, the daughter of a bank examiner. But she had attended Radcliffe on a scholarship in the early 1960s, and together with almost everybody else in her generation she had come to think herself deserving of everything in the world's gift—success, beauty, happiness, fame. The illusion of unlimited means had done the usual damage.

Having been married for some years to the producer, who was successful and often in California, the woman who once had wanted to be a poet had learned to weigh the meaning of her life against the prices paid for clothes, furniture and real estate. She had been unlucky in her assignment of milieu. The producer did business with people who could afford to spend $80,000 for a weekend in Deauville. His wife had learned to value the deference of sales clerks and hotel managers. If somebody else's wife owned a more expensive house in East Hampton, then somebody else's wife obviously had made a better deal with Providence. She no longer could bear to look in department store windows, and if she found herself walking on Fifth Avenue she took care to cross to the opposite side of the street before passing Bergdorf Goodman. Her wariness proceeded from a feeling of humiliation. If she wasn't rich enough to buy whatever she wished to buy, then clearly she was still poor, and what was the point of having any of it? Because she was poor, she was worthless, not fit to be seen in the company of dresses priced at $15,000 or diamond earrings marked down to $33,000 the pair.

In the arenas of academic or philanthropic affairs the complaint has a more decorous and muffled sound. I once heard the correct tone expressed at the Russell Sage Foundation in New York by a company of prominent scholars and journalists assembled to address the question of energy policy. The discussants had been invited because of their nominally earnest concern about the global distribution of heat and light. Both commodities at the time seemed to be going in disproportionate amounts to the rich and developed nations of the world. It was hoped that the study group might formulate an ethics of energy consumption whereby the less fortunate members of the international polity could find a place closer to the fire. The gentlemen talked in high-sounding abstractions for the whole of a morning and the better part of an afternoon. They worried about the shadow of famine falling across the map of the Third World; they counted the number of people dying of exposure in deserts that none of them had seen. At the end of the day the study director, an admirably complacent professor from Princeton, asked for specific suggestions. He reminded his guests that the foundation had allocated $250,000 for a five-year assessment of the dilemma, and he wanted to know what was the next step toward implementation. For about an hour various members of the group dutifully examined the question but failed to come forward with an idea that everybody hadn't already read in *Newsweek*. At last the delegate from Harvard, sharing George Amory's contempt for the meagerness of $250,000, said the sum was so small that it inhibited the surge of imagination.

"Who can do anything with $250,000?" he said. "The thing to do is to leverage it. Anybody with the right connections in the charity business ought to be able to run it up to $1.5 million before the end of the year. If we had $1.5 million, I'm sure we could come up with an idea."

Everybody applauded this initiative, and the seminar adjourned with the resolution to reconvene when the foundation had raised more cash.

The emphasis on what Wharton would have called "the external finish of life," extends across the whole of the social spectrum and accounts for much of the spending in the public as well as the private sectors of superfluous display. Early in 1985, writing in *The*

New York Times Magazine, Claude Brown, a student of the Harlem milieu and author of *Man-Child in the Promised Land*, recounted a conversation with a teenage boy convicted of murder who explained that he had wanted "to be somebody," to be able to "rock" (i.e., to wear) a different pair of designer jeans at least twice a week. "Man, it's a bring-down," the boy said, "to wear the same pants and the same shirt to school three or four times a week when everybody else is showin fly." The same spring *The Washingtonian* published a lead article entitled "Going Broke on $100,000 a Year," in which it was explained that a good many young and ambitious couples in Washington had been ruined by their taste for splendor. By way of illustration the magazine reprinted a number of household budgets as hopelessly out of balance as George Amory's.[15]

Two years later, in the spring of 1987, *The New York Times* raised, by 200 percent, the cost of pecuniary decency. On the front page of its Sunday Business Section, under the title "Feeling Poor on $600,000 a Year," a correspondent described the misery of the Wall Street novices "just buying their first $1 million co-ops" and beginning to feel intimations of immortality. The paper relied on the authority of Richard Zorn, an investment banker who retained the vestiges of a social and historical perspective.

"They can ape the styles of the rich and famous," Zorn said. "They earn $600,000 and spend $400,000 out-of-pocket. There's the house in Southampton and the nanny and entertaining and art and the wardrobe. But when the Joneses they are keeping up with are the Basses, it comes to the executive jet and the yachts and the sapphires and the million dollar paintings, and it's all over. What it means is that $10 million in liquid capital is not rich."

---

15. The nation's consumer debt (i.e., the sum borrowed by individuals) now stands at $2 trillion, roughly equal to the national debt (another $2 trillion); at least in the opinion of a number of respectable economists, this consumer debt presents a far more dangerous threat to the world's financial stability than the $1 trillion owed by the less developed nations of the Third World.

Talking to the same point, another banker cited in the same dispatch said, "I never knew how poor I was until I had a little money."

The federal government spends a large percentage of its income on the preservation of illusions no less foolish than Lily Bart's. Variations on the theme of dingy humiliation (scored for orchestra and brass band instead of solo flute) echo through the mournful statements of Caspar Weinberger, former secretary of defense, who wished to enjoy the privilege of conducting simultaneous wars, some nuclear and others merely conventional, on five continents and seven oceans. For this luxury that he perceived as necessity Weinberger asked that the trifling sum of $300 million a day be paid for five years into the Pentagon's account. Let Congress withhold any part of this allowance, and Weinberger would weep for the loss of Western civilization.[16]

Much the same tone of voice appears in the explanations of U.S. senators who say they cannot possibly keep up what they regard as a decent appearance on a miserable salary of $89,000 a year. Being accustomed to approving sumptuous military budgets and spending $2,453 for circuit breakers that cost $3 in less-refined parts of town, the senators ask their sympathetic retainers in the press how they can be expected to maintain at least two residences and attend, suitably dressed, all the civic occasions to which they owe the favor of their presence. Who will deliver them from the humiliation of having to give lectures in dingy halls? Of dodging like beggars for the coins of campaign contribution?

Ask an American what money means, and nine times in ten he or she will say it is synonymous with freedom, that it opens the doors of feeling and experience, that citizens with enough money

16. Few amenities in the modern world cost as much as a properly equipped military household. To present a decent naval appearance, the United States maintains a fleet of thirteen aircraft carriers, each of which costs $590,000 a day to operate. Each of the 500,000 American soldiers currently stationed abroad costs $88,000 to outfit in an impressively martial livery.

can play at being gods and do anything they wish—drive fast cars, charter four-masted sailing vessels, join a peasant rebellion, produce movies, endow museums, campaign for political office, hire an Indian sage, toy with the conglomeration of companies and drink the wine of orgy. No matter what their income, a depressing number of Americans believe that if only they had twice as much, they would inherit the estate of happiness promised them by the Declaration of Independence.

At random intervals over a period of thirty years I have conducted a good many impromptu interviews on this question, asking people of various means to name the combination of numbers that would unlock the vault of paradise. I have put the question to investment bankers and to poets supposedly content with metaphors. The doubling principle holds as firm as the price of emeralds. The man who receives $15,000 a year is sure that he can relieve his sorrow if he had $30,000 a year. The woman with $1 million a year knows that all would be well if she had $2 million a year.

All respondents say that if only they could accumulate fortunes of sufficient size and velocity, then they would ascend into the empyrean reflected in the best advertisements; if only they could quit the jobs they loathe, quit pandering to the whim of the company chairman (or union boss, or managing editor, or director of sales); if only they didn't have to keep up appearances, to say what they didn't mean, to lie to themselves and their children; if only they didn't feel so small in the presence of money, then surely they would be free— free of their habitual melancholy, free to act and have, free to rise, like a space vehicle fired straight up from Cape Kennedy, into the thin and intoxicating atmosphere of gratified desire.

It is precisely this belief that crowds them into the corners of envy and rage. Imagining that they can be transformed into gods, they find themselves changed into dwarfs. The United States provides life-support systems for the richest and most expensively educated bourgeoisie in the known history of the world, and yet, despite

God knows how many opportunities and no matter how elaborate the communication systems or how often everybody goes to Europe, the equestrian classes remain dissatisfied.

Nobody ever has enough. It is characteristic of the rich, whether the rich man or the rich nation, to think that they never have enough of anything. Not enough love, time, houses, tennis balls, orgasms, dinner invitations, designer clothes, nuclear weapons or appearances on *The Tonight Show*. This has been the urgent news brought to a sympathetic public for the past twenty years by the chorus of sensitive novelists, Norman Mailer as well as Ann Beattie, who publish the continuous chronicle of disappointment. Given the outward circumstances of their lives, their unhappiness sometimes approaches the margin of parody. There they sit, the wonders of the Western world, surrounded by all the toys available to the customer with a credit card, mourning the loss of innocence, the limits of feminism and the death of bumblebees.

Seeking the invisible through the imagery of the visible, the Americans never can get quite all the way to the end of the American dream. Even if we achieve what the world is pleased to acknowledge as success, we discover that the seizing of it fails to satisfy the hunger of spiritual expectation, which is why we so often feel oppressed by the vague melancholy that echoes like a sad blues through the back rooms of so many American stories. The poor little rich girl and the unhappy movie idol, like J. Gatsby, George Amory and the makers of the nation's foreign policy, compose variations on the same lament. Yes, we have everything anybody can buy in the department store of the free world: the Ferrari, the third husband, the F-16, the villa at Cap d'Antibes, the indoor tennis court, the Jacuzzi and the Strategic Defense Initiative. But no, it isn't enough. We aren't happy. Somehow we deserve more.

As portrayed in Ken Auletta's book *Greed and Glory on Wall Street: The Fall of the House of Lehman,* the partners in the firm could neither restrain nor appease their appetites for cash. They earned salaries of between $500,000 and $2 million a year, but for reasons that would have been self-evident to George Amory, nothing was ever enough, and everybody always needed more. "Greed was the word that hovered over the troubled partnership . . . Traders said the bankers were greedy because they were privately angling to sell the firm. Bankers said the traders were greedy to steal their shares and take such fat bonuses." Joan Ganz Cooney, the founder of Children's Television Workshop and the wife of Pete Peterson, one of the principal Lehman partners, explained to Auletta that her husband wanted to sell the firm so "we'd have no money worries." At the time her husband was receiving the equivalent of $5 million a year after taxes—a sum too small to suppress the feelings of anxiety and panic.[17]

Innumerable books by the sons and daughters of the rich remark on a comparable state of deprivation. Gloria Vanderbilt in her autobiography (*Once Upon a Time*, published in 1985) describes her childhood as a vacuum, empty of love or the merest sound of human recognition, as if she were "suspended in a bubble." Sallie Bingham, the reluctant heiress who in 1986 provoked the sale of her family's monopoly interest in the *Louisville Courier Journal*, speaks of being brought up in circumstances similar to those of a political prisoner. She was taught "never to ask the price of anything," but in return for this privilege she was obliged to maintain an attitude of decorous silence—never expressing her thoughts, never presuming to impose "undue stress or criticism" on the men in her family. The historian John A. Garraty noted in his study of *The New Commonwealth* that the unprecedented wealth and comfort of the *alte* nineteenth century in America resulted, paradoxically, in rising levels of exhaustion, anxiety and corruption. He went on to say that "the burgeoning

---

17. The arrest in February 1987 of Martin A. Siegel, a Wall Street *Wunderkind,* provoked his peers and confederates to exclamations of surprise. Siegel at the time was earning upwards of $1 million a year as a notable maker of deals for Kidder, Peabody. When it was discovered that he also was selling confidential tips for suitcases filled with cash, a broker said, "How many yachts can you ski behind at the same time?"

cities of the land expanded the opportunities and fired the imaginations of their inhabitants, yet seemed at the same time to narrow their horizons and reduce them to ciphers."

At college I was struck by the way in which heirs to even modest fortunes fitted their lives into small spaces. They had the resources to travel extensively, to underwrite the acts of the imagination (their own or those of others), to make the acquaintance of their own minds. Instead, they fixed their attention on the tiny distinctions between shirts bought at Tripler's and shirts bought at J. Press, between the inflections of voices in Greenwich, Connecticut, and the inflections of voices twenty miles north in Armonk. Their preoccupations were those of department store clerks or the editors of *New York* magazine.

Amory, in his senior year, shared a suite of rooms with a prepschool friend, a boy named Wainwright who barely could muster the energy to go to class. The boy had a talent for painting, but his parents had made a mockery of his ambition to study art, and he had learned at St. Paul's to suppress any sudden or suspicious movement of his imagination. He sometimes thought he would like to travel, maybe to India or Greece. But then he thought of the heat and the flies and what he called "the funny-looking people speaking funny-looking languages," and he decided he was better off seeing the world through the eye of an air-conditioned movie theater on Crown Street. His passivity anticipated the passivity of a subsequent generation brought up to sit in front of television screens, and his xenophobia was not too different from that of the foreign policy establishment that thought it could buy off its fear of Communism by staging a war in what it believed to be the air-conditioned movie theater of Vietnam.

Although I have no memory of a specific incident, I know that before I was eight I had begun to suspect that something was wrong with the local presumptions of grace. It was as if a magician at a child's birthday party had made a mistake with the rabbit, thus leaving at least one member of the audience with the awkward suspicion that what was being advertised as paradise might bear a closer resemblance to jail. Possibly it was something about the people waving their hats (not all of whom seemed to be smiling), or perhaps it was a remark overheard in a basement, or a chance encounter with one of Charles Dickens's novels. In San Francisco I had been brought up among people who owned most of what was worth owning in the city. At Yale I had been educated among heirs to certain affluence. In New York, Los Angeles and Washington I had met many of the people believed to have won all the bets—and yet, despite their ease of manner, hardly anybody seemed to take much pleasure in his or her property. What impressed me was their chronic disappointment and their diminished range of thought and sensibility.

Edith Wharton describes the asylum of wealth as a gilded cage, sumptuous in its decor but stupefying in its vacuity.[18] Lily Bart at least had the wit to know that by making money an end in itself she would be required to give up all but the enameled surface of her humanity. She would become a fly embalmed in amber, meant to be stared at, like celebrities in tomorrow's papers, by the crowd pressing its collective face against the windows of a Fifth Avenue jeweler.

Unlike widespread poverty, widespread affluence is something new under the sun, and the criminologists recently have begun to discover what was obvious to both Honoré de Balzac and Talleyrand—that is, that the relation between "subjective dissatisfaction and objective deprivation" is a good deal more complicated than anybody at Harvard previously had thought. Apparently it is not poverty that causes crime, but rather the resentment of poverty. This latter condition is as likely to embitter the "subjectively deprived" in a rich society as the "objectively deprived" in a poor society.[19]

18. Within a week of being acquitted of the attempted murder of his wife, Claus von Bülow, in an interview with *New York* magazine, observed, "A gilded life may, in many ways, become a gilded cage."

19. The statistical records show that in the United States in the twentieth century the incidence of crime has risen during periods of prosperity (before 1930 and during the 1960s and 1980s) and declined during the Depression, World War II and the decade of the 1970s.

In New York the masks of opulence conceal a genuinely terrifying listlessness of spirit. The equestrian classes promenade through the mirrored galleries of the media, their least movements accompanied by a ceaseless murmuring of praise in the fashion magazines as well as in *The New York Times*. Behind the screens of publicity, the mode of feeling is as trivial and cruel as the equivalent modes of feeling prevalent in the ranks of Edith Wharton's plutocracy or F. Scott Fitzgerald's troupe of dancers in the Jazz Age.

2. PROTOCOLS OF WEALTH

Money, not morality, is the principle of commercial nations.
—THOMAS JEFFERSON

It's 2:00 p.m.—do you know where your money is?
—Sign in a window of Merrill Lynch

THE HISTORY OF THE UNITED STATES IS SYNONYMOUS with the dream of riches. The first European explorers came looking for gold and the silk routes to the Indies; venture capitalists promoting the first colonies in Maryland and Virginia divided the landscape into the shares of a joint-stock deal. In Massachusetts Bay, the seventeenth-century founders of the Puritan enterprise believed that grace revealed itself as property. Together with John Calvin they assigned spiritual meaning to the texts of money and conceived of their New Jerusalem as a real estate development in which God and Mammon held equal interest. As early as 1690, having discovered that the North American forest lacked the gold and specie found by the Spanish in the south, the native transcendentalists relied on the abstracted forms of illusory credit. By 1750 the American colonists already were more accustomed than the Europeans to the sophisticated uses of paper currency. The divorce from England followed a long and bitter argument about taxes, and the first cry of rebellion was not Thomas Jefferson's "Life, liberty and the pursuit of happiness," but the Boston shipowners' "Liberty, property and no stamps!" The Revolutionary War was as much a financial speculation with the worthless paper issued by the Continental Congress as it was a gamble on the weather and the temperament of France.

Although I don't count myself a historian, I have read randomly enough in both primary and secondary sources to suspect that the gentlemen who wrote the Constitution in the summer of 1787 had it in mind to make their world safe for commerce, joining the moneyed interests of the merchant north with those in the planter South. Their prejudices were not dissimilar to those held dear by our contemporary members of the Business Round Table, the Council on Foreign Relations and the Cosmos Club. By the word "liberty" they meant liberty for property, not liberty for persons. At fetes in Colonial America the order of dancing was arranged in accordance with the net worth present in the ballroom. The principal guest, usually a British naval officer, danced first with the richest girl, then with the next richest girl, and so forth through the protocol of wealth.

Subject to the countinghouse atmospheres of the late eighteenth century (in which it was understood that every merchant was out for everything he could get and that no merchant could be overpaid for his services to mankind), the founders of the American republic could not conceive of human rights being established on anything other than property. The guarantee of freedom for economic forces took precedence over the guarantees of freedom to the powers of the intellect and imagination.

Madison worried about reckless agitation for "an abolition of debts, for an equal division of property and other wicked projects." Anticipating the suspicions of Attorney General Edwin Meese and Secretary of State George Shultz, John Jay observed that "the people who own the country ought to govern it." John Adams of Massachusetts thought that the "great functions of state" should be reserved to "the rich, the well-born and the able." Charles Pinckney of North Carolina suggested that no candidate be deemed fit for the office of the presidency unless he could prove a net worth of $100,000, which, in 1787, was enough money to buy, at current prices, a floor in the Trump Tower. His motion failed to persuade a majority, but it was indicative of the presiding sentiment. The Constitution didn't set a fee for admission to the polls—one of the remarkable achievements in Philadelphia—but many state constitutions required the voters in local elections to own property.

Most of the delegates to the Constitutional Convention feared what they called "the turbulent passions" of the common man, and they detested both the theory and the practice of democracy. They wished to confine the popular spirit let dangerously loose in the streets by the recent excitements of the Revolutionary War, and, like President Ronald Reagan's Justice Department, they assumed that the rabble couldn't be trusted with the gift of speech.[1] The argument of the convention had less to do with abstract ideals than with the division of interest between the financiers and merchants of seaboard towns and the farmers of the interior.

At the end of the summer in Philadelphia, the convention affirmed its belief in what Richard Hofstadter, in *The American Political Tradition*, defined as "an ideology of self-help, free enterprise, competition and beneficent cupidity." By and large these beliefs have remained safely in place throughout the whole of the American experience. With varying degrees of emphasis, they have informed the thinking not only of the Reagan administration but also the administrations of Andrew Jackson, Ulysses Grant, Grover Cleveland, Theodore Roosevelt, Woodrow Wilson, Herbert Hoover, Franklin Roosevelt, John Kennedy and Richard Nixon.

---

1. Observing the urban poor in the streets of New York, the young Gouverneur Morris was moved to remark, in the spirit of the contemporary editorials published in *The Wall Street Journal*: "The mob begin to think and reason. Poor reptiles! . . . They bask in the sun, and ere noon they will bite, depend upon it. The gentry begin to fear this."

Having established the sovereignty of property, the convention reluctantly granted the so-called people a voice in the government. The delegates did so not for reasons of high-minded principle but because they recognized in one another the rapaciousness of wolves and feared the despotism of which they knew they were entirely capable. They expected the rich to plunder the poor and the poor to prey upon the rich. The Bill of Rights was appended to the Constitution as a grudging concession to a loud minority that persisted in thinking of money as a commodity rather than as sacrament. The argument between these two unambiguous factions comprises the American dialectic and tells most of the story of American politics. The nation's history could be written as a long argument between opposed enthusiasms, an argument alternating between episodes of avarice and generosity, between spasms of orgiastic spending and sudden withdrawal behind the perimeters of guilt.

Conceived in bankruptcy, the new nation founded its capital city on a site convenient to the purposes of a real-estate swindle. The first American Congress addressed its first acts of legislation to the setting up of a national bank and a settlement of the war debt that enriched the speculators (most of them friends of Alexander Hamilton) who had bought up bonds at discounted prices. Recognizing the rule of money implicit in the American dream, the authors of the Tripoli Treaty in 1796 firmly declared, "The government of the United States is not in any sense founded on the Christian religion."

Before 1820 Thomas Jefferson knew that his hope of an aristocracy grounded in moral or intellectual merit had been outmatched by a plutocracy subservient to the rule of finance capital. In a letter to Du Pont de Nemours, he said, "We can never get rid of [Hamilton's] financial system. It mortifies me to be strengthening principles which I deem radically vicious, but this vice is entailed on us by the first error." He didn't know the names of the lobbyists still unborn, but Jefferson already could foresee his hopes for the American republic reduced to government by building inspector and military contractor, by kickback and tax exemption. Writing to another friend in 1810, not long after he had seen the surrender of the southern agrarian interest to the mercantile interest of the Federalist north, Jefferson observed, "Money, not morality, is the principle of commercial nations."

The American government from the very beginning willingly implicated itself in business, financing toll roads, canals, the first experiment in mass production (of rifles) and whatever else seemed likely to turn a profit. Throughout the nineteenth century the country borrowed extravagantly from abroad, providing considerably more of its well-advertised "freedom and opportunity" to foreign capital than it did to foreign labor. Most of the loans went bad. By 1845 the national preoccupation with money had become so virulent that Alexis de Tocqueville, the French politician and essayist commonly regarded as the wisest anatomist of the American body politic, devoted a good part of his *Democracy in America* to the fever of avarice. "In democracies," Tocqueville said, "nothing is greater or more brilliant than commerce. It attracts the attention of the public and fills the imagination of the multitude."

The primary American political disputes always have resolved into conflicts between different forms of property: between landed and financial wealth, between old and new enterprise, between Rust Belt and Sun Belt, between manufacturing and service industries, between large and small capital. The emergent commercial interests invariably campaign on the promise to get the government off the backs of the people, by which they mean, off the backs of their own profits. The ideas in which the arguments happen to be dressed remain matters of minor importance. Only the slogans change, but these, as every politician knows, can be bought and sold as easily as the ornamental drapery of the best academic opinion.

Jefferson's argument with Hamilton was superseded by a variation of the same quarrel between Andrew Jackson and Livingston Biddle on the question of the National Bank. The origins of the Civil War had less to do with slavery than with the southern hatred of the northern tariff against which, in 1832, John Calhoun first preached the doctrines of nullification and states' rights. By 1859 Lincoln understood that the United States was well on its way to becoming what Henry Adams later proclaimed "a banker's Olympus," and he accused the Democrats of adhering to the principle that "one man's liberty was absolutely nothing when it conflicted with another man's property." Between 1865 and 1914 the United States transformed itself into an industrial society, and the Gilded Age, much like our own, reveled in the glory of newfound wealth. Then as now, the press cast itself as unctuous sycophant, marveling at the sublime exploits of the financial magnates who breathed the life of capital into Walt Whitman's "factories divine." Most of the journalists then writing encomia to the glory of wealth would have been entirely content contributing the same sort of flattery to *Fortune, Forbes* or *Manhattan, Inc.* People took pride in their sharp practice, and they admired the figure of the small entrepreneur portrayed as Sam Slick, Yankee peddler.

The politics of the period revolved around the antagonism between the "money power" of the eastern seaboard and the populist sentiment of the West, between private property and "free grass," the cattle rancher and the homesteader, between the apologists for gold and silver currencies, between the nabobs and the small merchants, the manufacturing combinations and the Grange, Teddy Roosevelt and the trusts. For everybody on all sides of every argument the proofs of democracy were economic. Did the systems currently in place provide access to the ranks of property? Were the right sort of people (i.e., one's friends and allies) being admitted to the precincts of Eden?

No matter what their specific interests, the antagonists believed, with Daniel Webster, that "intelligence and industry ask only for fair play and an open field" and expected, with Henry George, that "the state would clear the ways and let things alone."

Every now and then the country's politics seem to fall into the hands of reformers eager to violate the protocols of wealth and bring down the walls of established privilege. But when these high-minded gentlemen manage to win an election and capture the insignia of office, their noble intentions somehow remain enbalmed in the tombs of rhetoric. Their supposed enemies ("vicious profiteers," "oppressors of the common man," "the resplendent economic aristocracy," etc.) somehow end up, much to everybody's wonder and surprise, with an even larger percentage of the spoils.

Both Teddy Roosevelt and Woodrow Wilson worried about the spirit of a nation lost to the swinishness of its appetite. Roosevelt complained of the "kind of moneymaker whose soul has grown hard while his body has grown soft," and Wilson, recapitulating the melancholy of Jefferson, said, "The truth is we are all caught in a great economic system, which is heartless." Neither President, however, could come up with a plausible counterweight.[2] Like the romantically dissident young men at the Hotchkiss School in the 1950s, they possessed no body of doctrine which they could oppose to the traditional principles of competition, self-help and the rights of property. They were too heavily indebted to their friends in Wall Street, and the proofs of the miracle of new wealth were too many and too spectacular. In the manner of modern neoconservative philosophers, Roosevelt comforted himself with little lectures to the plutocracy about the need for some kind of moral resurgence and a return to the old virtues that could rescue the country from its folly. He attempted to set vigorous military examples, and he presented himself as the implacable enemy of the trusts. But during his tenure in the

---

2. Henry Adams, writing to his brother, Brooks, about the likely election of William McKinley in 1896, observed, "The monied interest can't help winning and running the country. There is no other interest competent to run a hand cart." Of McKinley, Adams said, "a creature of the trusts . . . appealing to the bosses because he's a cheap article, like galvanized tin sheds." The same could be said of most of the politicians for whom I've been invited to vote during the past thirty years.

White House the trusts multiplied at a rate never equaled before or since, and by the end of the First World War, even as Wilson was mumbling his pious hopes for mankind over the recent dead at the American cemetery in Suresnes, the United States already had put in place the mechanisms of an industrial state most likely to prosper under the conditions of permanent war.

During the bleak interlude of the Great Depression the protocols of wealth were called severely in doubt, but Franklin Roosevelt's New Deal, denounced by a generation of Republicans as the prelude to the end of the world, proved to be the salvation of state capitalism. Even Jimmy Carter received the endorsement of the northern money interests because it was thought that he would play the part of a faithful Snopes, mouthing the acceptable pieties about the greatness of the human spirit while tending to the business of sweating the last dime of profit from the local sharecroppers. He disappointed his promoters because he proved to be too weak and girlish, too much given to moralisms in which, to everybody's disgust, he apparently believed.

Ronald Reagan campaigned on a promise to balance the federal budget; within six years he had run up the national debt to almost $2 trillion. Like his predecessors in office, Reagan understood that a successful American politician is a smiling and accommodating fellow who learns to put a human face on the imperatives of property.

Nothing in Reagan's presidency, least of all the crimes of pecuniary indecency committed by so many of his subordinates, served to dim the charm of his amiable improvisations on the theme of government. Standing firmly on the side of the family and the flag— against the officiousness of federal bureaucrats and the villainy of Soviet warmongers, against pornography, drugs, the ghost of Jane Fonda and the stale metropolitan sensibility of public television— Reagan gave the impression of being at his ease in Zion. He had about him an air of reassuring opulence, of a man familiar with the protocols of wealth and the comforts of Beverly Hills, accustomed to the safer suburbs, expensive cars, the scent of jasmine on a golf course, Bob Hope's geopolitics and the smiling camaraderie of Frank Sinatra. Like the late John F. Kennedy, whom he in many ways resembled, Reagan imparted to money the luster of something new and irreproachable.

Although money always has occupied an exalted place in the American imagination, never in the history of the Republic had that place been raised so high as in the years of the Reagan ascendancy. President Reagan's gaudy inauguration in 1981 cost $8 million and established the aura of vulgarity and conspicuous consumption synonymous with both his terms in office. The entertainments, reminiscent of those staged by the parvenu industrialists of the Gilded Age (William Vanderbilt, August Belmont, William Fahnestock et al.), lasted for four days and included nine formal balls, a fireworks display of 10,000 rockets, a reception for "7,000 distinguished ladies" and a vaudeville performance starring, among others, Charlton Heston, Johnny Carson, Donny Osmond and General Omar Bradley rolled onstage in a wheelchair as the personification of a conquering general. By 1985 the new style had congealed into a tasteless opulence expressed in fur coats for Cabbage Patch dolls and advertising copy that read, "Feel gloriously rich," "Satisfy her passion for gold," "It comes in 23 colors, including envy green," and "Rich is better." At a fashion show in Washington, the sponsors hired a ladies' room attendant to sprinkle carnation petals into the toilet bowls after each use; Tiffany & Company in New York advertised a $50,000 diamond necklace in a window display that presented a "bag lady" sitting in a cardboard box reading *House & Garden*.

Since the autumn of 1980 the nation has made no secret of its delight in money. The dreams of avarice glitter in the shop windows of every American city large enough to support a market in German engineering and Italian silk; college freshmen pin photographs of T. Boone Pickens and Donald Trump on dormitory walls once reserved for posters of Bob Dylan and Che Guevara. Among the parvenu real-estate magnates in New York with whom poor George

Amory felt obliged to maintain par value, it has become more or less "the done thing" to engage three jet aircrafts to the spring pilgrimage to Florida or the Caribbean—one for the principals, one for the children, one for the luggage and the servants. Aaron Spelling travels between New York and California in a private railroad car, and the wives of big-time stock salesmen spend as much as $20,000 a week on flowers, limousines and incidental porcelain. The media, both electronic and print, dote on the iconography of wealth. The magazines glisten with the display of opulence; the lists of best-selling books, both trade and mass market, attest to the public obsession with the beauty and power of money—who has it, how to groom and cherish it, what to wear in its presence, why it is so beautiful, where it likes to go in the summer.[3]

The obeisance to wealth takes so many forms that it would need a concordance to list them in hierarchical or alphabetical order. It is a matter not only of how people behave and to whom they show deference, but also what our society looks like, how it arranges its politics and expresses its feelings, what it talks about and how it administers its spiritual as well as its temporal rewards.

3. Passing a bookshop on Madison Avenue in the middle 1980s I noticed that the window display had been as reverently composed as an ode to Mammon. Among the new titles arranged on red velvet, presumably to suggest their resemblance to jewelry, I counted the following: *Hard Money; The Whims of Fortune*, Guy de Rothschild's autobiography; *Funny Money; An Innocent Millionaire; The Dreams That Money Can Buy; Old Money;* and *Very Old Money.*

Among the prices of luxury fixed by the tabloid *W* in May 1987, I was particularly drawn to the following:

— $300,000 to hold a wedding reception in Manhattan for 300 people.
— $23,000 a month to rent a two-bedroom suite at the Carlyle Hotel.
— $350 per week for a New York maid who "can't cook, won't walk the dog and wants weekends off."
— $1,000 for Glorious Food to cater dinner for four at home.

Across the whole of the American continent the talk of money is never quiet. Twenty-four hours a day it seeps through walls and shouts on the floors of the exchanges, whispers in darkened bedrooms and clatters in all-night restaurants, pleads and wheedles through telephone lines, takes up most of the space in the media, screams across kitchen tables, gloats in the windows of Madison Avenue and Rodeo Drive, drifts through bus stations and convention halls, worries in elevators, makes crazy the would-be artists in the gloom of the avant-garde. The papers print more advice on money than advice to the lovelorn; the tip sheets offer inside information in the manner of pardoners selling indulgences and tickets to paradise. Nobody can escape the insistent and commanding presence of money, and the unfortunate idealists who try to deny money's importance discover themselves doomed to embrace an attitude more fully centered on money than that of the greediest plutocrat. The language of commerce is the lingua franca that knits together all the jargons of the professions, the one national vocabulary in which people express the worth of their meaning.

Among the faithful in New York and Los Angeles not even the rumor of incest commands so sudden and respectful a silence as the mention of money in sufficient magnitude. Anybody wishing to recruit an audience, whether of insurance brokers or university professors allegedly Marxist, has merely to speak of his recent encounter with the sum in excess of $500,000. Maybe he has just had lunch with somebody who made a killing in real estate. Perhaps he ran across an author who just sold the movie rights for $2.5 million. Possibly he has fresh news of an expensive divorce or of a merger said to involve oil companies with combined assets of $8 billion. For a brief and luminous moment the money achieves the stature of celebrity, almost as if it were Robert Redford standing in a circle of klieg light. The audience listens with dumbstruck awe for as long as the messenger can clothe the apparition in the specific numbers of a deal. Once the tale is done, the vision fades, and the great spirit vanishes as mysteriously as it came. The guests rouse themselves from their trance, and resume, reluctantly, the familiar and languid gossip about the host's sexual indiscretions or the chance of nuclear war.[4]

A society's attitude toward its principal scandals offers an instructive measure of the society's order of value and obsession, and during the spring of 1987 Americans were entertained by a number of stories that allowed for ribald variations on the themes of eros—Gary Hart's presidential campaign destroyed by his liaison with Donna Rice, at least two Marines seduced by a Soviet temptress at the embassy in Moscow, the Reverend Jim Bakker fallen from grace in a Florida hotel.

In other countries, most notably England and France, the media and its many audiences would have cherished both the official details and the unofficial rumors of sexual intrigue. Who was seen with whom, and when, and in what states of undress? What was the color of the woman's chemise? From whom did the gentleman hire the chains or borrow the house in the country? Where was the gentleman's wife, and did the lady also know the Duke of Kent?

Within recent memory at least six British cabinet ministers have left the government in the midst of newspaper dispatches worthy of the Marquis de Sade. In France nothing so delights the public as the news of an archbishop's dying in a brothel, or the report of the President's romance with an actress, or the suggestion that the President's wife might have gone to Marseilles in the company of Algerian gangsters.

But in the United States the prurient interest attaches itself to money. The downfall of Gary Hart offered an especially instructive lesson in the presiding order of value. Under ordinary circumstances an American politician can keep as many mistresses as he can afford. Unless he stumbles into a crowd scene in the pages of *Playboy*, he can continue, without fear of contradiction, to make long

4. Money's arrival is always exciting, which is why all three television networks have traditionally devoted the first half hour of their evening prime time (i.e., the proverbial children's hour) to imbecile game shows. Money's departure is always as sobering as the news of a death in the family, which is why an awful silence falls on the table when the waiter presents the bill.

and well-received speeches about the need for the new awakening of a new American morality.

But Hart happened to be campaigning for the office of the presidency, and what was at stake was not so much a question of character as the immense sum of money—measured as political spoils, patronage, graft—that changes hands with the election of a new President from the other political party. Hart's indiscretion provided his competitors with a convenient way to eliminate his claim on the national fortune. The polls made it plain enough that the public wasn't much concerned with the gentleman's infidelity and sexual masquerades. What bothered people was his lack of business acumen. If a presidential election can be compared to a poker game, Hart had forsaken what looked like a winning hand for the sake of a woman's smile. Who could trust a man so stupid?

The press reflected the popular sentiment by dropping the lines of sexual investigation as soon as it was clear that Hart was a political bankrupt. A fair number of the nation's leading columnists, among them Anthony Lewis and Tom Wicker of *The New York Times*, felt obliged to apologize (on behalf of their profession) for having been associated, even tangentially, with such an indecent set of questions.

The Reverend Bakker's defeat at the hands of Satan allowed for a number of further questions—about a young girl maybe drugged, a minister conceivably well-versed in the art of seduction, a cadre of church functionaries possibly employed as panders—but none of these lines of inquiry excited the popular imagination as much as the hope of fraud. The primary concern centered not on the humor and sorrow implicit in the vagaries of human desire but on the cost-benefit analyses. How much money was the Reverend Bakker gathering from the credulity of his flock? Where did the money go? What would become of the financial enterprise?

If the libido can be employed in the service of commerce (as a kind of glossy varnish that improves the sale of cosmetics, office equipment, Caribbean cruises, television drama and second mortgages), then so much the better, and all well and good. But customers must remember to look, not touch, to give way to their impulses not in a cocktail lounge but in a department store or automobile showroom. Even the best-selling pulp novels that purport to expose the lasciviousness of the Hollywood gentry read like those self-help manuals that promise to teach typing or real-estate development. The characters don't go to bed with one another because they take pleasure in the encounter. They do so in order to advance their careers or because they want a better table at the Bistro.

In a rich man's culture the wisdom of the rich consists of what the rich wish to hear and think about themselves. Despite its occasional bouts of invective and melancholia, the American press is, and always has been, a booster press, its editorial pages characteristically advancing the same arguments as the paid advertising copy. Together with the teaching in the schools, the national media preserve the myths that society deems precious, reassuring their patrons (i.e., the thousands of separate audiences that constitute the American public) that all is well, that the American truths remain securely in place, that the banks are safe, our generals competent, our presidents interested in the common welfare, our artists capable of masterpieces, our weapons invincible and our democratic institutions the wonder of an admiring world.[5]

Again in combination with the schools, the nation's media reflect the character of a society impressed by displays of power and opulence rather than by the play of mind. The ancient Greeks admired in their art what they called the glittering play of "windswift thought." Pericles in his funeral oration boasted not of the weapons or statues collected in Athens, although these were many and beautiful, but of the character of the Athenian citizen—self-reliant, resourceful, public-spirited,

5. The media's long-standing alliance with the monied interests should surprise nobody except the youngest student at the Columbia School of Journalism. Among the 400 richest Americans memorialized in 1986 by *Forbes* magazine, 83 of them derived their fortunes from newspaper, television and publishing properties. Only the oil industry, which contributed 48 names to the list, could make even a modest claim to such pecuniary glory.

loyal, skeptical, marked "by refinement without extravagance and knowledge without effeminacy." "Numberless are the world's wonders," said Sophocles, "but none more wonderful than man."

Americans don't think so. We prefer the beauty and wonder of property. If asked to revise Sophocles along more contemporary lines, an American publicist, whether employed by *Newsweek*, a university or a corporation, could be relied upon to come up with a statement extolling the perfection of the profit margin or the value of the architecture donated by the alumni.

At the *San Francisco Examiner* the editorial staff observed the protocols of wealth by assigning prices to people as well as to objects and events. An executive known to earn $800,000 a year was entitled to more space in the paper than an executive earning $500,000 a year—unless, of course, the less opulent executive committed an especially atrocious crime. Actresses living in beach houses worth $2 million outranked actresses living in bungalows worth $1 million; aircraft carriers that cost $17 billion were more to be feared than aircraft carriers that cost $10 billion. The sums of money stood as surrogates for further efforts of imaginative definition.[6] The larger the number, the more magnificent the personality, the more necessary the corporation, the more deadly the weapon. Similar calculations governed the appraisal of press releases. If a messenger arrived carrying a paper embossed with the letterhead of some rich institution (the Ford Foundation, say, or the Mobil Oil Corporation), then clearly the message deserved to be read with informed gratitude. Let the same words appear typed on a piece of foolscap in the hands of an ordinary civilian, and the news was patently worthless. The deference of the city room aped the example of the stockbroker whom Heinrich Heine noticed one morning in the 1830s in the anteroom of the Baron de Rothschild's bank in

6. John Coltrane, the late jazz saxophonist, understood the convention as follows: "If you're bourgeois, money is *it*. It's all the questions and all the answers. Ain't no E flat or color blue, only $12.98 or $1,000. If it isn't money, it isn't nothing."

Paris. The establishment lacked the amenities of modern plumbing, and as a factotum emerged from the baron's inner office bearing a chamber pot, the broker rose to his feet, removed his hat and bowed deeply to the proof of the baron's mortality.

Over a number of years in the newspaper business, I dutifully took down notes of speeches delivered by people noteworthy for the titles and offices they held, not for their wit or intelligence. Most of what they had to say was bland or fatuous, but this didn't prevent their remarks from being prominently displayed on the front page of next day's editions. Banality in the mouth of a failed businessman or an unpublished novelist sounds banal; in the mouth of David Rockefeller or Philip Roth the same words acquire the weight of oracle.

Similar protocols regulate the size and duration of the applause meted out at fundraising dinners. Whether pledged to African orphans or victims of muscular dystrophy, $200,000 always gets a bigger hand than $50,000. On announcement of sums in excess of $500,000 the audience customarily rises to its feet like Heine's stockbroker, the warmth of its ovation appropriate to the welcoming of a newly elected President or the return of a triumphant general.

Speaking to a related point in January 1983, William Proxmire, senator from Wisconsin, explained the political variant of the rule to a reporter from *The New York Times* soon after he had ceased to be chairman of the Senate Banking Committee. Proxmire had held the rank of chairman by virtue of the Democratic majority in the Senate; when the Republicans assumed control of the Senate in 1981, Proxmire's annual lecture fees dropped from over $100,000 to less than $12,000. "If you're chairman of the Banking Committee," he said, "you don't have to speak at all. All you have to do is show up. You can read the phone book, and they'll be happy to pay your honoraria."[7]

7. Proxmire's point was confirmed by Stephen Hess in *The Ultimate Insiders*, a study published in 1986 of the way in which the national media follow events in the U.S. Senate. Hess noticed that the press pays attention to only a few obvious figures, primarily the chairmen of the prominent committees. The rest of the Senate goes about its business in the anonymous dark.

Prior to his appointment as Nixon's successor, Gerald Ford was known as an amiable but not very bright congressman from Michigan. Once arrived in office Ford was assigned, together with the Marine guard and the Great Seal of the United States, a reputation for sagacity. Not even *The New York Times* went quite so far as to describe him as a philosopher-king, but suddenly the paper's Washington correspondents recognized in Ford the lineaments of the homely wisdom traditionally ascribed to rural folk and singers of country songs.

At differing levels of intensity, this peculiarly American form of idolatry pervades the whole of the society. No matter what the venue—restaurant, newspaper office, hospital admissions office, department store, ballpark—the resident personnel reserve their deepest respect for the richest customers. Forever bowing to the Baron Rothschild's chamber pot, the nation pays homage to the sum of money in a room, not the people. Profit takes precedence over life and art and love; the freedoms of property take precedence over individual liberties.[8] Corporations—that is, money evolved to its highest and purest form of abstraction—enjoy more privileges than mere persons. The legal system rests on the necessary and fundamental premise that property rights remain absolute and supreme. Witnesses in a civil suit about a question of money can be forced to give testimony on pain of going to jail if they refuse to comply with a court's order. In criminal cases (i.e., those that address the lesser questions of human life), witnesses retain the right to keep silent.

At business conventions the rules of etiquette decree that the president of the richest corporation be accorded the places of honor

8. In the spring and summer of 1986 the abrupt rise in insurance rates provided an exemplary proof of the operative principle. Believing themselves suddenly poor the insurance companies doubled, tripled and quadrupled the premium payments required of amusement parks, county fairs, restaurants, Little League baseball fields, campgrounds and fireworks displays. It was decreed that a possible loss of money was a far more serious and important matter than the expressions of simple human pleasure.

at the banquet tables and the afternoon seminars, and if two businessmen otherwise unknown to one another meet on an airplane or at a wedding reception in the suburbs, the question, "Who are you with?" establishes their rank within the hierarchies of wealth and determines which one owes the other what measures of attention, notice and respect. The division of the prospective spoils in any venture capital deal (for a new electronics company, say, or first novel) awards the commanding interest to the man who puts up the money, not to the man who conceives of the idea, registers the patent or does the work. Adolescents embark on their rites of passage by proving their capacity to earn their own money, and within the desolate silences of failing marriages the arguments about money take precedence (i.e., they are angrier and more deep-seated) over the arguments about sex. On Wall Street people talk about the "size" of the money in a stock trade as if it were a measurement of sexual prowess, and on the terraces of the nation's better clubs the members find it difficult to believe that anybody can become trustworthy, or even decently human, on an income of less than $150,000 a year. Similar rules and procedures govern the manufacture of the nation's so-called arts and letters. The sum of a publisher's advance, together with the money allocated to promotion and distribution, determines the worth of a book. In Hollywood the liveliest dialogue and most inventive plot situations pertain to the preliminary structuring of the financial deal, not to the making of the subsequent movie or television series.

The protocols of wealth govern the distribution of the society's awards and punishments. People seeking redress for their grievances or compassion for their sorrow have no choice but to translate their grief into a specific sum of money. The nation's courts occupy themselves with problems in existential arithmetic. How much for a divorce? For a life? For lost arm or lost child? Given the current expectations among an increasingly rich and fastidious clientele it is entirely plausible to imagine a dissatisfied traveler to Florida bringing a lawsuit against the sun. If the plaintiff named as codefendants Eastern Airlines, Bloomingdale's and the manufacturers of Coppertone coconut oil—all joined in the conspiracy to deny plaintiff's right to a perfect suntan—the suit might enlist the eloquence of the ACLU as well as the guile of counsel willing to work for a percentage of the gross. After several years of lesser argument plaintiff's lawyers could bring their writs to the Supreme Court and demand a revision of the contract between an American citizen and the universe.

With respect to criminal cases, the sociological studies show that the judgments align themselves with a hierarchy of cash value. An offender is likely to be imprisoned if his or her status (i.e., net worth) is lower than that of the victim—for example, an unemployed youth who robs a prosperous citizen on a city street. But if the offender's status is higher than that of the victim—for example, a stock market swindler who steals from anonymous widows and orphans—then the offender is likely to be punished with a fine. The few well-publicized exceptions to the rule (Patricia Hearst, Paul Thayer et al.) sustain the mythology of a legal system founded on something other than the right of property.

As also might be expected of a commercial nation that has so long observed the protocols of wealth, the society possesses nothing that isn't for sale. This is as it should be, and, as Jefferson well understood, not an excuse for cynicism. Again with a few notable exceptions, it is difficult to think of anything in the United States that cannot be bought or sold—the presidency, a television network, longer life, *The New Yorker*, the Baltimore Colts, a municipal judge, an ambassadorial post, Revlon, justice, social rank.[9] Actors and popular athletes present themselves as billboards, paid as much as $300,000 per annum to wear Nike sneakers or tout the virtues of beauty creams and long-distance telephone lines. Once upon a time

9. In California during the state elections of 1986 a political consultant employed to rearrange the administration of justice in a small town said. "Give me $17,000, and I can defeat any sitting judge."

in West Los Angeles, in an elevator rising into the higher and more expensive atmospheres of Century City, I overheard a theatrical agent say to a friend, "There's nothing wrong with a quality piece of junk," and by the inflection of his voice I couldn't tell whether he was referring to a script, an actress or a politician.

Money paid in salaries and fees provides the first and most elementary measure of society's order of value. As answers to the familiar but always pressing question, "Who gets how much for doing what to whom?" the numbers establish the moral coordinates of the American dream. Because we value ourselves to the degree that other people stand willing to pay for our labor or our presence, money serves as the only acceptable collateral for speculations on the patents of an American self. The people who earn the most money are never those who advance the frontiers of knowledge or extend the reach of sympathetic imagination. With surprisingly few exceptions the highest fees are paid to the people who deal in the commodity of money. They might never become as rich as the entrepreneur who invents a new product or service, but the people who hold in their hands the vessels of power (i.e., the tax lawyers, corporate executives, investment bankers) enjoy the sumptuous living and the presumptions of grace granted the clergy in medieval Europe. Of the thirteen highest salaries (in excess of $1 million a year) paid to corporate executives in 1985, nine of them were claimed by senior partners in investment or brokerage firms. As explained by Peter Drucker in one of his astute essays on American corporate management, salaries reflect neither individual merit nor the workings of a market. They obey "the internal logic of hierarchical structure." All corporations delight in elaborate tables of organization; if the worker on the lowest tier of authority earns $15,000 a year, and if the corporation is large enough to boast thirteen intermediate grades of promotion, then the executive on the highest tier earns $300,000 a year—not because he is worth that much more than the man on the bottom but because it is necessary to preserve the proper order of deference.

The professions adhere to the principle that the best is the most expensive, the most expensive the best. A Wall Street lawyer cannot afford to charge less than $250 an hour because if he lowered his fee he also would diminish his reputation for guile. So also with the Washington lobbyists who, in order to convey an impression of sagacity, must be seen in the best restaurants, dressed in $1,500 suits, comforting themselves with oysters.[10] The lawyer and lobbyist might be fools, but their clients think that by paying a high price, they purchase an equivalent weight of intelligence. Comparable acts of blind faith sustain the fees charged by surgeons, literary agents and managers of investment portfolios. By the time the client discovers he has mistaken form for substance, he is either bankrupt or dead.

The protocols of wealth dictate the language of elections and define the nation's political ideal. All candidates profess their heartfelt belief in what might be described as Hotel America—that is, the earthly paradise that certainly would arise from the ashes of a corrupt society if all their promises could be redeemed and all their good intentions changed into the currency of law. Republican and Democrat, liberal and conservative, insurgent or incumbent, the candidates offer all but identical blueprints of the great, good American place. No matter what the differences in their policy positions (on foreign and economic affairs, racial prejudice, education, weapons, the deficit, etc.) the assumptions implicit in their texts reveal a uniform conception not only of the state but also of what is meant by the pursuit of happiness.

The narrowness of their collective political imagination leads them to conceive of the Republic as something very much like a resort hotel, in which the citizens receive the comforts owed them

10. In 1986 in *The New York Times* a prominent Washington lobbyist named Kenneth Schlossberg, remarking on the trouble that lately had befallen Michael Deaver, said, "The truth is that money has replaced brains and hard work as the way for a lobbyist to get something done for his client." The observation has become a commonplace of the nation's editorial pages.

by virtue of their status as America's guests. The subsidiary ideological arguments amount to little more than complaints about the number, quality and cost of the available services. Listed under the rubrics of a travel advertisement, the principal characteristics of Hotel America might be described as follows:

1. **The Electorate.** Another name for the clientele. The guests expect a good time, and prefer to leave the making of a moral effort at home with the laundry and children. Recognizing the popular vote as the personification of will and appetite, even the youngest candidates avoid the mistake of addressing their remarks to the nobler impulses in the crowd. To do so would require tiresome explanations as well as annoying exhortations to sacrifice, renunciation and self-restraint.

2. **The State.** The hotel management, deserving of respect in the exact degree to which it satisfies the whims of its patrons and meets the public expectation of convenience and style at a fair price. The candidates never speak of the state as if it were a cherished ideal embodying the history of the people.

    The guests have no obligation to the state except to pay their bills, preferably with a credit card and, if possible, under the heading of a tax-deductible business expense. This commercial definition of the state (as object rather than subject, as inanimate machinery instead of living organism) would have frightened both Aristotle and Machiavelli. It differs only slightly from the Mafia's designation of itself as Cosa Nostra, our thing.

3. **The Laws.** The rules of the hotel, subject to seasonal changes in the weather or the presence of trade conventions. The candidates construe the laws not as the permanent ethical code of the society but rather as tools with which to harvest the crops of wealth. It is assumed

by all parties that laws can be written or rewritten as easily as computer programs and that they serve at the pleasure of whatever transient majorities or special interests make the most trouble or pay the luxury rates.

4. **Politics.** A Greek word for the printed forms on which the guests can "take a few minutes" to jot down their complaints or suggestions. Every two years the hotel collects these memoranda about the freshness of the orange juice, the enthusiasm of the staff and the placement of the tennis courts. After submitting the results to the media and the opinion polls, maybe the management decides to replace the wine steward or change the furniture on the sun deck.

5. **The Good Life.** On sale twenty-four hours a day in the dining room and the lounge as well as in the international shops located in the mezzanine arcade. The management takes pride in its ability to maintain an Old World atmosphere that reflects a state of being rather than a state of becoming. The latter condition implies movement, which requires change, which creates friction, which causes pain, which is unconstitutional.

6. **Freedom.** Invariably celebrated as the supreme good and almost always confused with the license to exploit. The candidates never mention the use of freedom to create a higher order of responsibility or love. Every guest enjoys the inalienable right to indulge his or her holiday lust for goods and experience. The guarantee of happiness is included in the price of a room. Soon after their arrival, guests receive different grades of accommodations (first-class, economy, immigrant, etc.), but these may be revised upon payment of an appropriate fee.

To the extent that these assumptions underlie the political discourse, the vote-getting image of Hotel America bears an unhappy resemblance to the Marxist advertisement for a workers' resort on the shores of the Black Sea.

In a nation that makes a business its culture, and of its culture a business, the Constitution is customarily seen as a part of the boring paperwork preliminary to the closing of a real-estate deal, which is why Reagan and his attorney general could be excused for knowing so little about it. So can most of the nation's lawyers and elected officials. Among those whom I have met over a period of twenty-five years I think it fair to say that unless provided with a set of crib notes very few of them could name more than five of the constitutional amendments. The practice of government has more in common with the stock exchange than a civics class, but the news media's habitual piety seldom permits the discussion of politics in the language of commerce. In one of the few lapses into candor, William Greider, then an assistant managing editor of *The Washington Post*, some years ago described the acts of "buying, selling, swapping and hustling" as the fundamental means of expression occupying "the poetic center" of the national capital. Certainly this has been my own experience of the city. Traveling in and out of Washington on various assignments over the last twenty years I've noticed that I'm almost always in the company of people planning raids on the federal treasury. The politicians dress up the deals in the language of law or policy, but they're in the business of brokering the tax revenue. What keeps them in office is not their talent for oratory but their skill at redistributing the national income in a way that rewards their constituents, clients, patrons and friends. They trade in every known commodity—school lunches, tax exemptions, water and mineral rights, aluminum siding, farm subsidies, pension benefits, weapons contracts and prison uniforms—and they know that the simple act of writing a single sentence into a trade or housing bill can result in the making of fortunes. They work the levers of government like gamblers pulling at slot machines.

Nearly three in every ten Americans live in a household receiving direct payments from the government; four of the remaining seven probably work for an enterprise dependent upon a federal subsidy or dole. As has been pointed out by a number of alarmed observers in recent years, the cost of political campaigns has become so high that almost everybody in Congress spends most of his or her time begging money from would-be patrons. Senator Thomas Eagleton of Missouri, who retired in 1985 after three terms in the Senate, guessed that his colleagues were devoting 85 percent of their waking efforts to fundraising. Nobody, he said, could afford to attend committee meetings.

It is no wonder that in the United States people come to be valued for the money they command, not for their deeds or character. As their capacity to command money decreases, so also does their stature as human beings, which is why the advertising business has no interest in citizens beyond the age of fifty. Television sells to its advertisers an audience of women, aged eighteen to forty-nine, at a price of $16.50 per thousand. Older women and teenaged children sell for less. Elsewhere in the society anybody living on a pension trades at discount, on a par with the black, the crippled, the retarded and the insane; they remain of interest primarily to the doctors and travel agents who still can extract money from the wreckage of their health.

All societies judge by appearances, but the compulsion to do so becomes more urgent in those societies that depend so heavily on the external measures of success. To the extent that one's condition is oneself, the surfaces of that condition must be kept as bright and clean as a new shopping center. Americans cannot bring themselves to trust a poor man, and it is no accident that our Presidents appoint as Cabinet members and ambassadors men readily identified as the masters or servants of wealth. Although the media have made much of this tendency in the Reagan administration, noting the financial bona fides of such gentlemen as Donald Regan, Caspar Weinberger and George Shultz, the same principle governed the appointments in the Carter, Ford, Nixon and Kennedy administrations. Without money it is all but impossible to aspire to a public voice or persona in

American society, which is why a journalist who wishes to be heard or read must first attach himself to a wealthy media conglomerate and why it is much easier for incumbent politicians to raise campaign money.[11]

Even the more cynical and well-traveled Europeans, accustomed to seeing strange sights in Paris or the Malaysian Archipelago, admit to a degree of surprise when introduced to the American faith in cash. Perhaps this is because Europeans still tend toward a mercantile rather than a capitalist understanding of money. They think of the stuff as a finite commodity: any addition to the substance of A implies a subtraction from the substance of B. Americans take a more transcendent view. We construe money as an infinitely expanding resource, like helium or greeting-card sentiment or leaves on eucalyptus trees. In support of our faith we can offer so many miraculous proofs—of fortunes gained almost overnight in anything from California real estate to chocolate chip cookies—that it becomes easy to think of money not as a means but as an end.

Throughout the nineteenth century immigrants of all nationalities found it difficult to comprehend the American uses of money. Their letters and diaries express their confusion in a commercial society that wasn't held together by ties of family, by a monarchy, by tradition, by the secret police. They felt threatened by a capitalist dynamic that could so easily overturn moral certainties and so readily dissolve the stability of the land. Precisely the same fears haunt the recently arrived immigrants from points of origin as diverse as Guatemala and the Soviet Union.

The shock of recognition is most poignant among the Russians. Over the years I have encountered a fair number of exiles from Odessa, or Moscow or Tbilisi. Although grateful for the material

---

11. During a revision of *Harper's Magazine* in the winter of 1981 somebody suggested an advertising campaign, and one of the magazine's directors, formerly a publisher of *Life*, remarked that it cost "a minimum of $750,000 a year" to make even the smallest impression on any sort of significant public.

comforts of the United States and glad to escape the gray austerity of their own society, they cannot help noticing the crassness of the American market in human relations. Without exception they deplore the monetization of feeling. Alexander Solzhenitsyn made the point in a conversation with his biographer, Michael Scammell. "Absolutely everybody lives badly in our country," Solzhenitsyn said, "but you only have to call for help if you need it. For example, I was helped by dozens of people absolutely disinterestedly. And I never had to ask myself, 'Can I pay?'"

The newest immigrants cannot understand the substitution of cash transactions for the barter of love, sympathy, courage, neighborliness and honor. They never quite get it into their heads that in the United States the forming of loyalties and friendships requires the preliminary condition of commercial association or economic parity.

Without a deal or a business relation held in common, Americans discover they have little to say to one another. The pioneers moving west from Independence, Missouri, in the 1850s organized themselves into companies and elected their captains and treasurers for terms of no longer than a few weeks. Once arrived in California the transient conglomerate dissolved into its original subsidiaries. No matter what hardship people suffered together on the journey, they went their separate ways and disappeared into the void from whence they came. Much the same thing happens to people who change jobs and move to another city, corporation or marriage. They take down their prior loyalties as if these were little more than set decorations; within a week they have pitched the tents of their emotion on the ground lines of a new deal.

It is the monetization of human feeling that so enrages the women who resort to the furious speech of militant feminism. Ceaselessly reminded that the society reposes its trust in the personifications of money (i.e., in lawyers and captains of finance) women feel estranged from their natural roles as the protectors of society's values and the keepers of its rules. They see these prerogatives assigned to wealth, mostly to fairly dull-witted gentlemen who, despite their knack for money-getting, display an appalling ignorance of human feeling and priority. The feminists imagine that if only they could become presidents of companies, somebody would listen to what they had to say. They learn to trust what the literary agents and the divorce lawyers call "the sincerity of the final figure," and they come to believe that any sentiment not backed by cash must be deemed counterfeit.

The equivalence between money and feeling becomes increasingly apparent in the upper reaches of income and net worth. People who define their lives as functions of wealth display their affection, or lack of it, by withholding both the substance and symbolism of money. Between a rich man and his estranged son (or a rich mother and her alienated daughter) the *casus belli* almost always can be reduced to a precise sum: the inheritance the son expected but didn't get, the wife's fee for being cheated of her youth, the father's price for mortgaging what he thought was his own happiness to the speculation of his daughter's future. I sometimes think the only American story is the one about the reading of the will.

Howard Cosell once put the proposition in the fewest possible words. Together with Frank Gifford he was broadcasting a *Monday Night Football* game when the play on the field turned dull. Cosell lost interest in the score, and he began to talk to Gifford about the celebrities who had visited them in the booth during an earlier segment of the broadcast. Reggie Jackson had appeared briefly to acknowledge signing a $3 million contract with the Yankees, and Jimmy Connors had dropped by to report winnings of $80,000 the previous weekend at a tennis tournament in Las Vegas. Drifting into fond reverie, Cosell said: "Well, Frank, we've had a lot of money in the booth tonight." He didn't think it necessary to mention the names of the people to whom the money was attached. The names weren't important. Athletes come and go, some in triumph and some on stretchers, but the money lives forever.

3. THE GOLDEN HORDE

The American is nomadic in religion, in ideas, in morals.
—J.R. LOWELL, *Fireside Travels*

The greatest crimes are caused by surfeit, not by want. Men do not become tyrants in order that they may not suffer cold.
—ARISTOTLE, *Politics*

The rich are like ravening wolves, who, having once tasted human flesh, henceforth desire and devour only men.
—JEAN-JACQUES ROUSSEAU

FOREIGN OR LEFTIST OBSERVERS OFTEN MAKE THE MISTAKE of thinking the Americans a materialist people. British socialists like to remark on the gaudiness of American taste and the bulk of the nation's trash. The Soviet press presents a caricature of the United States as a nineteenth-century plutocrat—an obese gentleman in waistcoat and top hat devouring the fruits of honest labor as if these were truffles in the mouth of a pig. Variations on the same ideograph occasionally appear in the campaign literature of the Democratic Party as well as in the editorial columns of *The Nation, Mother Jones, The Progressive* and any other journal virtuous enough to ally itself with the victims of the interests.

The emphasis on greed misses the point. As Henry Adams noticed, Americans don't take much pleasure in material things. If we did, New York would more nearly resemble Paris, and the food in the better restaurants might at least be as artfully produced as the menu. Instead of being crowded into dirty and congested streets, the expensive real estate would lie along the rivers. Most American cities show to their best advantage when seen from a height or a distance, at a point where the ugliness of the buildings dissolves into the beauty of an abstraction. A television commercial is an artifact far more subtly made than the product it advertises; of the people who buy jogging shoes, 70 percent don't jog. The thing consumed isn't as important as what the act of consumption represents; it is the existential correlative that matters, the demonstration of what Thorstein Veblen called "pecuniary decency" and the proof of belonging to what John Calvin called "the company of the elect."

The American dream at any given moment accommodates itself to the spendthrift presence of two kinds of people living well beyond their means—the parvenu rich rising to the surface of their ambitions and the *ci-devant* rich sinking into oblivion. (Donald Trump represents the former constituency, George Amory the latter.) Both social orders within the equestrian class believe they deserve a good deal more than they possess, and neither order ever has enough money to sustain its definitions of self. The arrivistes spend in anticipation of Christmases yet to come; the departing notables spend to preserve the remembrance of Christmases past. Both sets of expenditure have less to do with physical necessity (food, clothing, shelter) than with the desired states of metaphysical well-being. It doesn't matter so much whether we like the taste of the creamed spinach at Mortimer's or the glazed turnips at the Bistro Garden, or even that we can be seen to pay $50 for a wilted salad and a bottle of overpriced wine, but rather that we can be assured, at least for the time being, that we enjoy the dignity of a name.

Unlike Europeans, Americans recognize themselves as pilgrims obliged to make and remake their lives with whatever materials come to hand. All status is temporary, all states of being conditional. It is the frenzied buying in the markets of self-esteem that distinguishes the American from the foreign rich. Knowing more or less who they are, the equestrian classes in England and France don't feel obliged to purchase the patents of their existence. On the grounds of an old and stately British house it is the old and stately duke who is likely to be seen wandering among the rosebushes in a seedy hunting jacket. He might be pitiably short of cash, but it doesn't occur to him to sell his land in order to present an opulent figure in London. A Frenchman can afford to be interested in a truffle rather than in what the truffle means.

A few among the American rich also affect shabby clothes and secondhand cars, but they do so because of their deference to money, not as an expression of their disdain. Being quite sure that money possesses supernatural powers (i.e., to bestow or rescind the freedom of movement), they don't wish to try its patience or insult its magnificence. Too prideful a display of worldly goods might excite the fevers of envy and subject them to the sufferings of Job.

What Tocqueville noticed as the peculiarly American dread of "sinking in the world" accounts for the seemingly irrational spending that prompts so many people to buy proofs of a salvation they cannot afford.[1] Maybe the weight of their acquisitions will prevent them from drifting off into the void, or relieve them of their

1. A variation of precisely this fear haunted John C. Calhoun, who perceived in the Northern tariffs of the 1830s the end of Southern political supremacy based on the economy of cotton. His cry to Congress was the cry of every dowager, every established class protesting the onslaught of the parvenu rich, of George Amory and the apostles of the Age of Scarcity, of the militant environmentalists and the authors of American foreign policy since the middle 1960s: "What! Acknowledge inferiority? The surrender of life is nothing to sinking down into acknowledged inferiority!" The firing on Fort Sumter turned out to be a proof of salvation that the South couldn't afford.

anxiety, or buoy them up against their fear of losing definition in the world.

The state of perpetual emptiness is, of course, very good for business. The feasts of consumption sustain the economy, keep up the volume in the stock markets, employ the unemployable, excite the fevers of speculation and stimulate the passion for political and sexual novelty. It isn't too much to say (as some of Reagan's apologists for supply-side economics have indeed said) that the safety of the free world depends on the size and violence of the American appetite. Deny the American public the chance to display its patriotic duty to consume the best of everything and within a matter of weeks the Communist host would stand at the gates of Paris.[2]

Whenever the economy runs into sufficiently serious trouble, the advice from New York and Washington shows a remarkable degree of bipartisan consent. Whether advanced by economists or politicians, by merchants, newspaper editors or corporate grandees, the pitch runs as follows:

1. Inject a massive dose of cash into the American bloodstream, and the economic leviathan (not unlike a movie actor braced for the camera with a line of cocaine) will rouse itself from recession and go stumbling through the world's markets with its accustomed voracity.
2. Put enough money in the consumer's fist, and the happy fool will come roaring back into Wall Street and the department stores, bidding up the prices of tractors and carrot cake.

2. Of all the subversive doctrines likely to wreck the American dream of paradise (more subversive than all the manifestos published by all the Marxist professors who ever graduated from Harvard), the most subversive is the one that the ancient Greeks expressed as the Golden Mean and the early Christians as the virtue of temperance. Were a majority of Americans suddenly to say, "I have enough . . . . No, I don't think I'll buy anything more this week," the country soon would fall into ruin.

3. The feasts of consumption ignite the blessed chain reaction that leads to more spending, more investment, more employment, more highways, more steel, more confidence, more traffic deaths, more missiles, more amphetamines, more forms to fill out, more firepower, more fear.

The advertising business plays with ingenious skill on the themes of perpetual discontent that haunt the citizens of an egalitarian society. When everything is more or less the same, and when everybody can compete on the same footing for the same inventories of reward, then the slightest variation of result produces a sickness of heart. The collections of goods and services testify not only to social status but also to an individual's worth as a human being. Small and shabby collections belong to small and shabby souls. The more equal people become, the more relentless their desire for inequality.[3] "The Americans," Tocqueville remarked in the 1840s, "clutch everything but hold nothing fast, and lose grip as they hurry after some new delight."

Our desperate haste has become more pronounced as the events of the twentieth century, its wars and dehumanizing bureaucracies as well as its invention of the atomic bomb, have conspired to remind us of our stature as dwarfs. To the extent that people feel themselves small they seek to enlarge themselves not only through the construction of immense organizations but also by their capacity as consumers. The motto on the T-shirt says "The man who dies with the most things wins," and the markets do what they can to sponsor the race. In the nineteenth century even a rich man could buy relatively few things with which to shore up the architecture of his identity. He could distribute his inheritance on gambling, women, furniture and horses. For his other amusements he had recourse to little else except his ambition and

3. The phenomenon is not new. William Dean Howells in 1866 observed that "inequality is as dear to the American heart as liberty itself."

largeness of mind. The educated aristocracy compiled volumes of commentary on butterflies and the roads in Abyssinia; it assembled libraries and commissioned works of art from Beethoven and Ingres; Tolstoy, himself a nobleman and owner of a thousand serfs, conceived of dramas on a scale commensurate with his lands and estates.

But the equestrian classes of the twentieth century, at least those with which I'm familiar in the United States, squander their talents on the arts of higher shopping. The principle of amassment unites the undermotivated rich with an undermotivated culture.

The most recent figures show that Americans now retain only 4.6 percent of their income as savings, the lowest percentage since the government began keeping records in 1959, and one that compares unfavorably with the Japanese, who retain 17.2 percent, with the West Germans, 12.9 percent, and even with the British, 11.7 percent. The banks serve the function of shills in Las Vegas casinos, hustling gold-plated instruments of short-term debt and setting up speculators with the funds necessary to make a play for an oil company or an airline. The stock market rises and falls on rumors of inside trading, and the states operate numbers rackets that compete with the gambling games run by newspapers.

Unlike their forebears in the late nineteenth century, the current heroes of finance display a talent for consumption but not production. The magnates of the Gilded Age—men like J.P. Morgan, Andrew Carnegie, Edward Harriman or James J. Hill—at least took the trouble to build railroads or steel mills. No matter how conspicuous their horses or their townhouses, their labors added to the sum of the nation's energy and wealth. The modern nabob is a parasite, and more often than not his story is the story of a stomach. Financiers on the order of Ivan Boesky, Carl Icahn or T. Boone Pickens begin by identifying a company that holds assets worth a good deal more than its purchase price. They then borrow the money to buy the property, but instead of trying to preserve it, they reduce its various productive organs to liquid forms of cash and tax manipulation.

The process is not dissimilar to flensing, boiling and trying out the carcass of a sperm whale. Occasionally the acquisitors keep one or another of the parts of the deceased enterprise (an insurance company, say, or a television station), but they do so for reasons of vanity—because somebody else's wife wants to broadcast the six o'clock news or transform a railroad station into a restaurant.

The predators repay their loans with the money distilled from the liquidation of assets; they also pay off the company executives who expedited the sale, ushering them safely off the premises with goodbye presents (i.e., "golden parachutes") often worth $10 million to $20 million. After subtracting these tax-deductible "opportunity costs," the acquisitors divide the remainder of the spoils and issue a press release about the great blessing they have bestowed upon the stockholders and the American people. Their deals, however, almost invariably result in the contraction rather than the expansion of wealth. The earnings of the new company service its debt to the past instead of its development into the future.

People who don't know what else to do collect things—not only objects but also the proofs of experience and emblems of status. Those who would set themselves apart from their neighbors remain perennial students of the self. The more intensely they feel their lack of presence, the more eagerly they buy tokens of personality—gold-plated golf clubs, CBS, cuff links heavily ornamented with initials, designer jeans and designer chocolate, TWA or Revlon, automobiles "especially crafted for Roger J. Straus."[4] Instead of asking "Who are they?" or "What is this?" they ask, much to the delight of psycho-analysts, dance instructors, cosmeticians, Wall Street arbitrageurs

4. The acquisitions can become fairly refined. In 1985 Saul P. Steinberg, an adept in the art of financial legerdemain, paid for the installation of the Metropolitan Museum's Christmas tree and créche. He also paid the losses of the literary evenings sponsored by PEN. Not enough acolytes showed up to listen, at $1,000 a ticket, to the musings of authors as renowned as William Styron and Norman Mailer. Steinberg's money allowed PEN to paper the house with a becoming crowd of penniless students.

and dealers in Hindu religion, "Who am I?" The market welcomes them as a golden horde, defining them as a collective of zip codes and demographic profiles to which it makes the ceaseless promise of escape into a better world. If only the customer will follow the instructions on the label, then maybe he will discover his true self on *Face the Nation* or in a bottle of Brut cologne.

The acts of consumption define the spirit of the age, and it would need a library of many volumes to catalogue the texts of extravagance. The more expensive fashion designers, among them Giorgio Armani, provide "mini-couture" for children under the age of ten; in Los Angeles it is possible to rent a stretch limousine equipped with hot tub and helicopter pad; the "nouvelle society" in Dallas and Chicago, as well as in New York and Washington, teaches its children the refinements of dressage and tells itself, in the words of one of its most impressionable ladies, "We're right now in our glory. We're at the peak of the Renaissance."

The reader surely can tell his or her own cautionary tales, and if I report a few observations from Manhattan, I do so merely to indicate the range of our current obsessions and not to cast any slight on the arts of opulence as practiced in Houston or Miami. On an otherwise ordinary Wednesday last November I received three communiqués from the markets in luxury, all of them tending to suggest that the feasts of consumption answer the appetites of the soul rather than the needs of the flesh.

The morning mail brought a postcard from a Madison Avenue butcher soliciting patronage from a clientele presumably grown bored and listless on a surfeit of steak, roast beef and rack of lamb. The butcher had gone to the trouble of acquiring more exotic commodities and was happy to announce he now could provide choice cuts of antelope, eland, mountain sheep, bear, elk, moose, beaver, hippopotamus, nilgai, cape buffalo, lion, opposum, chamois, llama, raccoon and yak. Being a man of delicacy and taste, the butcher passed over the cost of these items, but it is probably safe to assume that all would be expensive and that the prices would move upward in relation to the animal's rank on the Sierra Club's list of endangered species. In the event that none of these meats excited the curiosity of his patrons, the butcher was thoughtful enough to say he would gladly send his agent in search of any other beast anybody might have in view.[5]

Later in the morning, at breakfast in a coffee shop on the ground floor of the Pan Am building, I fell into conversation with a pilot who flew chartered jets for corporate grandees wishing to avoid the humiliation of traveling on common carriers. He had landed a few hours earlier at LaGuardia with one passenger on a plane configured to transport sixteen executives in elaborate comfort. His solitary passenger, an anxious gentleman who never removed his hat, had made the round trip to Los Angeles within the span of eighteen hours. While the plan was being refueled, the anxious gentleman hurried away in a limousine to Frederick's of Hollywood, a store that deals in the flashy sort of lingerie seen in the back pages of movie magazines. When he returned three hours later, looking like Santa Claus with a stack of packages that had cost him $6,000, the plane promptly took off for New York. ("If I had known he was into that kind of thing," the pilot said, "I would have worn my uniform.") It cost $25,000 to charter the plane for the passage to California, and the bill was sent to the corporation that regarded the passenger as a very important fellow. The pilot said most of the corporations that chartered planes did so not for reasons of convenience but for reasons having to do with somebody's vanity. He assumed that the corporation would pay for the lingerie, as well as the landing fees, but he was curious about the category under which it would list the expense.

5. The market for specialty foods in the United States now amounts to between $3 billion and $10 billion a year; the refinements of the table rank as high among the pleasures of the American equestrian classes as they did among their peers and namesakes in Imperial Rome. A farm in New Jersey last year offered, at $2.40 the dozen, nest eggs from "uncaged hens fed roasted whole grains."

At lunch I listened to a lawyer who for some months had been disbursing funds for the work of interior reconstruction in a large apartment overlooking Central Park. His client, a woman distracted by her ambition to become acquainted with "the best people," had already spent nearly $2 million, at least half of which had been allocated to the marble surfacing of the walls and floors. On first being shown the effect of the foyer, the woman pronounced it too cheap, too insufficient, too exposed to the condescension of the guests whom she expected to astonish at dinner. "They'll think I'm tacky," she had said. "They'll know I only spent $100,000 for the marble."

In order to make a bath and dressing room large enough to accommodate her self-esteem, her contractor had broken through three walls and joined what were once two bedrooms into a space that could bear decoration in the manner of Imperial Rome. Still the result was somehow too small. That morning she had instructed the architect to supply additional mirrors and to install an icebox in the wall next to the tub. "She needs the icebox to chill the cologne," the lawyer said. "She said that there's nothing so unpleasant as to step out of a bath on a warm day and have to wear tepid cologne."

At a dinner later that same week I encountered an NBC correspondent known for the purity of her political judgments who complained about the "obscene" and "outrageous" cost of Nancy Reagan's clothes. She had read in a gossip column that Mrs. Reagan had bought an evening dress for $8,000, and she was moved to make indignant references to Marie Antoinette. Her polemic seemed as fragile as her shoes. Being herself a woman of extremely modest attainments, she earned well over $150,000 a year for reading news bulletins on a teleprompter in a vocabulary configured to the understanding of a six-year-old child. It had never occurred to her that the cost of NBC's nightly news programming, most of it as subtle as the souvenirs sold in amusement parks, certainly exceeded what Marie Antoinette spent in six months for jewelry. In the summer of 1984 the national media sent 14,000 representatives to the Democratic convention in San Francisco (outnumbering the politicos by a ratio of three to one), and the sum of their travel and entertainment expenses over a period of four days would have paid Louis XIV's costs for the construction of Versailles.

Americans tend to prefer the uses of power to the uses of freedom. The heirs to the great fortune that fell to the nation's lot in 1945 assumed they had inherited not only the goods and chattels of the earth but also the spoils of intellect accumulated over centuries in the vaults of Western civilization. They wished to consume the products of the artistic imagination (somewhat comparable in the general conception to a vineyard in Bordeaux), but they had neither the patience nor the need to experience art. The study of literature, like that of any other art, offers as its reward freedom of mind and spaciousness of thought. Neither of these possessions makes much of a show in the world, and for the most part they are thought to be superfluous.

But even a society abandoned to an infantile delight in money needs something it can call by the name of culture. Books still furnish a room, and people excited by power like to go to opening nights, to wear pretty clothes and be marked present in a crowd of celebrities. The characters in the popular television dramas, like those in best-selling works of fiction and nonfiction, achieve their identities by virtue of their association with expensive merchandise. Novels by writers on the order of Judith Krantz or Danielle Steel or Dominick Dunne read like catalogues from Neiman Marcus. Nobody goes anywhere without drinking from a glass of Roederer Cristal, wearing a Cartier watch or picking up a Mont Blanc pen to write a check for the odd $2 million or $3 million while sitting at a table by William Kent in a suite at Claridge's.[6]

---

6. The protocols of wealth require the naming of almost every object worth more than $500. The authors dress up a sum of money in a label, and by so doing excuse themselves, like the reporters on the *San Francisco Examiner*, and *The New York Times*, from any further effort of the imagination. The bookshops report brisk sales of what is known to the trade as "designer fiction" dealing not so much with romance, or even lust, but with the headier fantasies of unlimited credit.

In nineteenth century France the newly enriched bourgeoisie crowded into restaurants invented for their amazement, and there, complacent under the chandeliers, they professed themselves astounded by the sauces of Escoffier. They took the food extremely seriously, not daring to express a naïve opinion for fear of making an atrocious blunder in the presence of waiters. The same air of uncertainty characterizes the *nouveaux littéraires* ennobled in the hundreds of thousands by university degrees in the past thirty years, solemnly consuming the *rôti de Styron*, the *mousse au Sontag* and the *prix fixe* offered by the Book of the Month Club. Rather than be proved ridiculous by what critics might say in *The New York Times*, the clientele makes itself sick on fantasy and nihilism in cream.

The pretext for an operatic or theatrical occasion (a kind of setting wealth to music) matters less than its exclusivity and expense. At the opening of its season in the autumn of 1985 the Metropolitan Opera staged what by all accounts was a truly dreadful performance of *Tosca*. Even the critic from the *Times*, defying the rules of decorum and risking the wrath of his editors, couldn't help noticing that Luciano Pavarotti's singing was poor, the production "heavy-handed" and "grandiose," the effect "lifeless" and "embarrassing." The paper's social pages, however, carried exuberant reports of the evening's spectacular success. About 750 notables, among them William F. Buckley, Jr., Helen Gurley Brown and Oscar de la Renta, paid $1,000 for a dinner lit with candles on the grand tier. Chanel arranged a fashion show and used the occasion to introduce its new perfume, Coco. Musicians in costume played trumpet fanfares for the arriving guests; the staircases had been tastefully decorated with actors dressed as Swiss Guards. Estée Lauder pronounced the opera "great."

In a rich man's culture, art is what sells and its price determines its worth. If the diamond bought at Tiffany's sparkles more brilliantly than a diamond of equal weight and size bought for $758 on West Forty-seventh Street, then even bad novels by Joseph Heller or E.L. Doctorow become masterpieces by virtue of the prices paid for the paperback and movie rights. Once an author or an artist has demonstrated his or her ability to earn money, he or she acquires, as if by court order, a reputation for genius. Under such a dispensation critics become indistinguishable from headwaiters or department store floorwalkers. They provide ready-made opinions and direct the customers to the newest lines of merchandise.

A prominent editor of *The New York Times* involved with the supervision of the paper's cultural pretensions supposedly once stated the commanding principle with a concision superior to that of my Hotchkiss English master. Explaining the protocols of wealth to a newly arrived subeditor, the editor is purported to have said, "A good author is a rich author, and a rich author is a good author." The maxim is possibly apocryphal, but its point is proved in the bias of the paper's cultural reporting.[7]

Twenty-five years ago a writer who wished to present himself as a serious or important artist was obliged to strike the pose of an outcast. The cultural convention of the period insisted on the image of the writer (or painter, sculptor or playwright) as a man against the system. Condemned because of his truth telling to stand outside the palace walls, the writer was presumed to have forsworn the corruptions of Mammon in order to receive the certificate of

7. I don't mean to single out the *Times* for special mention. The paper's cultural reporting is no better or worse than that in most of the nation's larger newspapers and magazines. Much of what can be said about the *Times* also can be said about *Newsweek*. Time, Inc., the networks and *The Washington Post*. I cite the *Times* because it is so earnest and so solemn, almost German in its obedience to the protocols of wealth. The paper's Sunday magazine consistently publishes long and fulsome profiles of individuals who, no matter what their other accomplishments, share the distinction of having made a lot of money. The magazine obviously cannot address itself to poor individuals because poor individuals lack expensive houses in Connecticut that provide the obligatory backdrops for the obligatory photographs.

genius. The critics looked more kindly on a writer's work if they could imagine him subsisting poetically in an attic, warming himself at the meager fires of a moral and aesthetic principle, directing a fierce guerrilla campaign against the overstuffed complacency of the bourgeoisie.

No more. The romance of the artist as an impoverished seer no longer commands belief. Under the new cultural dispensation, poverty is merely poverty, and behavior once attributed to the vagary of genius has come to be seen as being both boorish and subversive. The phrase "a poor artist" stands revealed as a contradiction in terms. If the artist were any good (i.e., "a real artist" and not a charlatan) he would meet that editor's criterion of being rich. If he isn't rich he has failed the examination of the market and deserves no sympathy. The bias explains why the literary press so seldom prints unpleasant reviews of well-publicized books. An angry review constitutes an attack not only on a writer or a work but also on money itself, which, of course, is blasphemy.

Although well known as an artist, the late Andy Warhol perhaps deserved to be better known as a businessman. He arrived in New York in 1949, son of an impoverished Pennsylvania coal miner, and within a remarkably short time established himself as the court painter to a plutocracy that didn't care to make distinctions between art and fashion. On his death in 1987 Warhol left an estate estimated at $15 million; he had become publisher of a successful magazine filled with successful gossip, the owner of precious Manhattan real estate and a corporate entity capable of leasing its name and likeness to, among other institutions, Sony, Braniff Airlines, Barney's and the rums of Puerto Rico. Invited to pose for a flattering portrait in the pages of *Manhattan, Inc.* (in October 1984), Warhol told the interviewer how he had happened to come upon the subject of his art: "I asked 10 or 15 people for suggestions . . . finally one lady friend of mine asked me the right question, 'Well, what do you love most?' That's how I started painting money."[8]

On reading the criticism in the *Times*, or in almost any other established catalogue of taste, I think of Mrs. Eddie Gilbert, who, during the bull markets of the 1960s, was married to a Wall Street financier said to be the equal of Maecenas or Bernard Baruch. Like his counterparts in the middle 1980s, Gilbert welcomed the flattering attention of the press. At the zenith of his notoriety in 1965 (about a year before he escaped to Brazil to avoid arrest on charges of stock fraud) Gilbert invited a few hundred well-advertised people, none of whom he knew, to a dance in his new apartment on Fifth Avenue. On the advice of their press agents, who also supplied the guest lists, the arriviste capitalists in those days believed that dances at home were more dignified than dances in nightclubs or hotels. Gilbert also wished to display his wife, Rhoda, to her best advantage, and he had gone to considerable trouble and expense to embellish her with a suitable sheen of manner. Rhoda, unfortunately, had been born and educated in the Bronx. Within a week of his marriage Gilbert sent his wife to finishing school. He paid for French lessons and studies in elocution; he encouraged her to follow the fashion and learn table arrangement. None of it achieved the intended effect. The speech lessons failed to soften the edge of Rhoda's voice; she knew the wrong gossip about the wrong people, and she never learned how to make

8. Better than anyone else, Warhol had understood that the art market in the 1960s answered the medieval alchemist's prayer for a philosopher's stone that could change lead into gold. Suddenly there were more millionaires in suburban Omaha than there were paintings by Manet or Titian. The gentlemen needed symbols of their economic triumph—something to place on the wall as a marker buoy attesting to the presence of a sunken treasure. The trendier museums acquired enough of the new art to establish a kind of Federal Reserve System for the canvas equivalents of junk bonds. Within a year of Warhol's death, Sotheby's auctioned his collection of cookie jars (most of them made of cheap pottery) for $247,830. Lead had turned to gold, and art was anything with Andy's name on it.

polite conversation with Arthur Schlesinger, Jr., or Marietta Tree. Her lack of an instinct for clothes forced her to depend on magazine advertisements. Occasionally tearing a page out of *Vogue*, she would carry it into a department store and ask a salesgirl to furnish her with everything in the photograph—the dress, the jewelry, the shoes, the Dalmatian.

On the evening of her husband's dance Rhoda took it upon herself to show off the rooms of the apartment to those guests who had come to admire Gilbert's net worth. With a woman she clearly didn't know, Rhoda adopted a manner she presumably had seen in a Katharine Hepburn movie. As they entered the library, Rhoda, standing in the doorway, said, with large and theatrical gesture, "And this, of course, is the library." Her guest returned the remark by making a comment about the books. The furniture in her own apartment had been assembled by the decorator who also had advised Rhoda, and the woman recognized the device of buying the works of standard authors in sets of colored leather.

"Oh yes," she said. "Those green ones there. Isn't that Thackeray?"

"No," said Rhoda. "Thackeray is always blue."[9]

The remark sums up the aesthetics of New York's cultural establishment. Rhoda, of course, intended nothing ironic by her observation. Like the producers of the evening news, she had as much sense of humor as a bank statement. She might not know Arthur Schlesinger, Jr., or Marietta Tree, but she knew what she had paid for, and she knew what things cost. She acquired her opinions at

9. In the New York of the 1980s Rhoda Gilbert's mantle of newfound magnificence apparently has descended upon Mrs. John Gutfreund, formerly an airline stewardess in Texas who married one of the city's richest men. Wishing to give a genuinely impressive party for her new friends, Mrs. Gutfreund two years ago hired Blenheim Palace in England and sent cards of engraved invitation stating, simply, "Mr. and Mrs. John Gutfreund, At Home, Blenheim."

retail prices, and she asked nothing more of them except that they conform to the current fashion. Neither does Dan Rather.

Once having acquired the correct opinions, it is relatively easy to acquire a commensurate social rank. The innumerable journals devoted to the celebration of expensive people estimate that anybody bent on important social climbing in New York must allot at least $150,000 a year (for clothes, dinner parties, tickets to charity balls, etc.) to the cost of the ascent. William Norwich, a gossip columnist for the New York *Daily News*, established a point system in early 1985 under the heading A TOUCH OF CRASS—250 points for knowing Paloma Picasso or Christine Biddle; 125 points for knowing Susan de Menil or John Kennedy, Jr.; additional points for living at 1020 Fifth Avenue, owning a Chinese Shar-pei, belonging to the Brook Club.[10]

Although I can appreciate the distaste of older and quieter money for its new and louder companions, I cannot see that the objection has much to do with the lowering of taste or moral standards. Social rank has always been one of the pricier commodities sold in the great American department store, and the ceaseless revision of what constitutes society gives rise to the great American comedy that has been playing continuous performances since the beginning of the Republic. As one generation of parvenu rich acquires the means to buy the patents of nobility, it looks down upon the next generation of arrivistes as clubfooted upstarts. An air of condescension comes with the country house and the charge account at Tiffany's. Because "society" in the United States rests utterly and entirely upon money, the comedy is always the same,

---

10. Before too long I expect to see one of the networks, probably ABC, mount a weekly broadcast entitled *Tuesday Night Dinner Party*. The correspondents in the booth— demimondaines beyond the charm of their youth—might provide a chattering commentary on the value of the names in attendance, the age of the wine and the freshness of the flowers.

deriving its humor as much from the slapstick repetitions as from the dialogue.[11]

In the first chapter of *Who Killed Society?* Cleveland Amory arranges a chorus of elegiac voices reaching backward in time, all complaining about the corruption of taste and the loss of a golden age. He begins with Emily Post, saying, in 1950, that "in the general picture of this modern day, the smart and the near-smart, the distinguished and the merely conspicuous, the real and the sham, and the unknown general public are all mixed up together. The walls that used to enclose the world that was fashionable are all down . . . There is nowhere to go." Through a series of similar laments, from arbiters as melancholy and well-placed as Frank Crowninshield (1945), Elsie de Wolfe (1935), Mrs. Jerome Napoleon Bonaparte (1929) and Henry James (1906), Amory eventually comes to George Templeton Strong, writing to his diary in 1864:

> How New York has fallen off during the last 40 years! Its intellect and culture have been diluted and swamped by a great flood tide of material wealth . . . men whose bank accounts are all they can rely on for social position and influence. As for their ladies—not a few who were driven in the most sumptuous turnouts, with liveried servants—[they] looked as if they might have been cooks or chambermaids a very few years ago.

Further on, Amory quotes John Adams, proper Bostonian and second president of the United States, remarking on the boorishness of New

11. Elsie de Wolfe stated the fundamental principle in 1935, in her autobiography *After All*: "If one wishes to be in society, one must have money and spend it . . . let society feed on it, drink on it and gamble on it. Then one can be anything, go anywhere and do most anything one wants." Aileen Miehle, a gossip columnist known to readers of the *New York Post* as "Suzy," reformulated the proposition last year in the pages of Andy Warhol's *Interview*: "Money doesn't talk anymore," she said, "it shrieks."

York while on his way to the Continental Congress in the autumn of 1774:

> With all the opulence and splendor of this city, there is very little good breeding to be found. We have been treated with assiduous respect, but I have not seen one real gentleman, one well-bred man, since I came to town.

The playing out of the social comedy turns on the humorous confusions between the attitudes characteristic of "old" and "new" money. Old money quite naturally prefers to construe its privileges as matters of divine right, as proofs of a just, safe, happy and well-ordered universe. The distinctions between the two classes of money give rise to the momentous questions posed in the nation's gossip columns. In precisely what tone of voice does money speak, and to whom? What attitudes does it strike and what clothes does it wear? In the presence of what kind of money is it proper to take off one's hat? When, after being introduced to what other kind of money, is it polite to take off one's dress?

The differences between old and new money sometimes become blurred in breathless transmissions from the fashion press, but the reader will be on safe ground if he or she can remember the fourteen cardinal points at which the two sensibilities diverge. As follows:

1. New money is more fun to be around. Not being inhibited by what it was taught in school, new money can send a limousine across town at three a.m. for a chicken sandwich, two bottles of champagne and a complete set of Marcel Proust. Cash has been acquired recently enough to retain an element of magical surprise; nobody has reason to believe that it won't endlessly replenish itself, like the leaves on the trees or the market in Manhattan real estate.

   Old money is niggardly and defensive, as besieged as a train of covered wagons drawn together in a circle.

The surrounding desert every day becomes increasingly expensive and difficult to understand. The slums get nearer, and foreign governments acquire more impressive collections of bombs.

2. Older money inclines to understatement and the color beige. The heirs unobtrusively come and go, secure in the knowledge that nobody will ask to see their identification. It is never necessary to scream or push; somebody will be around to take one's order, pay off the judge and clean the filters in the pool.

    Feeling a need for higher resolution, preferably in prime time, new money inclines toward louder colors and brighter magnitudes of movement and noise.

3. The possessor of old money finds it possible to say, speaking of Frank Sinatra, "What's his name? You know who I mean . . . the guy who sings." A man with new money finds it possible to say, speaking of paintings by Picasso, "I'll take two of the blue ones."

4. Assured of its prerogatives, older money seeks to establish its genuine humanity. Thus its diffidence and its striving to appear no different from ordinary people, subject to the same desires, appetites, weaknesses and fears.

    New money, all too familiar with those weaknesses and fears, seeks to put as much distance as possible between itself and the small-time sorrows of economy class.

5. The old rich recognize one another by faint and subtle signals—a tone of voice, a name in common, a summer at Fishers Island, the placement of a bunker below the thirteenth green at a golf course in Southampton.

    The new rich recognize each other by comparing possessions, like children matching Christmas presents or exchanging bubble-gum portraits of ballplayers. Thus they must specify the exact length of the motorboat, the engine capacities of the foreign cars, the name of the cabinetmaker who made the dining room chairs.

6. For a man accustomed to money, the prospect of its absence seems romantic. Not having money might give a person something to do. "If we were poor, Agnes, I might have written a play."

   New money knows that it would have written better plays if it always had lived in the south of France.

7. When dealing with servants, old money takes pains to treat them as equals. One tries very hard to remember where they live, the names of their children, what happened to the poor woman's first husband. The old rich assume that, were it not for their interest, the servants might not achieve human form.

   More recently excused from using the backstairs and the freight elevator, new money cannot avoid treating servants as equals. New money shouts, makes scenes and haggles over wages. The cook is still real.

8. Old money finds its exemplars of good taste in the trunk of its remembered childhood and youth—the paintings in the hall of grandmother's house, the way the lawn looked that summer of Didi's dance.

   New money replicates the rooms shown in *Architectural Digest* and the pets seen in *Vogue*.

9. New money believes its money is as good as anybody else's money.

   Old money disagrees. "I mean, after all, what's the point in having a club?"

10. Old money waits patiently in line at theaters and sporting events; it believes doing so is somehow democratic, that it associates itself, however briefly, with the lot of the common man. Neither do they demand the largest box at the opera nor the seat directly behind third base. It is sufficient that they came at all.

New money insists on a table near the band. At a charity ball they judge the evening a success in proportion to the number and quality of celebrities on the dance floor.

11. Old money reads the gossip columns with faint amuse ment, as if reading Restoration comedy or an account of some remarkable tribe in the uplands of New Guinea.

    To the new money the columns are as serious as the stock market reports.

12. Traveling in Europe, old money welcomes the opportunity to stay at a not very expensive hotel. For short periods it will endure cold water and bad food, thinking of the temporary privation as both adventure and penance.

    Having seen more than enough of real people, new money takes three floors at the Gritti Palace.

13. Old money associates the idea of the good with an idea of moral virtue. Thus the wish to appear convincing in an old duck-shooting hat while talking to a potato farmer about the prospects for an early winter.

    New money associates the idea of the good with an idea of power. Thus the wish to look convincing while on a dais at the Waldorf, preferably seated next to Barbra Streisand or Ed Meese.

14. New money defines a decent profit as all one can legally get, extending the qualification "legally" to any action not punishable by a jail sentence. Old money can afford the luxury of distinction: a 30 to 50 percent return is acceptable; 50 to 100 percent might be thought a bit grasping; anything over 100 percent begins to smack of bad taste.

Besieged by the incessant din of exhortation—to buy, to spend, to feed—it becomes increasingly difficult for people to carry in their minds nobler conceptions of themselves than those offered for sale in the show windows of the id. To the extent that people come to think of themselves as objects, their appetites become more unnatural, their definition of "consumable goods and services" more catholic. The personal notices in the intellectual journals begin to read like offerings from specialty food stores. The following announcement, published with a box number in *The New York Review of Books*, strikes what has become the preferred tone:

> AM I BEAUTIFUL? Some people say so. WASP brunette, 5'8", Ivy-educated, professional success, graceful, competent, serene, non-smoker, non-bitch, nicely proportioned in body and mind. Too intelligent and alive to be happy with a loser or a numbskull. If you're a civilized, solvent, emotionally available, spiritual, epicurean man over 40, who loves his work and himself, seeking multi-dimensional companionship with grown-up woman, please write.

The other notices on the page set the same kind of uncompromising standards ("trim," "intelligent," "caring," "fond of fall walks and classical music," "sense of humor," "rich") as those set by the buyers for Saks Fifth Avenue.

Under the terms of a success that entails the minting of the human personality into the coin of celebrity, the bargain has a Faustian component. Wittingly or unwittingly, the chosen individual becomes available to the public feast. The celebrity receives the gifts of wealth and applause; in return the gossip columnists and writers of high-minded editorials can do what they like with the carcass of his or her humanity. Over years of living in New York I gradually came to dread the vanguard of the golden horde (known to the press as "the jet set" and "the beautiful people") who inevitably showed up on opening nights, at benefits and charity balls, at the exquisite little dinners for Katharine Graham or Swifty Lazar.[12] They were the people who had to know everybody and go everywhere, their eyes glittering with the stare of the hunter and the hunted. So urgent was their hunger, so desperate their fear of the void, that it was pointless to speak to them of a feeling or an idea. With a single trite phrase they could leach the meaning out of a book, a love affair, a death in the family. They seized upon the artifacts of the human intelligence as if they were tasting the shrimp, turning the thing briefly on the tongue of money or publicity. Most of the time they couldn't remember what it was that they were seeing or eating. Last year's play is like this year's play because what matters is not the meaning of the play but its value as a comestible. The same people make the same round of the same parties not with the hope of human discovery but with the hunger of wolves.

Toward the end of the 1960s, in a dream that still comes vividly to mind, I discovered myself in the gallery of a museum much like the Museum of Modern Art. In the midst of an enormous empty space the entire repertory company had assembled for what clearly was an important event. Dressed in evening clothes, the beau monde talked to itself in its customary way, filling the silence with urgent gossip and grazing disinterestedly on the elaborate

12. The New York repertory company has remained remarkably stable over the last quarter of a century, largely because the members of the company, like the actors in the Italian commedia dell'arte, wear masks of easily recognized personae—famous novelist, rising politician, this year's richest Greek (or Arab, Japanese or Californian), the season's bravest director, the current suffragette or *enfant terrible*, most enlightened swami, ingenue, young and happy couple blessed by fortune. The troupe divides the calendar into the sequences appropriate to children, and during the summer and winter holidays it pitches its tents in the resorts familiar to the readers of *Town & Country*. Although some of its members practice professions (usually as actors, dress designers or politicians) the company consists for the most part of people merely rich enough to pay for the *son et lumière*.

hors d'oeuvres being handed around on silver trays. Three of the four walls served as giant movie screens, each of them showing a sequence of full-length films; the fourth wall opened through an arch into what looked like a dark closet.

Early in the dream it became clear that the guests could wander in and out of the films at will. The films were in various genres: Hollywood epics, pornography, foreign films, historical dramas, situation comedies. Once within the world of the film the guests acquired appropriate roles, costumes and lines of dialogue. They could stay as long as they liked, playing courtiers in Elizabethan England, gangsters in the Havana of the 1940s, cowboys or Indians on the old American frontier, James Bond or the heroine in *The Devil in Miss Jones*. Between appearances they could return to the party and pick up the lines of meaningless talk, remarking on the weather in Calais or Fort Laramie.

In the middle passages of the dream I understood that these excursions weren't merely idle. Everybody at the party was playing a macabre game. All the guests were looking for an answer to a question that never had been asked. They were allowed only one chance to whisper the answer into the ear of the master of the revels, a man dressed in a ballet dancer's black sweater and tights. If they were wrong, the penalty was severe—just how severe gradually becoming clear as the ranks of the celebrated host began to thin.

The arch opening through the fourth wall led into a surgical amphitheater where gaily costumed catering staff stripped the flesh from those guests who had failed the quiz. The victims were strung up on bars covered in red velvet. Their remains, cut into modish squares and triangles, were served, on toast or *encroûté*, to the surviving guests. What was terrifying about the dream was the insouciance of the ladies and gentlemen who continued to eat. They pretended not to notice that anything was amiss. Their talk was as bright and as empty as before, as if their absent friends had simply gone on to another party. For several months after waking from the dream I could still see in my mind's eye three well-known New York hostesses conversing about the season's new literary masterpiece while delicately choosing an hors d'oeuvre from a tray decorated with the flesh of the author in whom they professed to notice the stirrings of genius.

The restlessness of the American experience lends to money a greater power than it enjoys in less mobile societies. Not that money doesn't occupy a high place in England, India or the Soviet Union, but in those less liquid climates it doesn't work quite so many wonders and transformations. In the United States we are all parvenus, all seeking to become somebody else, and money pays the passage not only from one town to the next but also from one social class to another and from one incarnation of the self to something a little more in keeping with the season's fashion. The American ideal exists as a concept in motion, as a fugitive and ill-defined hope glimmering on a horizon. No coalition, no industry, no source of wealth lasts much longer than a generation and nobody dies in the country in which he was born.[13]

Across the span of an American life the landscape changes as suddenly as the truths voted in and out of office. Towns disappear as if they were circus tents. So do names, neighborhoods, baseball teams, stock market booms, political alliances, economic theories, celebrities and new fortunes. Men start out in one place and end up in another, never quite knowing how they got there or why, per-petually expecting the unexpected, drifting across the plains with the tumbleweed until they run up against a business opportunity, a woman or a jail. Against the transience of things, wealth seems to offer the last best hope not only of democracy but also of grace. What else but money guarantees a man's safety and existence? His place in the world? His identity? What else but money, radiant and godlike, can ward off the pursuing shadows of death and time?

13. The entire canon of American autobiography can be read as a set of variations on the melancholy theme of not being able to go home again, of the family farm and the old neighborhood vanishing into the mouths of progress.

The illusion of perpetual journey appeals to the restlessness of the American spirit, and the metaphor of a browsing horde coincides with the nomadic impulse that has been one of the dominant characteristics of American life and society since the seventeenth century. The American tends to believe that movement, in and of itself, means something, and the United States remains an immigrant nation, still largely populated by people not yet convinced that settlement is desirable or necessary. About 20 percent of the population shifts its household or habitation in a given year. The poor come north in search of employment or government largesse; the rich go south in search of easier taxes and eternal youth. Farm children drift into the cities in hope of finding fame or fortune; city children trek into the countryside in search of nature and philosophy.[14]

Even within the supposedly stable structures of American institutions (corporations, the Army, media, universities) the interior movement is as restless as water. Promotions fail to accrue to the accounts of people who stay too long in one place, who exhibit the virtues of patience and loyalty. Money attaches itself to velocity, to the changing of occupations or employers at least once every six or seven years. Accomplished bureaucrats travel back and forth between business, government and the media. The airlines depend not only on the salesmen en route to conventions but also on the wandering magi who come and go between conferences about the

---

14. Michel Chevalier, an astute and observant traveler in nineteenth-century America, noticed that American society had the morale of an army on the march. Albert Jay Nock, in his *Memoirs of a Superfluous Man*, thought the country "had the morale of the looter, the plunderer." Describing his boyhood in the 1870s. Nock remembered that the freebooters who had carried off the heaviest sacks of spoil "were held up in the schools, the press, and even the pulpit, as the prototypal of all that was making America great, and hence as *par excellence* the proper examples for well-ordered youth to follow. '*Go and Get It!*' was the sum of the practical philosophy presented to America's young manhood by all the voices of the age." The current generation has abbreviated the same advice to the phrase, "Go for it."

national debt or the future of the Democratic Party. The country swarms with the tribes of itinerant journalists, with strolling actors, baseball players and military officers, with people forever keeping their "options open," conceiving of democracy as a pastoral browsing.

In the popular culture the romantic idealization of the nomad appears in the character of the cowboy or private detective who has neither wife, children, friends nor obligations to the state. The archetypal man on horseback (sometimes taking the persona of John Wayne, at other times the persona of Sam Spade, Phillip Marlowe, Erica Jong or Ronald Reagan) rides into a dusty town and discovers evil in even the crudest manifestations of social organization. The villains inevitably belong to "the system" (i.e., the same system opposed by all aspiring politicians), which, as everybody knows, is corrupt. On foot or on horseback, by helicopter or automobile, the hero pursues his quarry through a Mexican desert or urban slum. No matter what the plot or set decoration (*The A-Team*, *Terminator*, *Miami Vice*, the James Bond and Clint Eastwood movies, *Star Wars*, *Beverly Hills Cop*), all the stories take place in a moral wilderness that resembles the ruin of Beirut. The brutalization of the nation's theatrical imagination over the last thirty years has reduced the media to the telling and retelling of a Bedouin's tale. Whether cast as detective or CIA agent, the wandering hero finds solace in violence, and his story always ends with a killing; it's the only plot he knows.

The rich American bedouin (i.e., the equestrian classes supported by the aerodynamics of money) live not so much in a world of thought and imagination as in the world of fantastic dreams, a golden horde traveling on golden credit cards in search of the soul's pasturage. Absolute truth, like the city of El Dorado, shines in the eternal sunlight just beyond the next range of abstractions. In New York or Los Angeles, as well as in Omaha or Cheyenne, it is impossible to avoid the man who passed through Freud on his way to Castenada and Zen and who, even now, is getting together his belongings for the journey into Dr. Buscaglia's Utopian empire.

Such people speak of ideas and religions as if they were places on a map. They comprise the mass market for manuals of self-improvement, as if the self were a tent on which they could make constant additions and repairs. A man gives up his profession, quits his wife and apartment, and moves ten blocks south to begin anew, in a new suit and with a new address. It is easier to tell the same stories to different people than to think of a new story to tell.

If he can afford the price of the ticket, the nomad comes and goes with the seasons of his desire. He has neither the time nor the inclination to think very much about the people standing by the wayside. The settled townsman makes art, science and law; of necessity he must understand something other than himself. The nomad merely gathers together his tent, his music and his animals, and wanders over the mountain in search of next year's greening of America.

Transported from place to place at high speeds, suspended in a state of dynamic passivity, the American equestrian classes devote themselves to questions of technique and the relief of boredom. They can concentrate their attention on the logistics of going to Pasadena for the Rose Bowl or to Japan for the cherry blossoms, on the ceaseless repetition of gossip and description of scene. But when, after prodigious labor, they find themselves on the fifty-yard line or standing under the trees in Kyoto, they can think of nothing to say. They have no idea of what any of it means, only that it is there and somehow very, very important, or very, very glamorous or very, very sad.

So much of what constitutes American society has a tentative and makeshift character, as if it had been put together for a season and was meant to be consumed at the point of sale. The presidential candidate traveling thousands of miles in pursuit of office presents himself to the American imagination as a romantic figure somehow reminiscent of a medieval knight-errant. The immense labor and hectic movement of the campaign excites sympathetic interest. But the administration of the public trust—unless discovered to be corrupt and therefore allied to banditry—inspires boredom. Within a year of a Senate or mayoral election hardly anybody can remember the name of the candidate who lost. The society devours its past and melts down its history into the commercial alloys of docudrama.

Americans can outfit expeditions—to Vietnam, California or the moon—but we haven't much talent for settlement, and we lack a sense of history. An author counts himself lucky if the subject of his book stays in the public mind long enough to attract even passing notice during its first week in the stores. Among all our celebrities we reserve our fondest affection for sports heroes because these are the most perishable, the most easily and quickly digested, names that can be left under the seats with the empty popcorn box.

If American cities have the feeling of nomad camps, littered with debris and inhabited, temporarily, by people on their way to someplace else, it is because we conceive of our cities as arenas or gymnasiums. It doesn't matter what the place looks like as long as the goalposts have been set at the proper height and angle. The pilgrims come to perform heroic feats of the imagination, to compete in the social and economic equivalents of the Olympic Games.

Our delight in all things transcendental gives the lie to our reputation as crass materialists. We would rather believe in what isn't there, and we imagine that material acquisitions serve as tickets of admission to the desired states of immateriality. The United States is a nation of dreamers, captivated by the romance of metaphor. American painting depends on theories that explain the absence of paint. The successful pornographic magazines—*Playboy, Penthouse* et al.—publish literary essays that nobody bothers to read, the texts appearing as symbols of an imaginary conversation. The television image, itself a metaphor, goes forth to an invisible audience. Ideologues of all persuasions carry on fierce discussions of social justice while blithely stepping over beggars lying in the street. Like the government in Washington, the economy floats on the market in abstraction—on the credulity of people willing to pay, and pay handsomely, for a domino theory, a body count, a stock market tip, or any other paper moon on which to hang the images of their desire.

The transcendental bias of the American mind can turn the whole world into metaphor. Entire vocabularies of symbolic jargon—academic, bureaucratic, literary, scientific—describe entire kingdoms of nonexistent thought. The eloquent theories of politicians and professors of sociology seldom withstand the judgment of practical result because, more often than not, they are meant to be appreciated as tropes. The politicians seldom see the things their laws describe. They talk about housing and federal health insurance, about poverty and schools and public transportation, but they don't ride the subways or wait in line for food stamps. Like the view of New York City from a helicopter, the idea of racial equality is beautiful when perceived from a height or a distance. But if somebody is fool enough to interpret it in a literal-minded way, mistaking the deed for the word—well, then, obviously somebody is going to get hurt. When *New York Times* columnist Tom Wicker some years ago spoke encouragingly to the prisoners at Attica about the "inequities of the system," he offered them a metaphor instead of information. He presented himself as a critic of the established order, but the inmates, judging by appearances and Wicker's obvious connections and influence, thought that he spoke on behalf of the established order. A number of prisoners died because they took him at his word. Nobody told them that journalism is a form of fiction.

The most celebrated American writers, among them Henry Thoreau, Herman Melville, Walt Whitman and F. Scott Fitzgerald, seek communion with the unknowable and lose themselves in what Irving Howe once described as "the sacred emptiness of space." Alone in the void each man becomes both performer and pioneer, inventing his spirit as he clears the wilderness of his mortality. The modern school of writing follows the tradition into the thinner atmospheres of surrealism. In the novels of Robert Coover, Donald Barthelme and Thomas Pynchon, the narrative exists only to be discarded. Like a first-stage rocket it boosts the author's circus of ideas into the metaphor of space. Except in a figurative way, as representatives of abstraction, the people in the novels possess neither meaning nor substance.

Who else is the American hero if not a wandering pilgrim who goes forth on a perpetual quest? Melville sends Ahab across the world's oceans in search of a fabulous beast, and Thoreau follows the unicorn of his conscience into the silence of the Maine woods. They establish the antipodes of American letters. Mark Twain sends Tom Sawyer floating down the Mississippi. Henry James and Ezra Pound travel backward in time, to Europe as well as to the personae of lost civilizations; Ernest Hemingway and F. Scott Fitzgerald go in search of the perfect sexual encounter, the perfect phrase, the perfect kill.

4. THE ROMANCE OF CRIME

There are crimes that become innocent, and even glorious, because of their splendor, number, and enormity.

—LA ROUCHEFOUCAULD

TO THE EXTENT THAT MONEY BECOMES SYNONYMOUS with freedom, Americans learn to think of it as preliminary to the fact of existence. It is no wonder we so seldom question the means of obtaining money. We might make a public moan in the newspapers about the decay of conscience, but in private conversation, no matter what crimes a man may have committed or how cynically he may have debased his talent or his friends, variations on the answer "Yes, but I did it for the money" satisfy all but the most tiresome objections. The desire for wealth may not be an attractive passion, but as an explanation it answers for most modes of conduct that otherwise might be construed as stupid, cruel or self-defeating.

In the spring of 1982 the news media blossomed with sensational reports of a trial in which Claus von Bülow, a European and vaguely aristocratic gentleman from Newport, New York City and points fashionably south, stood accused of twice attempting to murder his wife. The trial and retrial provided topics of speculation for many months, but not once did I hear any of the cognoscenti in Manhattan wonder what might have prompted dear Claus to behave in the tasteless manner suggested by the prosecution. It was understood by everybody who took an interest in the trials that Von Bülow would inherit roughly $14 million in the event of his wife's death, and for that kind of money even a clergyman could be pardoned for making a mistake of etiquette.

Convicted of attempted murder at the first of his two trials, Von Bülow within a week of the jury's decision found himself much in vogue on the summer social circuit. His European sang-froid recommended him to those hostesses who liked to serve raspberry sorbet in rooms slightly darkened by an atmosphere of intimate sadism. By September Von Bülow's presence at lunch was as necessary to the afternoon's success as its subsequent description in the gossip columns. Only when he was ultimately acquitted did his luster fade.

Nothing so excites New York society as the presence of a notorious criminal. During the few months before he was shot to death in Umberto's Clam House, Joey Gallo, a well-known Mafia figure and *bon vivant*, enjoyed a brief vogue in Manhattan as a fun sort of person to have around. He occasionally appeared at Elaine's, a restaurant frequented by media celebrities. His arrival there inevitably caused the talk in the room to abruptly die away into the stillness that constituted the establishment's highest mark of esteem. Under ordinary circumstances the company made it a point of pride to preserve an attitude of indifference even when confronted with the entrance of Jack Nicholson or Liza Minnelli. But Gallo never failed to quiet them. The presence of a man so closely acquainted with killing evoked the same hushed reverence that accompanies the first news of a political assassination or a $3 billion deal.

Explaining the uses of notoriety to *The New York Times* in April 1987, Reinaldo Herrera, a well-known figure in the New York social tableaux, said he would like nothing better than to give a dinner party at which he could parade the presence of Ivan Boesky and Jean Harris.

"They would add spice to the evening," he said, "because she was convicted of murder, and he pleaded guilty to robbing nearly the world. But most normal houses don't have the great names at their fingertips."

A contributing editor to *Vanity Fair*, and husband to Carolina Herrera, the dress designer, Herrera belongs to the well-photographed sector of society so admired by the city's gossip columnists. It is a fashionable *ton* that accommodates itself to so many expensively dressed thugs, whores and thieves that a strict moral constructionist (i.e., a person wishing to avoid consorting with criminals) couldn't risk joining the company at any sort of gala entertainment at the Metropolitan Opera or the New York Public Library.[1]

The definition of money as the sublime good—because it can be turned into all other goods—results in the depreciation of all values that do not pay. What is moral is what returns a profit and satisfies the judgment of the bottom line. Freedom comes to be defined, in practice if not in commencement speeches, as the freedom to exploit. The commercial reading of the text of human nature gives rise to a system that puts a premium on crime, encourages the placid acquiescence in dishonest thought or deal, sustains the routine hypocrisy of politics and proclaims as inviolate the economic savagery otherwise known as the free market or freedom under capitalism. It is no accident that in a society that presumes a norm of violence, whether on the football field or in the conduct of its business, people

1. The chairman of the popular culture department at Bowling Green State University in Ohio, Ray Browne, provided the *Times* with additional social commentary. "Never before have Americans been so desirous of brushing up against the notorious and the wealthy," he said. "We're mad to be in the same room with them, to let a little of the danger they engaged in rub off on us. If they're well-born, like Von Bülow or the Mayflower Madam, well, that makes it even more wonderful because we're trading up."

speak of deals as "killings."[2] No other modern nation, whether capitalist or socialist, shares the American tolerance for crime. The indices of murder and theft in the United States (whether measured in absolute numbers or percentages) dwarf comparative statistics in England, France, West Germany and the Soviet Union.

At this late stage in the history of American capitalism I'm not sure I know how much testimony still needs to be presented to establish the relation between profit and theft. It seems to me that even a cursory reading of the newspapers would incline a fair-minded reader to confuse the arts of crime with national policy and standard business procedure.

As published in innumerable books and journals over the last twenty-five years by innumerable witnesses of all denominations—reporters, sociology professors, federal investigators, political candidates, novelists and retired mobsters—the proofs of the American talent for criminal enterprise could take up all the space on all the shelves in the Library of Congress. Even so, maybe a few representative cases in point will remind the reader of the ways in which criminal practice has become a matter of habit and routine.

1. The annual profits accruing to organized crime amount to roughly $50 billion, revenues equivalent to 1.1 percent of the gross national product and larger than those earned by all the American companies manufacturing iron, steel, copper and aluminum. The occasional arrest of Mafia dons provides pulp for the newspaper mills but only slight reformations of the means by which criminal syndicates launder money, debase the labor unions, and operate gambling, loan-sharking and narcotics rings. Despite the countless "wars on organized crime"

2. An executive speaking to this point in *Fortune* magazine (November 1985) said, "I'd say we have a mature, responsible attitude toward our major competitors. We'd like to see them dead."

declared by political candidates arriving in office, the rackets continue to prosper and multiply—not because the police cannot find the avowed enemy but because the American public doesn't much care whether the wars are won or lost. Most people accept the pervasiveness of criminal enterprise as calmly as they accept rush-hour traffic.[3]

2. Within the ranks of nominally legitimate business, "inventory shrinkage" (i.e., theft by employees) now amounts to well over $100 billion a year, up from $16 million in 1970. Bank embezzlements yield losses five times greater than the losses suffered in bank robberies, and in 1981 the sum stolen from accounts listed in computers amounted to $200 million.

3. As of June 1985 the Defense Department was advancing criminal investigations against forty-five of the hundred largest defense contractors in the United States. General Electric was under indictment for fraud, and both General Dynamics and the Pratt and Whitney Engine Division of United Technologies were explaining their bookkeeping practices to grand juries. Bills of criminal particulars could be extended to almost the entire list of clients doing business with the Pentagon. Testifying before Congress in 1983, Admiral Frank C.

---

3. *The New York Times* in the autumn of 1986 endorsed the re-election to the U.S. Senate of Alfonse D'Amato despite its concession that the senator probably hadn't told the truth to a committee investigating his ethical conduct. Senator D'Amato had said he didn't know that the Republican political machine on Long Island—an organization with which he had been long associated—required its dependents to kick back one percent of their salaries to the cost of election campaigns. The *Times* deemed the senator's testimony "incredible" but then went on to say that he was a wonderful fellow deserving the confidence of voters.

Collins, executive director of quality assurance for the Defense Logistics Agency, estimated that half of the money spent on military procurement ($47 billion that year) reflected the cost of products that had to be remade or thrown away. Among defense contractors with whom I have had occasion to discuss the subject over a number of years, almost all of them say that they have no choice but to inflate their costs. They explain that the system is crooked, that if they were to act as if it were honest, they would go broke.

The Wedtech Corporation in New York City provided fairly spectacular proof of their cynicism when, in the winter of 1987, it declared bankruptcy as a result of a well-publicized criminal investigation. Organized as a small machine shop, the company in a remarkably few years evolved into a substantial military contractor doing a lucrative business with the federal government. At a Republican dinner in New York in 1984 President Reagan proclaimed John Mariotta, Wedtech's principal owner, "a hero for the 1980s" and praised him for his resourcefulness, hard work and "commitment to excellence." The investigation showed that the company had forged invoices, bribed assorted politicians (among them a former commander of the New York National Guard) and earned its profit from contracts bestowed without competitive bidding.[4]

---

4. The use of the federal government as a factotum of the special interests is as traditional as it is nonpartisan. In 1873 an observer in Washington, complaining of the spoils system, compared the House of Representatives to "an auction room" in which everything that could be sold (land, water rights, tax exemptions, tariffs, etc.) "passed under the speaker's hammer." Between 1875 and 1885 the Central Pacific Railroad paid its political agents in Washington the sum of $500,000 a year.

4. As has been made plain by the continuing disclosure of graft within the municipal government of New York, the criminal practices habitual to the nation's defense contractors also dictate the terms in which the nation's cities do business with their suppliers of goods and services. Although similar conditions pertain across the whole of the American continent, New York offers the gaudiest examples of civic misrule.

A few days prior to Mayor Koch's election for a third term in the autumn of 1985, *The New York Times* pronounced him an exemplary candidate: "He has hired first rate officials, provided honest government, and greatly improved municipal management." By the spring of 1987 at least eight officials in the Koch administration had been forced to resign on various charges of fraud and theft. Donald R. Manes, formerly Queens borough president, had died a suicide rather than answer questions about his administration of the public trust. Geoffrey G. Lindenauer, a failed bagman and quack sex therapist, complained in court that when accepting bribes he "never got the right amount." Bess Myerson, a once-upon-a-time Miss America and formerly commissioner of the city's cultural affairs, resigned because she had used her office to seek favors for her lover. Among the city officials appointed by Mayor Koch the crime rate of 50 percent surpassed that of any identifiable grouping anywhere in the world. Ronald Goldstock, director of New York State's Organized Crime Task Force, said that "corruption was so embedded" in the city's construction trades that it would need a full-time agency to investigate the rigged bids, bribes and payoffs that sustain the magnificence of the city's real-estate boom.

Writing in *The Wall Street Journal* in July 1985, William J. Stern, formerly chairman and chief executive of the

New York State Urban Development Corporation (and in 1982 finance chairman of Mario Cuomo's gubernatorial campaign), observed, with a somewhat wry gift for understatement: "'Doing contract' is the central theme of New York politics and government. There is next to no difference here in attitude and action between most Democrats and Republicans. The real issues are: Who is going to get the state or city contract? Who is going to be the law firm getting the fee? Who is going to be the investment banker handling the debt issue? The commercialization of public service has made political labels such as Democrat and Republican irrelevant. Party rivalries are often mere gigs to be played around election time. The efficient management of our state conflicts with the commercial and political agenda of the one political force that matters here—the force I call the 'state insider commercial party.'"

5. The drug traffic in New York City generates $45 billion a year in sales, which is nearly twice the sum earned by the city's retail trades. Given the amount of unreported and untaxed income loose in the streets, it's nothing less than miraculous that any of the city's policemen manage to stay honest.

6. As of March 1987, 111 officials appointed to federal posts by the Reagan administration had been accused of ethical misconduct. At least six special prosecutors were maintaining offices in Washington in order to direct investigations of Reagan's friends and colleagues, among them the attorney general.

7. The routine thievery in Wall Street shouldn't need much annotation. Despite the occasional and much advertised instances of financiers found guilty of "insider trading" (most notoriously the fine of $100 million imposed on the arbitrageur Ivan Boesky), the money

earned from privileged information continues to feed and clothe a sizable population of well-dressed embezzlers. Experienced traders on the floor of the New York Stock Exchange say they can see mergers and takeovers reflected on the ticker tape several hours, sometimes several days, before the public announcement. The Securities and Exchange Commission in March 1987 published a study of 172 tender offers brought to the markets between 1981 and 1985; in every instance abnormal rises in stock prices (of between 39 and 50 percent) occurred three weeks before the bid was announced.

Elsewhere in what is known euphemistically as "the investment community," the larceny takes more decorous forms. E. F. Hutton in the middle 1980s was discovered to have been writing bad checks in the amount of $250 million a day over a period of twenty months. A good many other prominent banks and brokerage houses delay interest payments on their customers' accounts—skimming (in the manner of bookies or bartenders) a fractional profit from the money passing through the institution. Asked to define the apparently arcane workings of an investment bank, a partner in the firm, more forthright than most, said: "The customers come up every spring like the grass, and we mow them."

8. During the inquiry following the explosion of the orbiter *Challenger*, it was discovered that NASA and its subcontractors had conspired for years in the routine falsification of reports. The price of the contracts took precedence over the value of the astronauts' lives. Equivalent orders of value inevitably show up in the investigations of pharmaceutical companies that manufacture drugs known (by at least some of the people in the company) to induce harmful side effects. The selling of goods requires a talent for meretricious argument,

and over the last decade an impressive number of leading business corporations have admitted to various charges of murderous deception. In most instances the presiding executives received sympathetic votes of confidence from their boards of directors.

9. The IRS estimates annual tax evasion at $100 billion. The "underground economy" now consists of transactions amounting to $300 billion a year, and many of the nation's more prosperous individuals store their wealth in Swiss banks and offshore tax havens.

10. Banks charge as much as 20 percent interest on credit, which comes close to the standards set by Mafia loan sharks, and willingly put up the funds necessary to the financial extortions known as greenmail. Executives rob their investors and employees by taking huge salaries and benefits as well as by voting themselves handsome settlements when they abandon the company to merger or buyout.

11. Motives having to do with money or sex account for 99 percent of the crimes committed in the United States, but those with money as their object outpoint sexual offenses by a ratio of 4 to 1.

12. Although as common as football cheers, the incidence of cheating at American universities is seldom reported or mentioned in dispatches to parents and alumni. According to a survey conducted at the University of Indiana in November 1983, 32 percent of the students looked at somebody else's paper during an exam, 12 percent used notes and 55 percent discussed the exam with a student who had taken it earlier. That same year at Princeton University two students made a brazen show of cheating during a physics exam. Despite the university's honor code, none of their fellow students took the trouble to report the breaking of the rules.

Given a reason to do so, I expect that I could fill another hundred pages with random instances—statistical and anecdotal—of the criminal behaviors deemed normal in American society.[5] But I don't wish to try the reader's patience or manufacture an occasion for moral outrage. Nor do I mean to suggest that every American entrepreneur is a criminal. The proposition, fortunately, is absurd. If it were true, the nation would cease to exist, wrecked by the stupidity of the criminal's belief that the future can be bought or stolen instead of earned. What strikes me as indisputable, however, is the nation's placid acceptance of the criminal ethic. Separated from the Puritan principles of restraint, the dynamics of finance capitalism reduce every transaction to the logic of a short-term deal. The lack of any noticeable connection between virtue and reward (i.e., between big money and habits of honesty or thrift) gives rise to the perception that moral scruples cannot withstand a cost-benefit analysis.

The media periodically announce a Christian reawakening across the whole of the American continent, but it is hard to know what modes of conduct still can induce, either among bystanders or within the minds of the principal characters, the feeling of shame. Who would have the effrontery even to use so archaic a word? On behalf of what ethical interest group or moral lobby? Imagine a man who wishes to acquire a reputation for villainy. What, as a practical matter, could the fellow do? He could deal in child pornography or indulge a taste for cannibalism. For these crimes against what remains of the public conscience he conceivably would be cashiered from the ranks of respectable society. Offenses of lesser magnitude

5. At the University of Indiana some years ago a professor of modern history lectured her class for an hour on the rise and fall of Nazi Germany and then asked her students for their thoughts on the topic. A sophomore said he thought Hitler was a success, somebody who "had it all for twelve years at the top of the charts," which was about as much and as long as even the biggest rock musicians had a right to expect.

merely would invite the usual offers from the television and publishing syndicates.

Within the society at large the emphasis on crime results in the melancholy effect often noted on the nation's op-ed pages by people who speak of "prosperity without tranquility" or "a great society without a good life." So also within the lives of individuals. The definition of money as the sublime good, and the depreciation of all values that fail to pay, results in the deadened spirit so often showing in the eyes of the members of the nation's better clubs. Most people would rather not be criminals; if given any kind of option they choose work in which they can take pride and love in which they can find meaning, but above a certain altitude of after-tax income (say, as a convenient rule of thumb, $500,000 a year) even the most saintly individuals find it difficult to avoid becoming criminals—if not in practice, then in the attitude of contempt with which they habitually regard their fellow human beings. The rich find few reasons for not taking what they believe is owed them by right of their wealth. It is too easy to rig the stock price or buy the girl. Wealth translates so readily into the pleasures of despotism that the rich come to imagine that they can ignore the civil as well as the moral law.

Under the rules of a society that cannot distinguish between profit and profiteering, between money defined as necessity and money defined as luxury, murder is occasionally obligatory and always permissible. I remember this lesson being expounded to me by a dying entrepreneur with whom I once spent several days in a house overlooking the sea at East Hampton. He was then a man in his seventies, wheezing and sly, married to a woman much younger than himself who sent him postcards from Paris and Antibes. He had undergone abdominal surgery that spring and didn't expect to live through the autumn. "She'll marry a novelist," he said, "and they'll talk about the unimportance of money." We sat on deck chairs, listening to the crying of gulls. The view of the horizon moved him to a series of last meditations on the nature of a successful business deal.

As a young man he had inherited, together with his brother, a large and prosperous drug company. Shortly after World War II he had grasped the possibilities of what later came to be known as the multinational corporation, and he traveled through the poorer countries of the world setting up dependent subsidiaries. "Whenever possible," he said, "seek out dictators and avoid doing business with democracies. They're unstable. You have to bribe too many people, most of them at least twice. If something goes wrong, somebody to whom you just paid $10,000 stands up in whatever they call a congress in those places and makes a speech about American exploitation. Nobody stays bought."

Most of all, he liked to tell his story about the Muslim state in which both partners agreed to take 100 percent profit from their enterprise. For a few years the owners of the subsidiary, together with their medical advisers, were satisfied with the division of spoils, but then they began to think that maybe 100 percent wasn't enough, that maybe the Aladdin's lamp of twentieth-century technology entitled them to 200 percent. Having no wish to disturb the American corporation, they proposed to increase the price to their own people of aspirin and simple pharmaceutical compounds. The minister of health objected to this on humanitarian grounds, and for a period of several months nothing could be done. The prospect of negotiation improved when the minister was taken to a hospital for a routine appendectomy. Soon after he arrived on the operating table, the surgeons informed him that the hospital had exhausted its supplies of anesthetic. They were terribly sorry, of course, but there appeared to be some difficulty about the cost of manufacturing morphine. The surgeon apologized for the inconvenience while holding the point of a knife to the minister's belly, explaining further that the pain of incision would be so great as to put the minister in a state of shock, which, although momentarily unpleasant, would in itself be a kind of anesthetic. The minister agreed to the rise in price.

The story was presented to me as a cautionary tale, and whenever the old man arrived at the moral of it he was seized by a fit of choking laughter, flapping weakly at his knee in a gesture meant to convey dramatic emphasis. "By God," he would say, "that's what business is all about." He died in October, and his widow married an ambassador to the United Nations.[6]

Over the years I have listened to a good many variations of the same lesson, but none impressed as much as the one told me in a bar in Brooklyn by a prosecuting attorney aspiring to political office. Earlier that same afternoon he had been informed that the mob had scheduled the murder of a young woman whom he intended to bring as a witness in a narcotics case. Stirring his drink and listening vaguely to the Yankees game, he developed a thought that had occurred to him that morning on the Verrazano Bridge. Maybe he wouldn't tell the girl that she was apt to be killed. The news might frighten her, maybe cause her to recant her testimony. It was always possible his information was wrong or that the murderers might fail their assignment. If, on the other hand, his information was correct and the girl was murdered, then he would have a much stronger case in court. When I left him an hour later, he was still stirring his drink and turning over in his mind the moral niceties of the proposition. The Yankees had two men on base in the bottom of the seventh, and Phil Rizzuto was saying something about what it takes to make a great ballplayer. On Thursday of that week the girl was burned to death in a car. The U.S. attorney made a technical mistake with his evidence and succeeded only in convicting her killers on a charge of violating her civil rights. They served three

---

6. The nation's business schools teach similar tactics and strategies; in a handbook entitled *Attacking the Competition* the students of marketing are advised to "select the optimum combination of weapons and tactics for a specific battlefield." The illustration on the pamphlet's cover showed a fighter plane transfixed in a gunsight. In New York the expensive divorce lawyers welcome their new clients by telling them, "You are at war," and advising them to cut off credit, hide assets, hire detectives and take sworn statements from the servants. The late Roy Cohn used to say, "What have we got on him?"

years in prison, but the U.S. attorney earned a newspaper reputation as a crusading enemy of organized crime and was elected, in the name of the people and of good government, to higher office.

Within the American scheme of things the romance of crime is as traditional as the singing of "The Star Spangled Banner" at Yankee Stadium. The grand predators celebrated in the tabloid press and on network television (J.R. Ewing, Alexis Colby, the Mafia) stand in a long and glorious line of criminal descent that begins with the earliest pioneers and proceeds, with mounting degrees of subtlety and firepower, through the depredations of the fur traders, cattle and railroad barons, wildcat oil-well operators, the Harding administration and the Teapot Dome, the Chicago criminal syndicates, Joseph Kennedy and Huey Long, Lyndon Johnson, Charles Manson, Richard Nixon, John De Lorean, Ivan Boesky and others, as they say at Academy Award ceremonies, too numerous to mention.[7]

As often as not the violent man proves to be the hero of the piece, and both the good guys and the bad guys, if they're worth the respect of their horses, show contempt for an abstraction as bloodless and chicken-hearted as due process of law. The conventional American hero proclaims himself the enemy of the society that reared him, shrugging off the restraints of law, art, science and family as he wanders farther west into the wilderness of the Dakotas or the sea. His descendants crowd through the turnstiles of the nation's gambling casinos and orgiastic spas, resentful of the obligations necessary to the survival of civilization.

The winning of the West was accomplished by greedy and ignorant men looking for something for nothing, governed by their basest instincts, "praised for courage they didn't possess and eulogized for

7. The American businessman has become prime-time television's most popular villain, appearing as often as fourteen times a week in the role of murderer, bandit and cheat.

moral principles utterly foreign to them."[8] When the James gang held up the Kansas City Exposition in 1872 the local paper described the robbery as being "so diabolically daring and so utterly in contempt of fear that we are bound to admire it and revere its perpetrators." Two days later the paper compared the gang to the knights of King Arthur's Round Table. The national press in 1960 hit upon almost the identical tone of reverence as well as on the same romantic legend when applauding the arrival of the Kennedy brothers in "Camelot."

Of the robber barons of the late nineteenth century, Thorstein Veblen observed, "It is not easy in any given case—indeed it is at times impossible until the courts have spoken—to say whether it is an instance of praiseworthy salesmanship or a penitentiary offense."

The distinctions usually turn on the size of the numbers and the dress and deportment of the suspects. In the 1920s Al Capone granted an interview to the press in which he said, "Everybody calls me a racketeer. I call myself a businessman." Were Capone still alive he probably could count on steady employment as a more or less permanent guest on the Letterman show. Our society admires the successful criminal, and Capone could play the part of elder statesman—talking about the old days in Chicago, remarking on the ways in which the rackets had changed over the last sixty years, offering his opinion on the most sensational crime of the week. Imagine a garrulous old man, comfortably smoking a cigar

---

8. The quotation is from John Terrel's *Landgrab*, but it is representative. D.H. Lawrence, in an essay on James Fenimore Cooper's *Leatherstocking Tales*, observed of the American frontier that "men murdered themselves into this democracy." The presidential commission appointed in 1869 by Ulysses S. Grant to look into the disappearance of the Plains Indians summarized its findings as follows: "The history of the border white man's connection with the Indians is a sickening record of murder, outrage, robbery and wrongs committed by the former as a rule, occasional savage outbreaks and unspeakably barbarous deeds of retaliation by the latter is the exception."

Contrary to the romantic encounters seen in the movies, most gunfighters in the Old West preferred to shoot their enemies in the back with a rifle.

and astonishing the audience with his cynicism and depravity. Soon he would be on the lecture circuit, commanding fees of $15,000 to address the Young Republicans at Princeton and Yale.

The contemporary novelist Louis Auchincloss, in an interview following the publication in 1985 of his novel *Honorable Men*, said of the country's morals, "We've fabricated a society of wolves and coyotes. Why does anybody think we are better than we were in robber baron days?" He was referring to the stock market, but he could as easily have been talking about the media, or the real estate markets, or the workings of what passes for New York society.

President Reagan, of course, made of his sentimental realpolitik the marrow of his politics and administration. Like his principal ministers and speechwriters, he imagined a world ruled by men on horseback, a world in which innocent homesteaders always need to be rescued by Clint Eastwood. Attorney General Edwin Meese reserved the right to interpret the American Constitution as he saw fit and to ignore the judgment of the World Court with respect to American intervention in Nicaragua. The National Security Council, whether under the direction of Robert C. McFarlane or Admiral John Poindexter, granted itself the right to violate any law that interfered with its delusions of geopolitical grandeur.

The vast ransom paid to the Pentagon's armorers, the lines of diplomacy set forth in the Middle East and Central America, the brass-band jingoism implicit in the government's language, the shows of military splendor in Grenada and off the coasts of Libya and Lebanon—all the instruments of power agreed that only by force or the threat of force can men be made to obey the dictates of conscience or reason.

This belief was neither new nor unique to Reagan. During the Eisenhower administration, John Foster Dulles, a corporate lawyer turned Secretary of State, formulated the precepts of unremitting war. President Kennedy sought to prove the validity of those precepts in South Vietnam, imagining that he could endorse the removal of Ngo Dinh Diem with the impunity of a Mafia chieftain ordering the death of a pimp. President Johnson chose civilian targets for bombing raids meant to prove the credibility of the American wish for peace. President Nixon invented the "madman theory of diplomacy" as a means of showing himself as dangerous as any Shiite gunman and as willing to touch a match to the nuclear fire.

Over the last thirty years, the makers of American art and government have gradually abandoned their faith in a democratic future and the hope of a world in which practical men could afford to take seriously something so wimpish as the rule of law. The intellectual mercenaries attracted to Washington since the late 1950s have prided themselves on their toughness of mind, their lack of effeminate compassion, their willingness to sacrifice other people's lives to the purity of an idea seen at Harvard or the Los Angeles Country Club. The fierce courtiers applauding the geopolitical *tableaux vivants* of the Reagan administration bore an unhappy resemblance to the claque of militant professors who took part in the imperial pageants staged by the Kennedy and Johnson administrations. Like the advocates of the old war in Vietnam, among them Maxwell Taylor, McGeorge Bundy, Walt Rostow and Dean Rusk, the preachers of a new war in Nicaragua, among them Caspar Weinberger and Elliott Abrams, derived their zeal for adventure from the reading of books. They fondled the weight and heft of their threats as if they were boys playing with guns.

In December 1983, Senator Daniel P. Moynihan told an audience in New York that the example of the United States nurtured the causes of terrorism. The American "inattentiveness" to the rule of law, he said, "allows other states to believe that we will not hold them accountable to standards of civilized and peaceable behavior." He reminded his audience that in February 1982, less than six months after an Iraqi terrorist group had set off a bomb in a West Berlin restaurant, the Reagan administration removed Iraq from the official list of nations that support international terrorism. Because the United States at the time favored the side of Iraq in its war against Iran, the imperatives of realpolitik in the Persian Gulf nullified any pious claptrap about moral or legal sanctions. Justice Felix Frankfurter concisely stated the operative principle when, in 1914, as a young lawyer in the War Department, he was asked to research the question of whether the American occupation of Veracruz constituted an act of war. He replied that he didn't need to look through the statutes. "It's an act of war against a great power," he said. "It's not an act of war against a small power."

President Reagan's speech eight days after the release of the hostages seized on the TWA plane in June 1985 confirmed the senator's pessimism and the justice's cynicism. Before an audience of several thousand lawyers attending a meeting of the American Bar Association in Washington, Reagan denounced a confederation of "outlaw states run by the strangest collection of misfits, Looney Tunes, and squalid criminals since the advent of the Third Reich." He named as members of this coalition the nations of Iran, Libya, North Korea, Cuba and Nicaragua. He pointedly omitted any impolite reference to Syria, which, like Iraq, had been counted in the list of the world's villains until it could perform a service to the United States. A few months later, of course, the President was himself engaged with his own cadre of fanatics (most notably Lieutenant Colonel Oliver North) in a secret arms deal with precisely those Iranian outlaws he so scornfully denounced.

The Iran-contra hearings in the spring and summer of 1987 proved beyond a reasonable doubt the Reagan administration's contempt for the law. In June of that year Representative Lee H. Hamilton, chairman of the House investigating committee, offered a summary of what had been learned over the first six weeks of the hearings:

> An elaborate private network was set up to carry out the foreign policy of the United States.
>
> Private citizens, many with divided loyalties and profit motives, sold arms and negotiated for the release of American hostages.

The President approved the payment of fines—or funds, rather—to terrorists, to secure the release of hostages. Senior officials did not know, and chose not to know, important facts about policy.

A National Security Advisor and an Assistant Secretary of State withheld information and did not tell the Congress the truth concerning U.S. involvement in the contra supply operation and the solicitation of funds from third countries.

When official involvement with the contras was prohibited, officials of the National Security Council raised money, helped procure arms and set up a private network to ship arms to the contras.

An official, designated by the Secretary of State as a loose cannon, carried out highly sensitive negotiations to obtain the release of American hostages. He gave the approval of the White House to a plan to depose Saddam Hussein [president of Iraq] and to go to war with the Soviet Union, in defense of Iran.

This same official participated with others in an effort to rewrite chronologies, altered critical documents and organized a shredding party to destroy those documents.

The Senate and House committees had taken testimony from a parade of witnesses, most of them as belligerent as they were inept, all of them claiming to have acted in the name of President Reagan's plenary power to do as he pleased. They might as well have cited the divine right of kings.

Reagan's remark about "misfits" and "Looney Tunes" drew loud laughter and long applause from the lawyers, who presumably were relieved to hear their president espouse a view of the world in which their services no longer would be required. The role of lawyers in the American wilderness always has been somewhat ambiguous, and the Bar Association continues to look for the proofs of its conscience. The effect is often comic. At its midwinter convention in

New Orleans in 1983 the ABA endorsed the principle of *omerta* traditional among partners in a criminal syndicate. By an overwhelming majority the delegates passed a rule requiring the membership to keep silent about the crimes of its clients. The rule applied to crimes committed in the past as well as those in which the client might currently be engaged. The ABA recognized only two circumstances in which lawyers might be permitted to speak: when the lawyer possessed prior knowledge of the client's intent to commit murder, and when the lawyer had no other means of collecting his fees. As now established by the ABA, the operative ethic permits a lawyer to hold his client to ransom but not to take actions that might prevent or discourage him from looting a corporate treasury or setting up a securities fraud.

Anybody who spends any appreciable length of time in the company of the rich becomes accustomed to their peculiar coldness. Once money comes to be understood as the staff of life, obviously nobody has enough of it to squander on anybody other than oneself. The rich object to the very thought of other people also becoming rich—crowding the golf courses, commanding tables at "21," taking up too much of the available light, space, air and publicity. Nothing comforts them as much as the reading of the obituary notices or listening to the reports of bankruptcy.

The old tycoon who expounded the ethos of capitalism that afternoon beside the sea in East Hampton always was glad to receive news of somebody else's misfortune. I still can see the glittering stare in his eyes when, on another afternoon, his nominal best friend, a Panamanian oligarch whom he had known at Princeton in the 1920s, told the story of his lost hacienda. The oligarch's estates were large. In the middle 1970s another general came to power as the presiding despot in Panama. Soon after his accession, he invited himself to lunch at the oligarch's principal residence, a ranch of 50,000 acres commanding a fine view of the Atlantic Ocean. They talked amiably of this and that, and then, as he was making his farewell, the general deigned to notice the beauty of the oligarch's estate. Almost as an afterthought, as he was stepping into his helicopter, the general said he thought so well of the place that he had decided to appropriate it for his own use and the greater glory of the newly revived Panama. The oligarch told the story with tears in his voice. The old tycoon listened without comment, his mouth drawn into a thin line, the expression on his face as cold as stone. The god had been made manifest in Panama, and the old tycoon's excitement was so intense that he didn't dare speak for fear of betraying his delight. To his friend of fifty years he could say only, "Too bad."

By and large the rich have the temperaments of lizards, and their indifference to other people's joy or sorrow bears comparison to the indifference of the stars in the constellation of Orion. Within the generation old enough to detest the enthusiasms of the 1960s—on the ground that the kids were letting their hair grow too long, taking too much pleasure in their sexual experiments and not showing enough respect for property—it was common for fathers to receive the news of their children's troubles with an air of contentment. At the Shinnecock Hills Golf Club in Southampton one afternoon in 1967 I heard a man say how happy he had been to learn that his son was in a Mexican jail. The father had decided not to try to make the boy's bail. "A few weeks in a goddamn jail," he said, "might teach him what's important." The club membership displayed much the same attitude when, on the day after Robert Kennedy's assassination, it was decided, by voice vote, not to lower the American flag to half mast.

Among people in the advanced states of the obsession with money, the symptoms of belief can also result in hysterical laughter. Though it isn't uncommon for women everywhere else in the world to calculate the net worth of their prospective husbands, the New York systems of accounting aspire to a precision that might be thought impolite in the suburbs. A woman I have known for many years who, in deference to the laws of libel, I will call R., required her third husband, twenty years older than herself and troubled by a heart condition, to submit to a physical

examination prior to their marriage. She took the further precaution of promising the doctor a percentage of the estate if she
could read a copy of the report. Satisfied that her new husband
would die within three years, she went gladly to the ceremony on
a yacht anchored off the coast of Florida. For eighteen months she
endured the life of exile in Miami Beach, sending notes on Cartier
paper to her friends in New York (most of them dress designers)
complaining about the heat and lack of first-rate merchandise in
the stores. Her husband did her the kindness of dying sooner than
had been expected, leaving her in the possession of five hotels,
an interest in the ownership of a dog track and an income of
$1 million per annum. So great was her joy at the coming to pass
of this miracle that when she telephoned her friends in New York
she could do nothing but giggle. For a week after the funeral her
friends would pick up the phone, and there would be R., chuckling
and gurgling to herself, as inarticulate as an infant.[9]

By way of idle amusements, the rich most enjoy the refined
forms of gossip that attain the sharpness of slander. Most American
gossip is about success, a means of putting clothes on money, but
slander subtracts from the reputation, and therefore from the net
worth, of the person under review. Skillfully deployed, the malev-
olent adjective becomes a knife with which to commit a bloodless
kind of murder. The willingness to believe the worst of people mur-
murs like a basso continuo below the flutelike melody of cocktail
talk. Everybody welcomes the news of failure—not only of their
enemies, which would be reasonable—but also of their clients and
friends. The rumors rise like the sighing of the wind. Who got killed

9. Bess Myerson, the former Miss America and commissioner of cultural affairs for
the city of New York, kept a diary during her second marriage to which she confided
the thought that if her husband "would die I would have the safety and security of
a house . . . and I would then reach out to new experiences." Speaking of the same
husband she also told her diary that he was "more like a thing I must manipulate."

last week in the market? Whose marriage has been destroyed? Whose children have been seized in the park by a divorce lawyer?

During the early 1960s I had occasion to attend a number of small dinners in New York for President John F. Kennedy; later in the decade I attended similar dinners for senators Robert and Edward Kennedy at the same Fifth Avenue address, and always I was struck by the aura of banditry that I also had seen flickering around the heads of Joey Gallo and Frank Sinatra.

President Kennedy pursued women with an obsessiveness that to his familiars was a matter of common knowledge and amusement from the first days of his administration. They spoke of his indiscretions with admiration and approval, their salacious gossip magnifying his image as Prince of the Realm. It was as if Prince Hal had brought with him into the White House the bacchanalia of the Boar's Head Tavern. In New York during the thousand days, it was impossible to go to dinner among the forward elements of society (i.e., with journalists passing through town on their way from Washington to Hyannisport, with White House advisers and Broadway directors, etc.) without listening to someone tell yet another amusing story about yet another actress who had discovered (much to her wonder and surprise) that politics wasn't always as boring as deficit spending or Berlin. The atmosphere of revelry, of the clamorous progress through cheering peasants in a hospitable countryside, so thoroughly pervaded the Kennedy administration that it was deceptively easy to think of it as frivolous. So many people were beguiled by Kennedy's charm that they neglected to remark on the grim rapacity of his desire or his resemblance to the Minotaur. From a distance I had admired Kennedy's strength and youthfulness. In a room crowded with the beau monde in New York, he seemed as absent as he was present, exhausted by the demands of his distracted appetite. It occurred to me that he might have aspired to a much nobler ideal of the presidency, and I thought of a stag brought down by hounds.

On the few occasions when I have come across Senator Edward Kennedy in a private circumstance I have found him, as in his public persona, besieged by a similar crowd of flatterers and hangers-on. In particular I remember a birthday party given for Senator Kennedy in the spring of 1963 by Stephen Smith, his brother-in-law and newly appointed campaign manager. Not knowing more than a few of the other guests in the room, most of them celebrities of large magnitude, I spent some time talking to a girl who had come to the party with the hope of making of herself a birthday present. As we watched Kennedy blunder back and forth across the dance floor in a game of bullfighting (the band playing the *paso doble* and Smith holding the jacket of his tuxedo as if it were the *capa torera*), the girl fretted about her clothes and hair. She had dyed her hair blonde for the occasion, but she had begun to think that this was a mistake. The senator's wife was blonde, and maybe he was tired of blonde; maybe he wanted something in a redhead or a brunette. No matter how often I reassured her, she refused to be consoled, worrying whether her dress was pretty enough, or the wrong color, or too obvious, or whether the senator had any known preference in fetishes. During the entire conversation she never took her eyes from Kennedy's person. The voracious emptiness in her face was as deadly and as terrifying a thing as I had ever seen. I understood what the Greeks had meant by the Gorgon turning people into stone.

This kind of adoration has an unhappy effect on the people subjected to it, and I can imagine that Senator Kennedy must be sick of being admired for reasons that have nothing to do with himself—because of his name, because people look to him for miracles, preferment or relief from boredom. Suetonius describes the Emperor Tiberius during the first years of his reign as a just and able administrator of the Roman state. But he soon became disgusted with the fawning of the court and with the business of governing a people who had so little respect for themselves that they could proclaim him a god. Corroded by self-loathing, he retired to Capri, where, during the last nine years of his life, he abandoned himself to the sexual atrocities for which he has been chiefly remembered.

In the iconography of his person, Senator Kennedy embodies the whole of his family's history and character—its courage and licentiousness as well as the ruthlessness of its ambition, its corruption, laughter, greed, wealth, privilege and cruelty. His place in the public imagination he owes to the death of three brothers, two of them assassinated. He can talk about the post office or the direction of the wind, but even the whisper of his voice brings to mind not only the despairing alcoholism of his wife and the drowning of Mary Jo Kopechne, but also the suicide of Marilyn Monroe, the drug addiction of the nephew for whom he stood as surrogate father, his own father's thievery and the rumors of sexual orgy that run like a soft counterpoint through the ballad of the Kennedys. The iconography has little to do with Senator Kennedy's own character or attainments. The armorers of the media force it over his head like a terrible helmet, both monstrous and beautiful. Senator Kennedy can do nothing to dislodge it. He inherits the reputation, the legend and the iron mask of power.

To the extent that Senator Kennedy remains invisible, he can be defined as a gravitational field, drawing to himself devotees who imagine that their own lives acquire meaning only insofar as they fall within the sphere of a magical object. The same kind of adulation attaches itself to rock stars, to celebrated criminals and to large denominations of money.

As a child growing up in the precincts of wealth, and later as a college student, newspaper reporter and resident of New York's Upper East Side, I got used to listening to the talk of financial killings and sexual misalliance that animates the conversation of the rich and the familiars of the rich. Partly this is a matter of precedent. Some years ago, intending to write a history of the great American fortunes assembled during the last decades of the nineteenth century, I made a preliminary study of maybe fifty families that had accumulated substantial holdings prior to 1900. Following the descent of the money through the lines of inheritance to the year 1960, I noticed that with notable but relatively few exceptions (among them the Rockefeller, Mellon and Harriman families) the lives of the heirs were marked by alcoholism, suicide, drug addiction, insanity and despair. The founders set up the financial pedestal for what, in a British or French circumstance, might have become a cultured and civic-minded oligarchy. But the mass of American wealth failed to combine in the forms of a European establishment. Only a handful of the heirs achieved, or even bothered to attempt, distinction in politics, the arts, medicine, literature, diplomacy or the law. For the most part they squandered the spoils in gestures of spectacular dissolution.[10] Which isn't to say that all the heirs lost all the money. Those families prudent enough to place their assets in the safekeeping of trusts prospered by reason of simple arithmetic. Between 1900 and 1960, in the midst of the most extraordinary prosperity known to the history of the world, the mechanics of compound interest and the accumulation of value in stock and bond portfolios guaranteed the preservation of sums sufficiently large to withstand even the most single-minded and fanatic raids on the principal.[11]

10. They continue to do so. Almost every week the newspapers publish reports of quarrels in which the heirs to the family fortunes succeed in murdering one another. In Fort Myers, Florida, a court convicted a young man of placing a bomb in his mother's car, in a Chicago suburb another angry heir hired a Mafia thug to dynamite his brother. 11. On examining the list of the 400 richest people in America as published in 1987 by *Forbes* magazine, Lester Thurow, dean of MIT's Sloan School of Management and a perceptive economist habitually curious about the arithmetic of social class, discovered that all of the 82 wealthiest families, and 241 of the wealthiest individuals, had inherited all or a major part of their fortunes. He also noticed that the $166 billion in business net worth held by the 482 families and individuals named in *Forbes* provided them with effective control over $2.2 billion in business assets—about 40 percent of all fixed, nonresidential private capital in the United States. The richest 10 percent of the American population (i.e., those families earning more than $218,000 a year) now hold roughly 68 percent of the nation's wealth.

In its more subtle variations the romance of crime is hard to distinguish from suicide. Because the rich regard themselves as their own most precious objects, they believe they can injure nothing more valuable than the masterpieces of self. The will toward self-annihilation is, of course, a familiar human characteristic. The plays of William Shakespeare and Sophocles, the history of the Roman Empire, the civil wars in Ireland and Lebanon, all attest to man's predilection for murdering himself. Even so, and without meaning to belittle the accomplishments of other nations at other times and places, I think it fair to say that something in the modern American spirit reveals a peculiar genius for the self-inflicted wound. When I read about the infant mortality rate in New York or Chicago, I think about the markets for pornography and the random violence in the streets. When I read about the poisonous chemicals flowing into the James River or consider the bitter effects of the American folly in Vietnam, I think of the enormous numbers of American schoolchildren who cannot look forward to a decent meal or a mediocre education. The parallel stupidities bring to mind Edith Wharton's terrible remark about the American plutocracy in the Gilded Age: "A frivolous society can acquire dramatic significance only through what its frivolity destroys."[12]

As a boy I occasionally watched my grandfather play bridge at the Pacific Union Club in San Francisco. He played for large stakes, but he thought it unsporting to look at his cards before making an opening bid. He never had trouble rounding up a fourth, and for the last twenty years of his life he lost—not only at bridge, but also at golf, cribbage and piquet—roughly $5,000 a day. He lacked the courage to resist the will to lose, and nothing pleased him so much as the

12. The American war in Vietnam, waged for almost no other reason than to sustain the heroic images of three presidents, resulted in 50,000 American dead and 300,000 American wounded. It also imposed on the economy a ruinous distortion from which it is yet to recover and destroyed a generation's belief in the legitimacy of the American government.

chance to dissolve himself in the acid baths of the polymorphous perverse, striking simultaneously at both time past (the money inherited from his father) and time future (the money he might otherwise have given to his children).

Again, as with so many other phenomena noted in this book, I thought my grandfather's talent for losing was an aberration confined to a particularly angry individual belonging to a particularly careless social class. During the decade of the 1960s I learned to associate the impulse—expressive of an otherwise inarticulate rage—with the prerogatives of wealth. The assassination of John F. Kennedy offered the first of many demonstrations.

Kennedy appeared before the public as the *beau ideal* of the American dream. Handsome and charming and young, he represented everything that could be said in favor of inherited privilege. The adulation bestowed on his person had less to do with his character and intelligence than with his joyful consumption of the world's goods. So gracefully did Kennedy devour the best of everything the society had to offer—women as well as houses and sailboats and Harvard professors—that he restored to the magazine advertisements a sense of redeeming social purpose. Although warned of a probable attempt on his life in November 1963, Kennedy refused the unsporting precaution of a bullet-proof limousine on his last motorcade through Dallas. Like the heirs to so many other American fortunes, he died in defense of the proposition that money buys an option on immortality.

In New York in the 1960s the feats of self-annihilation performed by the children of affluence kept pace with losses inflicted on the American troops, most of them poor, recruited to fight the war in Vietnam. At about the time that Kennedy was killed in Dallas the New York repertory company of "beautiful people" began to sustain heavy casualties. The heir to an automobile fortune died of an overdose of heroin in a transient hotel west of Columbus Avenue; a woman known for the trendiness of her political views was hacked to death in London with a blunt knife by the eighteen-year-old son whom she had seduced in the stoned aftermath of a Beatles concert. A reporter whom I had known at the *Herald-Tribune* began riding the uptown subway in search of his final story. He made it his practice to walk into bars in the vicinity of 125th Street, and then, in the silence attending the arrival of the only white man seen on the premises in ten years, he would say, while loudly slapping a $20 bill on the bar, "I want to buy a drink for every nigger in the house." To the reporter's wonder and disappointment, nobody ever assaulted him or even chided him with a harsh word. In all the bars in which he offered himself as a victim over a period of five years the patrons unanimously refused the bait of blood sacrifice. Mostly they thought the gentleman crazy, a kind of holy fool with whom it was proper to deal as gently as with a customized Cadillac. Somebody always found him a taxi; sometimes one or two people rode downtown with him to make sure he didn't present himself as Christ in a really dangerous neighborhood.

The sense of something going very wrong made itself felt in communiqués from every sector of the existential front—not only in the reports from Saigon and Watts but also in the gossip current in New York's more expensive drawing rooms and restaurants. The trendiest hostesses entertained a succession of prophets announcing ways out of what had come to be seen by 1968 as a cul-de-sac. The decade had opened on the prospect of limitless horizons, but in less than eight years the long vistas of idealism had shown themselves to be so many *trompe l'oeil* painted on the walls of the media. The counterculture's music of love and flowers was transposed into a theme for police sirens; the promise of "freedom now" tethered the faithful to the posts of sadomasochistic sexual fantasy or led them into the cages of drug addiction (no less cruel than the tiger cages reserved for political prisoners in Hue). The dream of social reform ended with the mean-spiritedness of a government bureaucracy eager to punish the poor for their indolence and presumption.

The decade failed to make good on its promises, and the children of affluence (by then numbering in the many hundreds of thousands) found themselves forced back on the diminished sensibility and chronic disappointment characteristic of their class. In the joy of self-destruction, of course, the victim discovers that over the kingdom of his own spirit and his own flesh he can exercise the powers of a god. Given a decent allowance he can buy enough props and hire a large enough cast of supporting players to stage the long-running and unabridged production of his own Götterdämmerung.[13]

It's a matter of substituting the lesser for the greater pleasure, accepting the excitement of the moment of dissolution in lieu of a long and patient working toward the architecture of an idea, a marriage or a life. The *jeunesse dorée* at the Hotchkiss School in the middle 1950s summarized the deception in the phrase, "If you don't think you can win, make it look as if you didn't try." The pleasure of undoing is more delightful in the company of other people bent on the same purpose, especially if everybody present has something of value to lose—money, reputation or force of intellect. They talk about their prospective ruin as if they were children going to a birthday party. Most self-regarding American cities provide innumerable sets and locations for the ritual performance of self-sacrifice, but the commercial anonymity of most bars and massage parlors discourages patrons who understand, if only dimly, that the entertainment doesn't have very much to do with drugs, alcohol or sex. They seek the company of their peers, to whom they can say, by implication if not in so many words, "We are all in this together, if I get drunk, then so will you get drunk, and tomorrow we will

13. The psychoanalysts have noticed that people brought up in rooms empty of feeling often turn their rage inward, directing it against their more human selves and imitating the forms of cruelty particular to the authority who did them the most harm. The observation pertains both to the Harlem slum child, borrowing the methods and sensibility of the police, and to the children of the rich indoctrinated in the techniques of withholding love. In 1986 American police departments reported 40,000 teenage suicides, most of them committed by children born into relatively comfortable circumstances.

know we have wasted an equivalent value and committed the same crimes against our hope of the future." The orgiasts in Beverly Hills play sexual charades in large houses, or arrange variations of a treasure hunt through a sequence of cars, apartments and hotel suites. Their counterparts in New York have a talent for abstraction, and they distill the essence of orgy without having to go to the trouble of getting undressed. In the bars and nightclubs frequented after midnight by trendier crowds, the guests study one another across the white tablecloths, their eyes cold under the often-glittering surfaces of their paranoia. The talk drifts across the chronicle of defeats— marriages dissolved, contracts canceled, children lost. Even those among them who have become famous in the eye of the world (i.e., to the readers of "Page Six" of the *New York Post*) do not think they have been granted permission to exist. Whether men or women, they have about them the air of the lost boys in Peter Pan. As the night gives way to the early hours of the morning, the inmates watch the door with mounting desperation, as if waiting for the arrival of somebody to give them birth. The sadness of three o'clock in the morning consists in its primitive superstitions. The watchers in Soho, or in any other of the thousand vantage points offered by the nation's roadhouses and gambling casinos, have returned to the smoke of the Neolithic cave. The time is 3000 B.C. and the half-men crouched over their fires and listening to the wind from the glaciers feel themselves worthless, outcast, unredeemed. They await the arrival of a god.

5. SOCIAL HYGIENE

Money, which represents the prose of life, and which is hardly spoken of in parlors without an apology, is, in its effects and laws, as beautiful as roses.

—RALPH WALDO EMERSON

Fresh air and innocence are good if you don't take too much of them, but I always remember that most of the achievements and pleasures of life are in bad air.

—OLIVER WENDELL HOLMES, JR.

AT THE PACIFIC UNION CLUB IN SAN FRANCISCO the kitchen staff scours all the coins brought into the building by members tainted with the commerce of the streets. Only after the coins have been thoroughly polished do the waiters presume to offer them as change on silver trays.

Rituals similarly devout obtain in every quarter of American society—not only in the better banks, where the tellers always present new currency, but also in every financial institution subtle enough to disguise the provenance of the numbers so primly arranged on balance sheets and computer screens. The laundering of money is a large and profitable industry, employing hundreds of thousands of workers (accountants, lawyers, investment managers) who, like their colleagues in the criminal trades, send millions of dollars every day to the purifying baths in Switzerland, Grand Cayman and the Bahamas.

I cannot think of any other people as obsessive as Americans about the ritual washing of money. It is as if we know, somewhere in the attic of our Puritan memory, that money is a vile substance—ungodly and depraved. To an Italian, as to a Czech or Brazilian, the fine distinctions between clean money and dirty money belong to the chemistries of the absurd. Money is money, and there's an end on it.

Americans worry about money's deportment because not only do we believe one's money is one's self but we also believe that an American is by definition always and forever innocent. The Puritans arriving in Massachusetts Bay thought they had regained the states of innocence lost to Satan by generations of corrupt and inattentive Europeans. Their heirs and assigns still hold to that presumption. Foreigners commit crimes against humanity. Americans make well-intentioned mistakes. Foreigners incite wars, manufacture cocaine, sponsor terrorists and welcome Communism. Americans cleanse the world of its impurities.[1]

True, our corporations occasionally might prosper because of our talents for price-fixing, theft, loan-sharking and fraud, but such crimes, being American and therefore subject to our special arrangement with Providence, can be understood as temporary breakdowns in the otherwise flawless machinery of the American soul. The fault is never one of character or motive.

---

1. The presumption is traditional. The earliest Americans believed they embodied what subsequent generations would call "the last, best hope of mankind." In the words of a characteristic speech delivered at Covington, Kentucky, on July 4, 1850 by William Evans Arthur, apprentice congressman and judge, America was "the ark of safety, the anointed civilizer, the only visible source of light and heat and repose in the dark and discordant and troubled world."

So extraordinary a dream of innocence condemns us to the ceaseless rituals of purification that set the terms of the national political debate, shape the contours of the language and define most of what passes for American literature and education. If the laundering of money is the most conspicuous of the nation's rituals, it is the practice of philanthropy that most vividly expresses the American genius for the arts of ablution. Having granted ourselves the power to purify the world, we further assume that by our works and good intentions we can change even money into a detergent. Our generosity is both legendary and undeniable. None other among the world's peoples gives so much to their fellow men. A good part of the contribution, conceivably the bulk of it, undoubtedly meets the standards of purity set forth by the metaphysical equivalent of the Food and Drug Administration. But a considerable sum of the largesse serves to clothe the criminal nakedness of the donor in robes of virtue.

On advice of public relations counsel, John D. Rockefeller, in the early years of the twentieth century, undertook a program of large-minded philanthropy in order to revise his image as a small-minded scoundrel. Generations of speculators in the issues of immortality have imitated his example. Without their continuing enthusiasm the country would be hard put to maintain its schools, museums or concert halls. Even so recent a Croesus as Ivan Boesky used a fraction of the money acquired in rigged stock deals to bestow gifts on Harvard University and the Jewish Theological Seminary in New York. When he was indicted for fraud, his money once again was seen to be soiled, and Boesky felt obliged to resign from the seminary's board of trustees and to ask that the bronze letters of his name be removed from the wall of its library.

In its refined state money becomes, in Ralph Waldo Emerson's phrase, "beautiful as roses." Still, it is never wise to take too many chances with its dark and terrible enchantments. We prefer to handle money in the purified form of a credit card—that is, something decorously abstract that doesn't arouse the suspicion of hotel clerks who might look with disdain on any prospective guest so vulgar as to offer cash.

Given the belief that one's money is one's self, it is no wonder that Americans should be obsessed with the cleanliness of their persons. The nation spends as recklessly on soap and cosmetics as it does on weapons, the object of both expenditures being the protection of the American body politic against the contamination of foreign substances.

Every drugstore in the country stocks hundreds of sprays, perfumes, disinfectants, creams, fresheners, lotions and scents—all intended to preserve a specific part of the anatomy in a state of sweet-smelling innocence. American food comes wrapped in plastic, supposedly cured of its impurities and often decorated with artificial colorings that disguise the baseness of its origin.

Among the well-to-do, especially the Protestant well-to-do, too close an acquaintance with money, or too much of a concern about its comings and goings, cast on one's character the shadow of unseemly doubt. The late Nelson Rockefeller never carried cash on his person. He traveled on his own planes, and he owned houses in most of the places he had reasons to visit. His credit was sufficient to any emergent occasion in a store, and if he unexpectedly had need of some trifling sum (for a newspaper or cup of coffee), he borrowed the money from somebody following along in his retinue. Nor did he bother to make indecent inquiries about the extent of his holdings. During his campaign for the presidency in 1968 I remember him making a speech to a crowd of Puerto Rican steelworkers in a slum near Cleveland, Ohio. Exuding his familiar optimism, his arms raised in a gesture of brotherhood, Rockefeller addressed the crowd in well-meaning Spanish, promising that if he was elected President of the United States he would do everything in his power to distribute justice, fiscal responsibility and pieces of the American pie. The crowd cheered him with shouts of *"Arriba, Arriba,"* never knowing, as the candidate himself didn't know, that Rockefeller owned the steel mill. He didn't own it outright, of course, in the way that a man owns a house or a dog, but through a series of intermediate interests that obscured the low-caste nature of its function.

I have known quite a few people who think it demeaning to look at a bill or to ask, when buying razor blades or a fur coat, what the item happens to cost. One of my uncles in California took pride in saying that he never looked at his disbursements. During the first week of January every year he signed in blank all the checks in three large checkbooks, allowing his secretary to fill in the numbers as the bills came due.

"I never know how much I've got," he often said. "I let the tax guys subtract what I owe the government every month, and I tell them to give me whatever it is that I can spend."

Transferred into the political arena, the doctrines of social sanitation oblige all candidates for public office to feign the clean-limbed idealism of college sophomores. Even the meanest of politicians has no choice but to present himself as one who would remove the stains from capitalism's bloody clothes and wash the sheets of the American conscience. The pose of innocence is as mandatory as the ability to eat banquet food and endure the scourging of the press. No candidate can say, with Talleyrand, that he is in it for the money, or that it is the business of politicians to add to the wealth of their handlers.[2] The system in place is always assumed to be corrupt, and the electorate expects its once and future Presidents to tell wholesome lies—to present themselves as honest and good-natured fellows (not too dissimilar from high school football coaches) who know little or nothing of murder, ambition, lust, selfishness, cowardice or greed. The more daring members of the troupe might go so far as to admit having read about such awful things in the newspapers. But the

---

2. Ronald Reagan campaigned with the backing of the comfortably rich. Quite appropriately he rewarded them with profitable military expenditures, astringent monetary policies and reduced taxes. Gary Hart neglected to maintain the pose of blameless innocence, and within a matter of five days his presidential campaign vanished as abruptly as a traveling circus.

incidents in question invariably have to do with a foreign country or with somebody belonging to the other political party.

Generations of reformers—whether liberal or neoliberal, conservative or neoconservative—come forward with plans to remove the politics (i.e., the sordid bargaining) from what they prefer to describe (as if the abstract phrase were a kind of bathroom scent) as "the political process." They campaign on the preposterous notion that if only all the smoke-filled rooms in Washington could be thoroughly aired and fumigated, then all the deals could be done on public television by civic-minded officials appointed to presidential commissions and shuffling their papers with white gloves.

The country's domestic politics oscillate between different theories of what constitutes a proper detergent. Within recent memory the antipodes of this dialectic have been well and fairly represented by Jimmy Carter and Ronald Reagan. In the election of 1980 President Carter cast his politics in the form of a coroner's report. Presenting himself as an innocent betrayed by circumstance, he spoke of poisoned seas and dwindling stores of light, of blacks and Jews doomed to rage at one another in second-class hotels, of Russians armed with invincible weapons. He proposed to redeem the country, not to govern it, and he offered the faithful his own example of having been twice born, thus renewing his innocence with the spiritual equivalent of a second mortgage.

Against Carter's melancholy divinations, Reagan presented himself as the candidate bringing hope, faith, freedom and prosperity to an audience desperately wishing to hear tales of paradise regained. He held out the promise of an illusory future, but it was a lot better than the prayerful silence in the loser's locker room. As required by the conventions of the American political theater, Reagan also played on the themes of innocence—but in a major instead of a minor key. The sweetness of his actor's voice confirmed the palpable sincerity of his belief. Somehow he had persuaded himself that all the dreams come true and that the script of every American life is written by the kindly mythographers at

Warner Brothers. Like his most enthusiastic supporters, Reagan had no wish to see or govern an America that didn't confirm the press releases put out by a studio publicity department.

His training in Warner Brothers movies of the 1940s and 1950s fortified Reagan with ideal qualities for the political theater of the 1980s. The Hollywood of Jack Warner's day insisted on a fairly narrow range of permissible behavior, and our movies, unlike those of any other country, upheld the social and political conventions of the America pictured in the postcards. Women couldn't be seen in bed with men; nobody could admit to having heard of Freud or the unconscious mind; the heroes and the villains were cast as unalloyed images, and it wasn't proper to suggest that in most human beings the elements of good and evil were so evenly mixed that a man's life could be portrayed as a deadly combat within the wilderness of the self.

Reagan carried his repertoire of golden commonplaces from one microphone to another. He couldn't make a mistake with his lines even if, as often happened, he neglected to read the script and observed that to see one redwood tree is to see them all, or that the slums of Los Angeles would be improved by an epidemic of botulism. The failure of his own imagination corresponded to the failure of the public imagination. Not that he is an unkind or unsympathetic man. He wouldn't harm anybody—not a Chicano or black or Arab, not even a Russian. He counts Sammy Davis, Jr., among his closest friends, and he wept when the Polish ambassador told him the story of his escape from the Communist golem. Every now and then Reagan's aides would usher into his presence a delegate from the anonymous community of the weak, the sick and the poor. Reagan responded with a genuine surge of emotion, amazed to discover what the poor woman had suffered, astounded by her tale of misery and injustice. But once the apparition had been removed from his sight, she vanished as mysteriously and as suddenly as she came, withdrawn into the void from whence hideous images (of Buchenwald or a little Vietnamese girl blazing with the light of napalm) sometimes escape from captivity and float across the screen of the news.[3]

Reagan was elected precisely because he couldn't see the other side of the postcards, because he wished to know as little as possible about an America in which illiterate children commit murder for the price of a secondhand radio, in which, contrary to the publicity appearing in *Fortune* and *Vogue*, most business ventures end in debt and failure, in which hospitals resemble prisons, and the prisons have become as crowded as resort hotels—a nation inhabited not by smiling faces on the postcards, but by people so frightened or intimidated that they have no choice but to sell, in a falling market, what little remains to them of their dignity and self-respect, and who, to their sorrow, all too easily find a buyer in a corporation, police official or pimp.[4]

During the momentary alarm about the high incidence of drug addiction among the American people in fall 1986, President and Mrs. Reagan set the standard of virtuoso performance in the art of ritual expiation. They appeared in concert on network television to announce "a national crusade" against the use of drugs. Reagan said, "Let us not forget who we are. Drug abuse is a repudiation of everything America is." Mrs. Reagan, with whom the president was holding hands, said, "There is no moral middle ground. Indifference is not an option."

If their concern hadn't been so unctuous, and their voices not quite so false, their announcement might have seemed less like the scattering of incense and the tinkling of tiny bells.

3. On being asked about the photograph of the Vietnamese girl several years after the Vietnam War had been lost, General William Westmoreland said he had been told, and always had thought, that the girl was burned by a hibachi stove.
4. Quite a few of Reagan's California friends, among them Frank Sinatra and the late Alfred Bloomingdale, have proved themselves intimately acquainted with the moral underworld. Apparently they say nothing of their adventures to the president.

A few months later the President asked the Congress to reduce the budget appropriation for the drug program that he himself had proclaimed, thus demonstrating the ritual nature of his concern. In New York Mayor Koch asked for troops to defend the city's perimeters, but stationed patrol boats in the harbor for only seven days. Elsewhere in the country the voices of pious incantation recommended shooting suspected drug dealers on sight. An eleven-year-old girl in Los Angeles reported her parents to the police when she found a marijuana plant in her family's garden. An editor highly placed at *The New York Times* was heard to remark that it might not be a bad idea if somebody's Christian air force bombed the coca plantations in Colombia.

In the midst of the singing of psalms nobody had the bad manners to ask why it is that Americans have become so fond of drugs. Nor did anybody embarrass the choir by pointing out that:

1. The attempt to suppress drugs by punitive means is as futile as the wish to teach cooking to an ape, and
2. The government—whether municipal, state or federal— has little or no intention of doing anything to reduce the crime implicit in the drug traffic.

The simplest arithmetic demonstrates the lack of honest intent. New York City currently assigns six judges to hear 20,000 narcotics cases a year, which means that roughly 19,400 cases become matters for plea bargain, and the average length of time spent in jail as a result of a drug arrest amounts to seven days. The city obviously hasn't got the money to hire enough judges, deploy enough police spies and build enough jails. The same arithmetic pertains everywhere else in the country. If Congress or the Reagans meant what they said, they would be obliged to amass a defense fund on the order of $50 billion to $70 billion a year, almost all of it directed toward education and the manufacture of antidotes. But they don't mean what they say, and almost everybody with any experience of drugs knows they don't mean what they say. Every district attorney understands that the laws cannot be enforced; so does every judge, detective, addict, literary agent and brothel-keeper. Marijuana is now one of the principal American cash crops, comparable to corn or wheat or soybeans. (Pursued to its logical end, the realpolitik suggested by the editor of *The New York Times* would entail the bombing of California.) The number of people addicted to drugs of all description reflects the prevalence of fear and unhappiness through all ranks of American society. Like the hiring of additional customs agents, or the launching of more heavily armed Coast Guard boats, the making of vindictive laws inflates the price of drugs and increases the profit margins in the smuggling trades.

If either the government or the society were serious in the desire to reduce crime and human suffering supported by the drug trades, the Congress, at very little cost, could transform narcotics into substances as legal as alcohol, pornography or tobacco. Deprived of its romance as well as of its profit, the drug business might follow the steel and textile businesses into bankruptcy. Fewer people would commit fewer crimes, and the courts could take up more difficult questions of justice.

But the Reagan administration, like the vast majority of the American people, preferred the purity of its illusions. The society chooses to believe that the world's evil doesn't reside in men but exists, like the air, in the space between them. To the extent that drug addiction can be defined as a foreign conspiracy—a consequence not of ancient human predicament but of new export strategies in Bogotá—Americans can take comfort in their righteousness. Like the late Howard Hughes hiding on a roof of a Las Vegas hotel from the armies of invading bacteria, the innocent nation affects a sensibility grown too refined for the world.

The media cater to the affliction by their incessant dwelling on the fear of disease, crime, foreigners (chiefly immigrants and

Russians), drugs, toxins (in earth, air, fire and water), poverty and death. Urgent bulletins about these seven deadly contagions constitute most of what passes for the news. During the spring and early summer of 1987 the media promoted the fear of the AIDS virus into a near panic. The best evidence seems to suggest that in the United States the virus seldom accompanies the act of heterosexual love. Between 1981 and 1987 no more than 18,000 people had died of the virus (as opposed to 90,000 people who die annually from tuberculosis), and of the dead, all but a tiny fraction (.012 percent) were homosexual, intravenous drug users or persons infected by blood products. The media nevertheless insisted on an epidemic certain to affect the general population.

The concern with pollutants of all kinds—in the atmosphere, the sea, the slums, the Third World—also governs the shaping of American diplomacy. If a foreign country doesn't look like a middle-class suburb of Dallas or Detroit, then obviously the natives must be dangerous as well as badly dressed. The inhabitants of any alien landscape—whether drug addicts standing on a street corner in Harlem or a crowd shouting slogans in a Latin American plaza—acquire the unreality of apparitions in a tale told by Steven Spielberg. To the United States the Third World often takes the form of a black woman who has been made pregnant in a moment of passion and who shows up one day in the reception room on the forty-ninth floor threatening to make a scene. The lawyers pay the woman off; sometimes uniformed guards accompany her to the elevators.

During the whole of the twentieth century the continental United States fortunately has escaped the ravages of war, and so it is easy enough for heirs to the American fortune to believe they have been anointed by Providence. In their eager innocence they make of foreign policy a game of transcendental poker in which the ruthless self-interest of a commercial democracy (cf. the American policy toward the Plains Indians and the Mexicans) gets mixed up with dreams, sermons and the transmigration of souls. In Europe people may not know very much about foreign affairs, but at least they can recognize the subjects under discussion. They know enough to understand that the dealing between nations is a dull and sluggish business, unyielding in the financial details and encumbered by the usual displays of pride, greed, nastiness and spite. But the Americans, like Woodrow Wilson talking to David Lloyd George and Georges Clemenceau in Paris in the spring of 1919, prefer to imagine themselves playing cards with the Devil.

The will toward innocence requires the Americans to make even of war a bloodless enterprise. Napoleon often warned his generals against the stupidity of such a sleight of hand, reminding them that in the conduct of war the cardinal sin—to be avoided at all costs and on pain of certain defeat—was the habit of "making pictures." Officers who chose to see what they wished to see, as opposed to what might be taking place on the field of events, marched their armies into the enfilading fire of oblivion.

But the man who has inherited a great fortune does nothing else except make pictures. Unlike the poor man, who must study other people's motives and desires if he hopes to gain from them, the rich man can afford to look only at what amuses or comforts him. He believes what he is told because he has no reason not to. What difference does it make? If everything is make-believe, then everything is as plausible as everything else. Asian dictators can promise to go among their peasants and instruct them in the mechanics of constitutional self-government; the Shah of Iran can say he means to make a democratic state among people who believe that they have won the blessing of Allah by burning to death 400 schoolchildren in a movie theater. The rich man applauds, admires the native costumes and sends a gift of weapons. He believes that, once inspired by the American example, the repentant Asian despot will feel himself inwardly changed and seek to imitate the model of behavior established by Henry Cabot Lodge. Dictators don't really want to be dictators; they were raised in an unhealthy social environment. If given enough tractors and a little moral encouragement, they will renounce the pleasures of sodomy and murder.

The absurd political presentations that have found favor in Washington over the past thirty years resemble the farfetched rationalizations with which New York art dealers sell the latest school of modern painting to the *nouveau riche*. Assuming that the world is so much painted scenery, the patrons in Washington assign all the parts and write all the last acts. Other people make exits and entrances. Thus President Carter, on the last night of 1977, offered a toast to the Shah of Iran in which he described the Shah as his "great friend" and Iran as an "island of stability" in the Middle East.[5] A year later Iran was in the midst of revolt and Washington was advising the Shah to abdicate in favor of any government, civil or military, that could restore production in the southern oil fields. In 1941 the Soviet Union appeared on the stage in the role of brave friend and courageous ally; six years later, the script was rewritten and the Soviet Union appeared as the villainous éminence grise, subverting the free world with the drug of Communism. China remained an implacable enemy of human freedom for the better part of thirty years, but in 1972 President Nixon announced the advent of democracy, and in 1978 President Carter proclaimed the miracle of redemption. Following the

---

5. It is instructive to quote Mr. Carter's toast at some length because it so nicely illustrates the somnambulism of American statesmen content to see whatever they wish to see. Mr. Carter explained that he decided to celebrate New Year's Eve with the Shah because he had asked his wife, Rosalynn, whom she wanted to be with on that occasion, and Rosalynn had said, "Above all others, I think, with the Shah and the empress Farah." The President then went on to say: "Iran, because of the great leadership of the Shah, is an island of stability in one of the more troubled areas of the world. This is a great tribute to you, Your Majesty, and to your leadership, and to the respect and the admiration and love which your people give to you . . . . We have no other nation on earth who is closer to us in planning for our mutual military security. We have no other with whom we have closer consultations on regional problems that concern us both. And there is no leader with whom I have a deeper sense of personal gratitude and personal friendship."

example set by the wall posters in Peking, the American press blossomed with praise for a regime previously celebrated for its brutality. The stage-hands of the media took down the sets left over from the production of *Darkness at Noon* and replaced them with tableaux of happy Chinese workers eager to buy farm implements, military aircraft, and Coca-Cola.

The American debacle in Vietnam followed from the picture-making habit of mind. The American commanders, both military and civilian, substituted the data bases of a preferred fiction for the texts of inconvenient fact. The end was implicit in the beginning, in the fatuous dream of innocent omnipotence to which the American equestrian classes succumbed after the victory of World War II. All the best people in all the best places believed that the United States was invulnerable. Because of its wealth and technical capacity the country was free to do as it pleased in the world. As might be expected, it was Henry Kissinger who distilled the presiding delusion into resonant nonsense. In one of his treatises on American realpolitik, Kissinger said: "A scientific revolution has, for all practical purposes, removed technical limits from the exercise of power in foreign policy."

Such a comfortably materialist view of the world confirmed the working prejudices of advanced capitalism. As William Gibson painstakingly demonstrated in a book entitled *The Perfect War*, we set up our war factory in Vietnam as proof of our talent for "managerial science and scientific production." Transposing the war into a currency of debits and credits, our leaders spoke of "kill ratios" and "body counts," of "assets," "quotas," "lucrative targets," "short term-dividends" and "acceptable rates of return." Few of them knew the Vietnamese language or anything about the Vietnamese people. Nor did they care to know. They conceived of the enemy as raw material to be processed into the commodity of victory. Their factory operated on a simple formula—"If it's dead and it's Vietnamese, it's VC." What was the point of learning to talk to an object as inanimate as a bale of hemp or a barrel of oil?

The production model of war, like any other mechanism of advanced capitalism, doesn't recognize the values of allegiance, loyalty or honor. In place of the military virtues it substitutes numbers and public relations slogans. American soldiers were carried on the books as costs of production, like flares or radios or boxes of ammunition. Artillery units bombarded abstract spaces defined as free-fire zones, their effectiveness measured not by any tactical result but by the number of rounds delivered. Aircraft dropped bombs on symbolic targets, again not for any particular military reason but to send a "bomb-o-gram" to other war managers in Moscow, Washington and Hanoi about the high-quality of American courage and resolve.

By their own lights and measurements, Americans won the war. Certainly they met their quotas of munitions exploded and ears collected. If, in the end, the world of event stubbornly refused to conform to their expectation, it was, as usual, not their fault. Even after taking casualties of 58,000 dead and 300,000 wounded, after laying waste to three countries and killing probably as many as 2 million Laotians, Cambodians and Vietnamese, the American techno-bureaucracy insisted on the perfection of its technique and the innocence of its motive.

Retreating under cover of euphemism, all the best authorities agreed that the war had been a well-intentioned mistake—"a quagmire," "a morass," "an accumulation of small but unavoidable errors of judgment," "a swamp," "a nightmare." It fell to the lot of Arthur M. Schlesinger to pronounce the pious benediction. "The story of Vietnam," he said, "is a tragedy without villains."

The proofs of innocence coincide with the assumptions of grace habitual among people who believe themselves ennobled by the patents of property. Like a twice-born Christian, the rich man likes to believe that he exists in a state of perpetual blamelessness. When anything goes wrong, it is never money's fault. Perhaps money makes mistakes, but these belong to the category of technical miscalculations or temporary lapses of judgment; the mistakes never have anything to do with anger, egoism, ambition or stupidity. If fault must be found, then it must have something to do with a public misunderstanding rather than an improper action.[6] The equestrian class, like the innocent American republic, invariably discovers itself betrayed—by events, by parents or doctors or servants, by Russians or Afghans or Israelis, by the Japanese interfering in the credit markets or a collision of oil tankers off the coast of Peru, by terrorists and travel agents and unseen trolls manipulating the levers of history.

Over the last twenty years the American masters and commanders have noticed that otherwise profitable or patriotic acts have unpleasant or unforeseen consequences. The corporations prosper, and the arms merchants sell their goods to illiterate tyrants, but the whales languish, and somebody always gets killed or sent out to sea in a boat. This disturbs people who prefer not to have anything to do with the killing, or, to put it more precisely, who like to think that any killing done on their behalf falls to the lot of the hired help (the South Vietnamese, the Shah of Iran, the Chilean junta, the contras) or remains safely in the past—buried with the glorious dead who paid the debt to the future at Concord, Gettysburg and Guadalcanal, and who bequeathed to their descendants the trust fund of freedom.

It is no accident that environmentalism in its more militant phases is a rich man's cause. The Club of Rome discovered the limits of growth while gathered on the terrace of a villa overlooking a vineyard that belonged to its founder. Throughout the 1960s and 1970s the most diligent advocates of the movement tended to possess substantial wealth and property, and their expressions of concern about the natural world had a way of sounding like the pleasant condescensions of landowners asking tenant farmers about the goats.

6. Precisely this line of reasoning informed the Reagan administration's explanation of its illegal arms deal with Iran. The chronic lack of imagination of men who serve the interests of money leads them to think themselves incapable of evil intent. They cannot understand how they can be accused of employing illegitimate means to acquire what belongs to them by right.

Their earnestness invariably reminded me of a lady who, making a show of her innocence, was nearly stabbed to death on a beach at East Hampton. From the deck of a glass house, at about noon on a Sunday in August, the lady noticed a company of fishermen dragging a heavy net through the surf. It had taken them six hours to set and haul the net, but the lady apparently wasn't aware of their labor or their need to sell the fish for something so loathsome as money. The piteous sight of so many fish gasping on the sand moved her to politics. Arming herself with garden shears, she rushed forth to cut the net. One of the younger fishermen, not yet accustomed to the whims of intellectual fashion, had to be restrained from driving a knife into the woman's stomach. He didn't understand that he was watching a dramatization of the lady's innocence. Presumably she didn't object so much to the killing of fish (later that same evening I doubt she had much difficulty eating smoked salmon); she objected to bearing witness, and therefore becoming an accomplice, to the killing. As long as the fish were killed in cold and distant seas she could pretend they arrived on her table of their own free will. Like mine workers and cleaning women they chose their places in the universe for the sheer joy of doing what they always had wanted to do.

A similar attitude of dreamlike trance informed the American media's response to "the energy crisis" of the early and middle 1970s. Citizens in the lower reaches of society accepted the crisis as another Washington entertainment, or they didn't pay much attention to it one way or another. Apparently they figured that when the dark night closed down they would do whatever was necessary to stay alive. If they couldn't afford to pay for gas and oil, they would burn wood, light candles and roast animals in the park. The letters to the editors of newspapers confirmed this impression. The correspondents didn't drive expensive cars; they didn't own twenty-seven household appliances, and they couldn't remember having had enough money at one time in their lives to worry about heating a ski lodge.

But among the equestrian classes the news of the crisis carried the weight of biblical judgment. In Greenwich, Connecticut, people spoke of nothing else. At the Ford Foundation and in the pages of *The New York Times* the resident oracles published ominous prophecies. The degree of a man's sensitivity to the crisis could be calibrated to the size of his income. The more prominent his place in the hierarchy, the more likely he was to talk about the crisis as if it were a plague visited upon him by the undeserving poor.

Even so, despite what can be said for the whales and the Third World, it is in the arenas of big-time sports that the acts of ritual purification achieve their highest and most visible expression. The American public chooses to look upon sports as a form of civic religion, and the ceremonial scrubbings-out of sin that attend any athlete's fall from Heaven surpass in their pomp and solemnity the comparable acts of contrition imposed on lapsed financiers or politicians.

First the repentant sinner—mumbling inaudibly into the television cameras, apologizing to his mother and his coach, saying what he is told to say about how he didn't mean to desecrate the name of so noble a sport. Secondly, the alarmed commissioner—Peter Ueberroth or somebody equally wholesome—imposing a fine and a penance, which, if the player knows what's good for him, he gratefully and promptly accepts. Finally, the choir of owners and sportswriters—proclaiming in pious unison the next generation's need of exemplary heroes, explaining that once again and thanks to the courage and high character of all concerned, the game has been restored to a state of grace.

Big-time sports is a big business—more precisely, the entertainment business. The numbers on the bottom line, like the numbers on the bottom line of most other businesses, have little to do with ethics or morality. But, unlike any other business in the United States, sports must preserve an illusion of perfect innocence. The mounting of this illusion defines the purpose and accounts for the immense wealth of American sports. It is the ceremony of innocence that fans pay to see—not the game or match or bout, but the ritual portrayal of a world in which time stops and all hope remains plausible, in which everybody present can recover the blameless expectations of a child, where the forces of light always triumph over the powers of darkness.

The playing field is more sacred than the stock exchange, more blessed than Capitol Hill or the vaults at Fort Knox. The diamond and the gridiron—and, to a lesser degree, the court, the rink, the track and the ring—embody the American dream of Eden.

On the other side of the left-field wall the agents of death and time go about their dismal work. Wars fester and explode; the family business fails, and somebody's boyfriend wrecks the car; widows and orphans fall prey to lying insurance salesmen; banks foreclose on farm mortgages, and children die of bone cancer. But inside the park the world is as it was at the beginning. The grass is as green as it was in everybody's lost childhood. Nobody grows old, and if only the game could last another three innings, or maybe forever, nobody would ever die.

If the wisdom of the rich consists in what the rich want to hear and think about themselves, it is not surprising that a rich nation confers its richest rewards on those writers who can preserve the illusions of innocence. Like the bureaucrats who formulate government policy, the artisans of the media make elaborate and cosmetic use of euphemism. They have a talent for blurring and softening the meaning of words, for not calling things by their right names, and the best of them can change even the plainest words into face powder.

As a child I learned from listening to the conversation of my elders that it was permissible to use plain words only when speaking about foreigners and members of the lower social orders. About one's friends and peers it was necessary to speak less bluntly. The drunkenness of longshoremen (i.e., people whom one didn't know) could be described as "stinking" or "degenerate." Although given to the same habits, one's friends were said "to be having a little trouble with booze." Of an acquaintance conducting a sexual liaison with somebody else's wife it was proper to say that he was "having a little thing with Ginny." Gossip columnists who printed rumors of scandal involving one's friends were denounced as notorious liars, wretched hirelings of the yellow press. But if the same rumors were brought against a politician or a movie actress, then one was free to talk about the sordidness of their illicit lust. The photographs published in the papers (preferably of the women in tears and the men with hats pulled down over their faces) offered examples of the wickedness into which the country might sink unless something was done to correct the public morals. Among the poor and socially remote, the discovery of sin provided occasions for uplifting sermons.

Always it was important to remember that about oneself and one's friends it was never correct to use the words "rich" and "poor." Both words were too emotional and therefore in bad taste. The people one knew were "affluent" or "comfortably fixed." Other people might be said to be "rich," but always in a tone of disparagement indicating that they were so base and unrefined as to be "interested in money." To say that somebody was "poor" implied an attitude of pity or contempt.

Later in life, making the rounds of the several spheres of society open to the curiosity of the press, I learned to recognize the equivalent desire for vagueness in the languages of government and law, of business and diplomacy and the academic professions. The discussion of money itself took place in the antiseptic vocabulary of "nonperforming assets," "comparative advantage" and "negative returns." The Central Intelligence Agency never asked its operatives to commit murder, it issued requests for "terminations with extreme prejudice." The deadliest street drugs went by the names of angel dust and snow. When American troops in Vietnam killed every man, woman and child in an undefended village, their commanders called the process pacification. Doctors spoke in code, and the War Department preferred to go by the name of the Defense Department, which, in 1984, defined the act of war as "violence processing." The jargons of advertising, sociology and economics were so elaborate as to require the use of phrasebooks.[7]

Under any circumstances it was important to refrain from indulging the impulse toward wit or direct statement. The country that had taken upon itself the persona of a rich man didn't like to hear people making jokes that threatened the pomposity of its new-found magnificence. Matthew Troy, a New York politician convicted in the middle 1970s of accepting bribes from his public-spirited constituents, paused to answer a reporter's question outside the courtroom in which he had been sentenced to three years in jail.

"What is politics?" said Councilman Troy. "I'll tell you what politics is. Politics is men who kiss ass for money and women who fuck for it."

The newspapers thoughtfully omitted the remark in the next day's editions, possibly because it was too vulgar, more likely because it was too insulting to their self-esteem. If this was what politics were about, what would become of their Sunday commentary? Of the people's right to know?

So many people have written books and treatises about the weakening of the American language since the end of the Second World War that it would be superfluous to recite the customary list of examples. The reader can refer to the morning newspaper, to

---

7. Remarking on the pervasiveness of scientific gibberish as early as 1924, G.K. Chesterton observed, "Science in the modern world has many uses; its chief use, however, is to provide long words to cover up the errors of the rich."

The National Council of Teachers of English presented its Doublespeak Award for 1987 to NASA for the following account of the *Challenger* disaster:

"The normal process during the countdown is that the countdown proceeds, assuming we are in a go posture, and at various points during the countdown we tag up the operational loops and face to face in the firing room to ascertain the facts that project elements that are monitoring the data and that are understanding the situation as we proceed are still in the go direction."

almost any public speech, government document or recently published textbook. Despite the profusion of pornographic images in
movies and magazines, our language becomes increasingly timid
and antiseptic. The newspapers publish never-ending accounts of
crimes and misdemeanors, which allow editorial writers to rise
to the daily occasions of moral indignation. But if the investigations seldom seem to get anywhere, it is because the indignation
is largely ceremonial. The media perform the rites of purification,
rehearsing the formal cries of protest in order to assure their audiences that the crimes under review represent an aberration from
the norm of innocence. The impulse to smother and correct, to
smooth out the edges of experience and tell wholesome and well-
groomed lies, shows up in all genres of American writing.

With the approach of a presidential election, the cadences of
American political speech and writing become indistinguishable
from those of the Puritan sermon. The candidates use the press conference and the photo opportunity to teach abbreviated lessons on
the reclamation of the American purpose and the redemption of the
American soul. Newspaper editorialists exhort their congregations
to acts of repentance and reform. Television celebrities renounce the
comforts of Beverly Hills to endure the mortifications of the flesh in
Kansas City shopping malls. The dinner conversation in New York
and Washington turns on points of doctrine as obscure and as furi-
ously dissected as the medieval ranking of the saints.

During the first hundred fifty years of the American settlement,
the sermon, especially the jeremiad, served as the principal means
of literary expression among a people who enjoyed the favor of
Providence. To write was to preach. Colonial stationers printed in
devout quantity the texts of Cotton Mather and Jonathan Edwards;
booksellers stocked their shelves with travelers' guides to perdition.
As long ago as 1670, in New England towns that through the glass
of time seem as virtuous as postcards, the resident divines already
were bemoaning the degeneracy of the age. When ascending the
pulpit they affected the gesture of rubbing hideous sights from their

eyes, as if they couldn't believe the extent of the folly and wickedness to which, reluctantly, they bore witness.[8] By 1780 Hannah More
could say, speaking of the polite table talk acceptable in Salem, that
it was always "the fashion to make the most lamentable *Jeremiads*
on the badness of times."

Throughout the nineteenth century the American genius for
lamentation showed up in the essays of Henry Thoreau and Ralph
Waldo Emerson, in the novels of Herman Melville and Nathaniel
Hawthorne, in Walt Whitman's poems, in the speeches of John
Calhoun, Andrew Jackson, Daniel Webster and Henry Clay. No
matter what the victories on the temporal frontiers, the badness
of the times could always be seen along the spiritual sectors of the
front, and it was incumbent on the writer of sensibility to despair
of the state of the union between God and his chosen apostles. The
world was not the world unless it was coming rapidly to an end.

The twentieth century took up the theme with the speeches
of Woodrow Wilson, the writings of the Progressive movement,
the social criticism of the 1930s and the homilies of Jimmy Carter.
Even now, toward the end of a century supposedly secular, in
an industrial state pleased to style itself modern, no newspaper
would deem itself respectable without an editorial page that could
be sung by a church choir. The bookstores wallow in commercial
visions of the Apocalypse—environmental, moral, thermonuclear,
chemical, economic, social and political. The season's best-selling
tracts, whether Bob Woodward's biography of John Belushi or
Peter Collier and David Horowitz's meditation on the Kennedy
family, invariably tell the popular folktale of Satan coming to
seize prideful souls made corrupt and vainglorious in Sodom.
Any author worth his weight in tears tries for a title in which the

8. Both President Reagan and New York City Mayor Ed Koch employed this device in
1986 to great effect—Reagan on learning of the Iranian arms transfers, Koch on being
told about corruption among his own appointed city officials.

prefix "The Last" modifies "Day," "Waltz," "Train to Paris," "Exit to Brooklyn," "Convertible," "Hurrah," "Gentleman" or "Unicorn."

The procedures of social hygiene require the authors of orthodox economic treatises to resolve a set of primary contradictions. How is it possible for a man to be both a good Christian and a successful capitalist? How does a man join the necessity of pitiless self-seeking with the obligation of meekly turning the other cheek? How is it possible to hold the simultaneous beliefs that what is moral doesn't pay, but what pays is, by definition, moral?

The founders of the American republic seemed to have had less difficulty with the questions than the heirs to the enterprise. Being Christians, the patriots assembled in Philadelphia in 1787 still believed men were by nature predatory creatures, rapacious and sly, obedient to their appetites. They identified the economic cause as the *primum mobile* of the world's secular sequences, and stipulated a scheme of things in which a man's economic interest always preceded his political, artistic or sexual interest. Being merchants, they understood that merchants left to their own devices tend invariably to the comforts of monopoly and the economies of crime.[9] In the writing of the Constitution they sought

9. They could cite as their authority Adam Smith, the political economist whose *Wealth of Nations* was published within a few months of the Declaration of Independence. Smith detested aristocrats, distrusted capitalists and grieved for the laboring poor. He was pressed into service by the apologists for Reagan's triumphant plutocracy as an almost biblical spokesman for unlicensed greed. Anybody who takes the trouble to read Smith can marvel at the resulting travesties of his texts. For example, Smith on the plutocracy: "All for ourselves and nothing for other people seems, in every age of the world, to have been the vile maxim of the masters of mankind." On the military-industrial complex: "The Sovereign, for example, with all the officers both of justice and war who serve under him, the whole army and navy, are unproductive workers." On monopoly: "People of the same trade seldom meet together, even for merriment and diversion, but the conversation ends in conspiracy against the public, or in some contrivance to raise prices."

to pit interest against interest, ambition against ambition, vice against vice; by so doing they hoped to establish a set of rules that yoked the plurality of base impulses into the harness of the higher good. Accepting the Hobbesian dynamic of unceasing combat between implacable factions of selfishness, they wished men to be as free as possible to engage in that combat. Because they were clear about the mechanics of the marketplace, they had little use either for a theology of money or the ceremonies of innocence. They could afford their clarity of mind because they enjoyed at least three advantages no longer available to the current generation of heirs.

First, they could rely on the bulwark of religion. Like most of their countrymen in the late eighteenth century, the Founders took seriously the injunctions of Christianity, and they rendered unto Caesar the things that belonged to Caesar without pretending that they also belonged to God. Secondly, the population of the thirteen colonies was small enough to permit the unity of coherent discourse among the still smaller unity of the monied and educated classes. The gentlemen gathered in Philadelphia spoke much the same language and had read more or less the same authorities. Thirdly, the Founders could count upon the emptiness of the frontier. The citizens likely to cause trouble could leave for points west, carrying their disappointment, their bankruptcy and their sedition through the gaps in the Alleghenies and down the broad reaches of the Ohio River.

Given these hedges against domestic discontent, the Founders didn't need the unctuous piety that became increasingly urgent as the eighteenth century passed through the industrial transformations of the nineteenth century into the postindustrial combinations of the twentieth. Andrew Jackson still could afford to be clear on the topic of money; so could Nicholas Biddle and Collis Huntington. Speaking to a newspaper reporter in Philadelphia in 1833, Biddle, in the midst of his quarrel with Jackson about the charter of the National Bank, observed: "I can remove all the

Constitutional Scruples in the District of Columbia [with] half a dozen presidencies, a dozen cashierships, fifty clerkships, 100 directorships to worthy friends who have no character and no money." Fifty years later, in another era but the same moral venue, Huntington kept a meticulous record of the bribes paid to congressmen to forward the interests of his Southern Pacific Railroad. In 1876 Huntington remarked to a friend that the members of the Senate divided into three classes—"the clean" (those who did as they were told without asking for favors), "the commercial" (who were paid) and "the communists" (who resisted both logic and money). Certainly John D. Rockefeller, Sr. was clear about the ruthlessness necessary to the success of financial enterprise. He may not have been especially interested in the magical properties of money, but he had a passion for his grand design, and if he had to dynamite a few trains or hire a few thugs to discourage his competitors, well, that was what free markets were all about. To a congressional committee in 1887 he explained that business was like growing roses and that the gardener who wished to raise a perfect American beauty rose had no choice but to crush the buds of the lesser roses intruding on its light. A few years later, to another committee investigating another rumor of monopoly, Rockefeller, becoming irritated by the tedious line of questioning, said, testily: "The Lord gave me my money."

The American public in the late nineteenth century was inclined to take him at his word, acknowledging without rancor the truth in the observation that behind every great fortune stands the brooding presence of a great crime. The grand predators of the Gilded Age, among them James Fisk, Cornelius Vanderbilt and Jay Gould as well as Rockefeller, basked in the adulation of a newspaper audience that followed their exploits with the avidity it now bestows on the newly rich entrepreneurs celebrated in the pages of *Fortune* and *Manhattan, Inc.* Then as now, the gentlemen in question might be cheats and swindlers, but as long as their stratagems were successful, the audience remained free to imitate or envy their opulence.[10] During the panic of 1894, at a time when people literally were killing one another in the streets outside the New York Stock Exchange, the press sent a delegation of reporters to receive a statement from E.H. Harriman and J.P. Morgan. The reporters waited for three hours in the anteroom, their hats balanced politely on their knees. A secretary eventually brought them a single sheet of paper bearing the message, "The United States is a great and growing country," and then, below the signatures, the further advisory, "This is not for attribution." The reporters accepted the news with the humility becoming their station, much in the manner of Heine's stockbroker bowing to Baron Rothschild's chamber pot. Finding their ways back to their offices through crowds rioting in the streets, the reporters reassured their readers that prosperity was at hand.

With the advent of the twentieth century, the fiction of the innocent millionaire became somewhat more troublesome to sustain. The frontier closed down; the expanding crowd of immigrants embraced a babel of languages and moral systems; the Christian religion softened into Sunday school irrelevance. Clearly it was true that capitalism promoted ambition, encouraged hope, inspired invention and provided the rewards of fortune. Unfortunately, it was also true that unless harnessed to principles of moral restraint, capitalism yielded bountiful fruits of greed, fraud and crime. It was this darker side of the American moon that had to be denied. What was needed was some kind of theology adjusted to the plutocratic circumstance, a means of changing the faith in money into the coin of a secular faith. Possessors of great wealth found it prudent to acquire newspapers and public relations counsel. A choir of authors and journalists outbid one another in their eagerness to compose hymns to Mammon and sing odes to the personifications of cash. If some

10. Before his indictment for insider trading on Wall Street, Ivan Boesky, the arbitrageur known for his best-selling autobiography in praise of greed, was constantly in demand as a commencement speaker at the nation's universities.

of the older magnates didn't have the patience to sit for flattering portraits, their heirs and assigns (whether constituted as blood relations or corporate boards of directors) commissioned a gallery of hagiographies in which the ancient highwayman appeared in the ennobling light of philanthropist, art collector, humanist, saint. What once had been honestly seen as a pit began to be transformed into the disembodied and vaguely benign "free market."

The current generation of choristers stands in the long line of profitable succession that began with the cupbearers hired by Vanderbilt and Rockefeller. Their books fall into one of two classes—the tract, in which the author teaches the reader how to get rich; and the fairy tale, in which the author explains the divine and blameless origin of the American economic miracle.[11] The second genre is more difficult, possibly because the practice of American capitalism so seldom conforms to cherished theories of individualism, open markets and boundless opportunity. Obliged to preach the virtues of thrift and hard work to a congregation that lives off its rents and dividends, the writer has to make up in poetic fervor for very small businesses—for rock singers and professional athletes as well as the owners of pizza franchises. In its larger movements—the federal government, broadcasting networks, companies listed among the Fortune 500—the national economy depends on systematic price-fixing, monopoly, noncompetitive bidding and a sophisticated degree of state planning.[12]

11. Among books of the first class, all of them derived from P.T. Barnum's *The Art of Money-Getting* published in 1840, I think of *Iacocca*, *In Search of Excellence* and *The Seven Minute Manager*. Books of the second class include *Wealth and Poverty*, *Losing Ground* and *Two Cheers for Capitalism*.

12. Nor does the entrepreneurial temperament prosper within the institutional restraints of a gigantic corporation. Anybody who has any doubts on this score needs only to read the accounts of the disagreements between Roger Smith, chairman of General Motors, and H. Ross Perot, the Texas computer magnate who bought a large block of the company's stock. Perot served for several months on the company's board of directors and then quit in disgust, baffled by the company's stupidity.

That this is so should be obvious to anybody who takes the trouble to think about the American military budget (currently $350 billion per annum) or ask a few elementary questions as to why American workmanship is so poor or why so many American products cannot be sold in the world market.

How, for instance, could the defense industries stay in business, much less employ a substantial fraction of the population, without the assurance of contracts over long periods of time and unless their products were exempt from the proverbial test of utility?[13] In a society supposedly distinguished by its individualism and diversity, why do all the hotels and office buildings and suburbs look the same? Why does so much of the food taste the same, and so much of the television news sound as if it had been written by the same committee of ten? Why has the vast expenditure for public education over the last twenty-five years resulted in a declining standard of literacy? Why has the easing of government regulation driven into bankruptcy so many of the smaller and presumably "innovative" enterprises that the new rules were meant to encourage and sustain? Why has the legislation intended to provide health care to more people at lower cost yielded precisely the opposite result?

The answers to most of these questions can be traced to the preference for the beauty of dogmatic belief over the nuisance of unsightly fact. John Kenneth Galbraith was at some pains to point out the disparities as long ago as 1965 in *The New Industrial State*. In an essay published at the end of 1985 Galbraith observed that the Reagan administration had raised the power of rhetoric to the degree of mystical faith. Supported by a claque of sophists (among them George Gilder, who defines capitalism as another word for altruism, and by Michael Novak, who equates the indifference of the market to the redeeming purity of Christian love), Reagan and his friends proclaimed their uncompromising commitment

13. In 1986 the Defense Department estimated it had paid $50 billion for equipment that didn't work.

to free enterprise and their steadfast determination to get the government off the public back. The events of the Reagan era betray the ritual phrases. The government has been used almost exclusively to the benefit of the equestrian classes—intervening in the steel industry, subsidizing American exporters through the Export-Import Bank, rescuing the Chrysler Corporation as well as hundreds of banks (most notably Continental Illinois), guaranteeing farm prices and farm credit institutions, approving the inside trading preliminary to corporate mergers and takeovers, sustaining the defense industries and protecting the insurance companies.

Throughout the whole lexicon of American political journalism since 1945, the apologists on all sides of all arguments tend to agree on a division between good and evil that can be reduced to the following schema:

GOOD	EVIL
private	public
the self	the world
feeling	thought
simplicity	complexity
expression	art
the country	the city
innocence	experience

By and large this same system of value defines the cosmology of recent American literature, which, with few notable exceptions, constitutes another of the American rituals of innocence. Throughout the nineteenth century and well into the twentieth, the country's better writers (among them Mark Twain, Ambrose Bierce, William Dean Howells, Henry Adams, Edith Wharton, Theodore Dreiser, Thorstein Veblen, John Dos Passos, H.L. Mencken and Dorothy Parker) still could discuss the mechanics of money. The sardonic spirit was never dominant, but prior to 1945 it still could reflect the temperament of a people who didn't take themselves too seriously, who could afford to laugh at their own absurdity. After the war, and more obviously through the decades of the 1960s and 1970s, the voices became muffled in abstraction and overlaid with the gloss of metaphor.

Like any other crowd of arrivistes, the newly rich society wished to put as much distance as possible between its place of residence and its place of business. Polite opinion became too solemn to tolerate affronts to its dignity, and it was as impolite to discuss money in "serious fiction" as it was to mention the subject in the drawing room. Among writers applying for membership in the company of immortals a well-bred lack of knowledge about money, or anything else that stunk of the marketplace, served as proof of a refined sensibility.

Beyond the flowering borders of John Updike's prose, the country recklessly abandoned itself to a frenzy of conspicuous consumption. All kinds of vulgar people went about the vulgar business of making vulgar fortunes. The booms in real estate matched or surpassed the booms in electronics, in the record and publishing industries, in television, in professional sports, in oil and arbitrage. Excited herds jostled to get into the best deal, the most prestigious resort, the most expensive store. In Washington the government joined the orgy of speculation. Through a sequence of Democratic and Republican administrations the government inflated the currency to float the bubble of prosperity. Congressmen ordered new suites of offices and assistants. President Lyndon Johnson pronounced the country rich enough to afford both the luxury of peace and the sport of war. The Defense Department approved cost overruns amounting to many billions of dollars for weapons so ornate and ineffectual as to bear comparison to the poodles kept by the plutocracy in the Newport of the 1890s. Vulgar journalists, of course, were allowed to talk about such things; such was their métier, and they were expected to provide the stuff of gossip—about deals, mergers, the gold and credit markets. So also the commercial authors who, like Harold Robbins, could talk about the so-called real world with as much license as the anonymous chroniclers at *Forbes, Newsweek* and *The National Enquirer.*

But in the spheres of writing specifically and self-consciously literary none of the acquisitive frenzy of the period intruded upon the solemn contemplation of the self. Most of the writers were themselves rich. Having been well brought up in the better universities, they had learned to repress the expression of their monetary needs and desires in much the same way their Victorian ancestors had repressed offensive sexual impulses. The paradigmatic work of fiction, taught for a quarter of a century in the nation's schools of creative writing and published unremittingly in *The New Yorker,* achieved their most brilliant effects in the precious metals of symbolism. More often than not their protagonist is a sensibility, not a person.

Variations on the descent into the devouring maw of time and age account for the bulk of American literary fiction published between 1960 and 1980. The theme is so persistent that I sometimes wonder why so many writers of my generation and acquaintance regard themselves as tourists traveling in an alien wilderness. If they could be asked to fill out a passport stating their metaphysical place of origin, I suspect it wouldn't occur to them to give their nationality as American. Probably they would identify themselves by region or degree of sensibility—as Southerners, or Catholics, or structuralists, or Marxists—but always as discerning visitors from a better world (frequently confused with childhood) passing through town on their way to Cannes or the English Department at Berkeley.[14]

For as long as I have been going to the *levées* of the New York literary salons I don't think that I have met more than two or three

---

14. As editor of a magazine that continues to publish informed writing, I'm happy to say that I still can find a good many exceptions to the general rule of narcissism. Among the writers whom I think especially good, I would list Evan Connell, Walker Percy, Robert Stone, Larry Heinemann and Joan Didion.

people who know much about the specific weights and measures of economics, medicine, history, law, finance, physics or human anatomy. Even reading in these subjects apparently has become distasteful, as if they constitute too ominous a reminder of the world's rigor and contingency. I once spoke to a critic who reported he had seen a child drown in a flood. The child's death impressed him as being faintly vulgar. Not so much frightful or shocking as a transgression against the canons of good taste. He went on to explain that what has become inconceivable for both the writers and readers of "serious" fiction is the possibility of anybody becoming implicated in the realm of action. Even the smallest of actions might prove catastrophic—if not to oneself then possibly to a cousin or a newt—and so it is best to do nothing at all. The characters define themselves by virtue of their moral and aesthetic attitudes and by the mutual recognition (or, more often, nonrecognition) of states of refined feeling.

Prior to the twentieth century, the bulk of the world's literature was written by men who had some knowledge of business or the state. I think of Sophocles and Thucydides (both military commanders) of Seneca, Cicero and Caesar (all politicians), of Montaigne, Bacon, Donne, Pascal, Fielding, Gibbon, Burke, Jefferson, Franklin, Tocqueville, Trollope, Stendhal, Lincoln, Huysmans, Marx, Bismarck, Keynes, Cavafy, De Gaulle, Malraux, Churchill and Freud. The enormous wealth of the United States had made possible the existence of a verbal class that need do nothing but produce objects of language as ornate, and often as lifeless and heavy, as the jeweled chalices and gold figurines contrived for the greater glory of medieval popes. Organized into subsidiary guilds, the members of this class talk chiefly to themselves—weapons analyst to weapons analyst, historian to historian, public relations counsel to public relations counsel, lawyer to lawyer, novelist to novelist, and so forth through the hierarchy of intelligible discourse. The guild makes a profession of reading books and forming opinions; it feeds off itself, writing about the act of writing, producing commentaries on commentaries.

Every now and then I go to one of those melancholy seminars at which, almost continuously for twenty years, the well-known authors of the moment ask each other ponderous questions about the fate of American letters. Everybody talks about the transmigration of the American novel, about the quality of truth found in journalism, about the decay of criticism. When listening to the set speeches, I ask myself who reads the novels of William Burroughs except the people who have reason to write about the novels of William Burroughs? Is it conceivable that the physicists at the Livermore laboratories look to the stories of John Updike to inform their speculations about the nature of the universe, or that George Shultz, en route to yet another disappointing exchange of views with an Islamic tyrant, rummages through the novels of John Irving in the hope of finding some hint as to the purpose of diplomacy?

The questions reduce themselves to absurdity, and the writers of the present generation, well aware of the absurdity, come to think of themselves as guests of the management. What else can a poor scribbler do but sing and dance and play with the toys of words? Joseph Heller makes bleak jokes about the inanity of Washington, D.C., because he has no choice in the matter. Knowing nothing about why or how the government functions, he makes a virtue of necessity and presents his ignorance as wit. Other writers seek to curry favor with their unseen hosts by transforming themselves into clowns or prophets, offering parodies and self-parodies, never knowing what will endear them to the audience behind the screen—an audience that, for reasons unstated, may or may not be amused. Thus the vogue for autobiographies on the part of so many writers still in their twenties or thirties. Surely the managers must also have been children once; surely they will listen to the confessions of a young girl's youth and early sorrows. Although brought to the highest pitches of sentiment by the woman diarists, the genre also embraces the novels of middle-aged English professors. Even at the age of forty they send postcards from Europe or academia. Being observant lads, they notice sexual comings and goings in the dormitories or on the lawns, and somewhere in the drunken summer darkness they're sure there lurks the answer to Donne's question about who cleft the devil's foot. But they still don't know what Daddy does when he gets off the train in New York or Washington, or how he gets the money that pays for the divorce lawyer, the new bicycle or the library's complete edition of Proust.

Rather than being ashamed of their ignorance, the literary guilds take a perverse and willful pride in what they regard as their spiritual cleanliness. If they remain ignorant of the evils abroad in the world (choosing to see them as symbols and abstractions instead of as specific cruelties inflicted on specific individuals for specific reasons), so also they can disclaim any responsibility for the casualty lists. None of it is their fault.

6. THE PRECARIOUS EDEN

To not get in is to die.
> —Young woman on being refused admission to Area,
> a New York discotheque

Whoever expects to walk peacefully in the world must be money's guest.
> —NORMAN O. BROWN

CHANGING THE COIN of their innocence into the prices of real estate, Americans conceive of the world as being divided, unevenly but along only one axis, between a nation of the rich and a nation of the poor. The geopolitics of money transcend the boundaries of sovereign states. The frontiers run between the first- and third-class cabins on a Boeing 747, between private and public schools, between the right and wrong tables at Le Cirque. The Upper East Side of Manhattan belongs to the same polity as the Seventh Arrondissement in Paris; the yachts moored off Cannes or the Costa Brava sail under the flags of the same admiralty that posts squadrons off Newport and Palm Beach. The American plutocrat traveling between the Beau Rivage in Lausanne and the Connaught Hotel in London crosses not into another country but into another province within the hegemony of wealth. His credit furnishes him with a lingua franca translated as readily into Deutschemarks as into rials or yen or francs, buying more or less the same food in the same class of restaurants, the same services in the same class of hotels, the same amusements and same conversation, the same politicians, dinner companions, newspaper columnists and accordion music.

Despite the systems of modern communications (or possibly because of them), the hierarchies of international capitalism resemble the old feudal arrangements under which an Italian noble might swear fealty to the Holy Roman Empire and a Norman duke declare himself the vassal of an English king. The lords and barons of the modern corporation become liegemen to the larger fiefs and holding companies owing their allegiance not to Britain or the United States but to BP, IBM or Citibank. A corporation's trademark, apparent nationality or address no longer offers a reliable indication as to the nature of its ownership. Even within the narrow confines of an industry as small as publishing, the names seldom mean what they say. Doubleday, arguably the most jingoistic of American publishers, belongs to the Bertelsmann Publishing Group, a West German media syndicate. Another German syndicate, Verlagsgruppe Georg von Holtzbrinck, recently acquired *Scientific American*. Rupert Murdoch, the Australian press magnate, owns, through a combination of holding companies, several British and American newspapers (among them the London *Times*, the *Boston Herald, New York* magazine, and the *New York Post*), as well as Harper & Row and 50 percent interest in the Fox television network. More sophisticated arrangements, all of them feudal in character, govern the tables of corporate organization in oil, banking and retail.

In the American mind the amphictyony of wealth assumes the ecumenical place once occupied by the medieval church. Within this favored estate everybody obeys the same laws and pays homage to the same princes.

About the qualifications for admission the gatekeepers of the media attempt to be precise. In the spring and summer of 1982

Architectural Digest published a series of advertisements for itself characterizing the magazine's 550,000 subscribers as residents of an exemplary suburb identified as "Affluence, America." A drawing executed in the Art-Deco manner of the 1920s showed a handsome man and an attractive woman dressed in costumes reminiscent of a movie derived from *The Great Gatsby*. They stand against a background of horses and lawns, the accompanying text proclaiming them peers of a privileged realm and attributing to them characteristics presumably held in common by all the other happy citizens of Affluence, America:

- Average household income of $114,000 per annum
- 8 of 10 buy fine arts and antiques
- Average home entertains 65 guests per month
- 5 of 10 own two or more cars
- 1 of 5 worth at least $1 million
- Average house worth $250,000
- 3 of 4 go abroad every 3 years
- 2 of 5 buy wine by the case[1]

Nor do the media mince words about the comforts found within the compounds of the precarious Eden. The real-estate offerings published in the nation's better magazines and newspapers achieve a breathless tone of voice appropriate to a second-grade reader recounting the adventures of Dick and Jane. All of them sound alike, but the prospectus for apartments costing between $500,000 and $10 million at the Trump Tower in Manhattan sets the standard for

1. The advertisement quite properly omits any reference to the less flattering aspects of Affluence, America. The apologist doesn't seek out statistics on the other side of the coin—for example, 2 of 5 in the hands of a psychoanalyst; 1 of 2 divorced; 8 of 10 estranged from their children; 3 of 4 complain of chronic depression; 4 of 8 addicted to cocaine; 1 of 5 under indictment for theft or fraud, etc., etc.

the genre. Describing the property as "the world's most prestigious address," the realtor begins the sales pitch as follows:

> Imagine a tall bronze tower of glass. Imagine life within such a tower. Elegant. Sophisticated. Strictly Beau Monde.
>
> It's been fifty years at least since people could actually live at this address. They were Astors. And the Whitneys lived just around the corner. And the Vanderbilts across the street.
>
> You approach the residential entrance—an entrance totally inaccessible to the public—and your staff awaits your arrival. Your concierge gives you your messages. And you pass through the lobby.
>
> Quickly, quietly, the elevator takes you to your floor, and your elevator man sees you home.
>
> You turn the key and wait a moment before clicking on the light.
>
> A quiet moment to take in the view—a wall-to-wall, floor-to-ceiling New York at dusk. The sky is pink and gray. Thousands of tiny lights are snaking their way through Central Park. Bridges are becoming jeweled necklaces.
>
> Your diamond in the sky. It seems a fantasy. And you are home.
>
> Maid service, valet, stenographers, interpreters, multilingual secretaries, Telex and other communications equipment, hairdressers, masseuses, limousines, conference rooms—all at your service with a phone call to your concierge.
>
> If you can think of any amenity, any extravagance or nicety of life, any service that we haven't mentioned, then it probably hasn't been invented yet.[2]

2. As of April 1986, the two residents of the Trump Tower who had been most in the news (i.e., titular heirs to the aura that once drifted around the heads of the Astors, the Whitneys and the Vanderbilts) were Johnny Carson and a notorious madam.

The prospectus mentions the principal points of interest deemed essential to the American dream of Eden. First and most importantly, the place is exclusive. Not just anybody gets past the concierge. Secondly, the place is secure—an enclave on a high floor, at the end of a long driveway, over a bridge, beyond a gatehouse, surrounded, if not by moats and battlements, at least by lawns, beach front, walls, golf courses and a privately owned regiment of police. Lastly and most interestingly, the place bears comparison to a child's nursery, sustained by a system of services as satisfyingly complete as those provided to an infant in the womb.

The desire for exclusivity is as American as the sentiment in favor of democracy. Once having proclaimed our loyalty to the abstract idea that all men are created equal, we do everything in our power to prove ourselves unequal. Among the world's peoples, none other belongs to so many clubs, associations, committees and secret societies. The obligation to invent ourselves prompts us to the ceaseless manufacture of class distinctions, as if the collections of our emblems, memberships, insignia, keys, passwords and club ties might somehow make the weight of an English title. Anybody who has had the misfortune to serve on an admissions committee for a reputedly exclusive club, or, even worse, to serve on the board of directors of a cooperative apartment building in New York, can testify to the national longing for what the Trump organization calls "an entrance totally inaccessible to the public." The co-op committees insist on examining the balance sheets of prospective buyers and argue for hours about the possibility of a stain on the linen of the applicant's social or commercial credit. In the more exclusive buildings the buyer not only must put up the entire price in cash (often as much as $5 million), but he must prove additional assets of a safely larger amount.

For the last fifty years Mrs. Joseph Reed has presided over the society gathered at Jupiter Island, Florida, possibly the most exclusive of the winter resorts frequented by the Protestant rich.

Established in the 1930s on a narrow sandspit a few miles north of Palm Beach, the resort prides itself on its indifference to the gaudy spectacles of the *nouveau riche*. Unlike the residents of the Trump Tower, the owners of property on Jupiter Island have transcended the need to display their wealth. The men wear button-down shirts frayed at the collar, and the women seldom entertain in a manner that could be construed as opulent. The gentry prefer old, wooden station wagons (affectionately known as "woodies") to the showiness of a Mercedes Benz, and the butlers, reflecting the customs of the household, incline to place journalists and celebrities in the same class of undesirables with IRS agents and terrorists.

It's no good going to Jupiter Island unless one also owns a house and belongs to the Jupiter Island Club. Both these privileges remain firmly within the gift of Mrs. Reed. The prospective candidate for admission first must pass three probationary winters on the island, allowing Mrs. B. the opportunity to observe an applicant's deportment. If at any time during those three winters Mrs. Reed finds anything amiss, she sends her butler to the candidate with the gift of a new cashmere sweater. The sweater is for the trip north.

Lest the reader think that such rituals occur only among the very rich, consider also the ordinance passed a few years ago by the township of River Edge, New Jersey, forbidding those of its residents who happened to be tradesmen (carpenters, house painters, television repairmen, etc.) to park their vans in the driveways of their own homes. The town council decided that the signs, licenses and commercial decals on the sides of the vans spoiled the illusion of suburban ease. Any strangers driving through the town might come to scornful conclusions about the kind of people occupying the real estate. The mayor was quoted as saying, "Trucks do depreciate property values," and the town council advised owners of such vehicles to cover them with tarpaulins, to paint out the lettering on the doors or to exchange the vans for station wagons. The ordinance didn't specify "woodies."[3]

With regard to the security of their precarious Eden, the American equestrian classes stand willing to bear almost any inconvenience or expense. The heirs to even modest fortunes exist in a perpetual state of dread. Because they seldom know how to earn money, they come to think of it as a magical stone or idol in a bank vault. For reasons they never quite manage to understand, the money was provided by a djinn who happened to be crossing the tracks of the Southern Pacific Railroad on a warm afternoon in 1884. To different families the djinn appeared at different times in different disguises—as an old prospector who gave away his claim to the Comstock lode, as a mother who could dance or a father who hit it big in the movies, or as an immigrant engineer, kindly but shabbily dressed, who invented a process for smelting steel but then sold it for a pittance to the founder of the fortune. Under no matter what circumstances the title to wealth was conferred, the heirs know one thing for certain: the djinn has come and gone and won't be coming back. Foolish heirs sometimes forget this great truth, and so they squander a few million in schemes advanced by promoters who persuade them that the djinn still lives, that he can be found in the depths of a real estate deal or on the sunny heights of a high-tech stock.

Prudent heirs shun the folly of such temptation. They have been taught to mistrust the illusions of the world, the flesh and the Devil, and they know that without money they are lost. The abyss looms

---

3. Magazines practice similar acts of exclusion when they prune their subscription lists of readers who inhabit the poorer zip codes. Advertisers pay higher rates for affluent audiences, and they don't wish to associate their products with buyers of an inferior class. The Chubb Insurance Group places its advertisements only in those magazines that can claim readers with an average net worth of $500,000.

on all sides—in the trees beyond the croquet lawn, in the tall grass behind the hedge, in the bar downstairs from the grand ballroom, across the street under the treacherous neon light. Their awareness of the abyss makes them fearful of shadows. Dependent upon a magic they don't know how to replenish, they feel themselves threatened by enemies of infinite number: thieves, journalists, tax agents, blackmailers, debauched women, unscrupulous grocers, Third World dictators, terrorists, Communists and populist sentiment in Detroit. They remain certain that nobody would help them in their distress, that nowhere in the bleak waste of the universe could they find any human hand willing to stay their fall into ruin and disgrace. Thus they huddle together like alarmed cattle in the enclaves of Fifth Avenue or Palm Beach or Beverly Hills—"wherever it is," in F. Scott Fitzgerald's phrase, "that people go and are rich together." Fitzgerald missed the point of his own observation. What he thought was a matter of choice is a matter of necessity. Where else except among their own kind can the rich feel safe from what they feel is the justifiable envy and resentment of the less fortunate? No wonder they conceive of their money as an idol in the basement, from which, from time to time with trembling reluctance, they chip away a fragment of the living rock.[4]

Assessed in the scale of median family income, the two richest cities in California are Rolling Hills (population 2,076) and Hidden Hills (population 1,812), situated at opposite ends of Los Angeles County. Both of them are entirely enclosed by walls. Countless other communities across the United States crouch behind defensive perimeters patrolled by dogs. The owners of property in places like Greenwich, Connecticut, and Grosse Pointe, Michigan, rely on spiked hedges, weight sensors, electronic surveillance and saturation floodlights. In 1984 the nation's equestrian classes spent $29

4. When Americans travel abroad they carry with them their passion for security. The oil company compounds in Saudi Arabia, like the military enclaves in South Vietnam and the expatriate colonies in Paris and Rome, replicate the safe houses of the American rich.

billion for various calibers of armed protection—private police, burglar alarms, bulletproof cars, bodyguards.[5] During the same year the nation as a whole (i.e., via its federal, state and municipal governments) allocated only $15 billion to public law enforcement. All corporations of any size or pretension maintain security systems as elaborate as those deployed by the Pentagon, and it is as difficult to gain entrance to *Newsweek* or *The New York Times* as it is to pass through checkpoints into East Berlin.

As might be expected, the heaviest security defends the perimeters of money. In 1986, Richard Laermer, a writer for *Manhattan, Inc.*, toured the nine-story building in which Shearson Lehman houses its computers and stores the records of its financial transactions. He noticed the usual sober-minded precautions:

> . . . but the security system is what is most overwhelming. For my escorted tour, I come in through the front doors and go up an escalator leading to the mezzanine/lobby/security entrance, where overhead cameras gaze at me. A security person, one of a half dozen or so posted in the lobby, directs me to a "checkpoint" where I sign in and get the visitor's card that must be attached to my lapel in order for me to be admitted through the turnstile by another security person. Employees, I am told, are issued cardkeys, bearing only their photographs, that allow them to pass through the turnstile. Cameras follow my progress to the elevator bank and when I get off upstairs. An employee would now have to pull out the card-key and insert it into a slot to enter what is referred to as a "people floor." (Only specially coded cards can get one near the floors that house the data-processing

---

5. The citizens of California support 1,654 alarm companies, and in Miami a mechanic charges $50,000 to equip a Cadillac with gunports, floor armor and the capacity to release tear gas. When interviewed by *The New York Times* in the spring of 1983 the mechanic had so many orders on hand that he couldn't promise delivery for six months.

machines and the emergency generators. Those areas have cameras *and* guards.) A door opens, then locks shut. When I ask why it locks, I am told, "So the next card can properly function." Sure enough, I'm now trapped between two doors. To get through the next one, an employee has the choice of either putting the card in yet another slot or inserting it into a contraption that looks like a microwave oven with a coin changer. A sign instructs: Look into the mirror. If the facial features match the ID photo, one is allowed to pass. If not, an alarm goes off and a guard arrives on the scene.

American celebrities routinely employ armed escorts, and when invited to speak at a university or business convention Henry Kissinger insists that his expenses cover the cost of first-class travel and hotel accommodation for two bodyguards.[6] Most Hollywood actresses go to some trouble to disguise themselves in shabby sweatshirts, old sneakers and dark glasses when appearing in the demilitarized zones otherwise known as the real world. They dress in their personae of film stars only when making well-photographed entrances into heavily fortified positions.

Raised to the power of public policy, the national obsession with security becomes the military budget (as said before, $370 billion a year). What is the theory and practice of American isolationism if not the wish to keep the nation safe within the walls of fortress America? The Pentagon appropriates vast sums in its mystical quest for the invincible shield of Achilles (a.k.a. "Star Wars"), and the Congress passes increasingly severe immigration laws. Just as the makers of locks and burglar alarms do a land-office business in every American city and suburb, so also the nation's defense contractors sell the dream of hiding the country under a bubble of bulletproof

6. When the late William Casey, formerly director of the CIA, played golf at Palm Beach, he ambled around the course in the company of two Secret Service agents armed with machine guns.

glass. The White House has been reinforced with concrete revetments, and in 1986 Secretary of State Shultz asked Congress for $2.8 billion to fortify American embassies abroad.[7] The Congress in 1987 armed the nation with more stringently protective tariffs, and the Justice Department under the nervous direction of Edwin Meese proposed a battery of laws to defend the American people against the impurities in their urine and their speech.[8]

Together with the promise of bodily ease and safety, admission to the precarious Eden behind the walls of money holds out the hope of the great American escape. It is the feeling of suspension in a world outside of time the American rich define as happiness. They wish to believe the season is always summer, the hour always six o'clock in the evening (i.e., the traditional "children's hour" or the hour when the adults permit themselves their first drink), the instant always the instant just before the curtain goes up on the Christmas performance of *The Nutcracker Suite*. Imagining that time remains static and fixed within the enchanted gardens of money, the leisure classes see no reason to grow up, much less grow old. Nor can they imagine why everything shouldn't remain precisely as it was in the sunlit memory of their first romance, their first million, their first toy.[9]

Both the Republican Risorgimento of the early 1980s and the countercultural insurrection of the middle 1960s proclaimed allegiance to the manifesto of Peter Pan. The manner of dress had changed, and so had the age of the malcontents, but the habits of mind were similar. Both revolutions excited the passions of the

7. Testifying before the Senate Committee on Foreign Relations, Shultz characterized American diplomats as "front-line troops" in the war against terrorism. "They are," he said, "being shot at." When traveling in Bogotá, Colombia, in 1985, Shultz was accompanied by 151 bodyguards.
8. In 1980 tariffs protected 20 percent of American goods; by 1987 the favor had been granted to 35 percent of American goods.
9. Among the rich the worst quarrels occur during the summer or Christmas holidays. Everybody is supposed to be having a good time, and it's annoying to be interrupted at one's games or be reminded of one's mortality.

radical bourgeoisie—"revolutions from above," instigated by rich people believing they were entitled to more than they already possessed. Like the admirers of Jane Fonda's political attitudes, Ronald Reagan's partisans cast themselves as rebels against "the system" and posed as romantic figures at odds with a world they never made, a world encumbered with the sins of death and time.

What else is the promise of the Republican Risorgimento if not the dream of American individualism regained, of capitalism unbound, of rescue from the vultures of federal regulation, of freedom to go plundering through a world in which the spoils properly belong to the rich, the strong and the well-connected? The promises aren't so different from those of the open road traveled by Jack Kerouac and Bob Dylan, except that El Dorado is now to be found on the temporal instead of the spiritual frontier.

The new movie required remarkably few revisions of the old script. During the Age of Aquarius it was impossible to trust anybody over thirty—unless the poor wretch held tenure at a university and was willing to wear a beard and sign petitions on behalf of Consciousness III. By 1981 it was impossible to trust anybody under the age of thirty—unless the stout fellow had already made his first million and owned a seat on the stock exchange. George Gilder's *Wealth and Poverty* replaced Charles Reich's *The Greening of America* as the holy text of reaction. One troupe of arcadian Californians superseded another on the stage of the national political theater. Orange County displaced the Woodstock Nation as the railhead of crusade, and the locus of the earthly paradise moved from a commune in the White Mountains to a golf course in Palm Springs.

Declaring time to be circular, apologists for both revolutions announced the great truth that nothing ever changes in the land of perpetual summer. The counterculture found its converts among people who didn't wish to grow up; the Republican Risorgimento recruited its congregation among people unwilling to grow old.

Innumerable teachers and school administrators have remarked on the loss of historical memory among the current generation of

American students. A poll conducted during the bicentennial year showed that 20 percent of those asked couldn't remember what had taken place in 1776; among an audience of college students at the University of Michigan in 1981, nobody in the classroom knew what was meant by the word "Nazi."[10] The effect is much amplified by television, which sustains the illusion that nothing takes time. The television screen presents a world of Platonic forms and metaphors, a world in which history is meaningless and memory irrelevant, where instant fame (reflected in the fleeting smile of a talk-show host) leads to instant eclipse, where politicians come and go in a matter of minutes and a woman's life can be transformed between commercials.

The juxtaposition of images aspires to the simplicity of moral fable. The news footage is reliably grim—riots in the slums of Uganda or Mexico City, murder victims being loaded into police ambulances in Brooklyn. Scenes of poverty and human wretchedness alternate with the advertisements for vacations in sunny Florida, for $20,000 automobiles and unlimited credit, for skin cream and perfume and cleansing lotions, all guaranteed to restore the bloom of eternal youth.

The disorientation in time allows people to imagine themselves resident in a magical present. Because the viewing audience seldom can remember what it saw yesterday, the politician, like the actor or the advertising salesman, has no choice but to tell the crowd what it thinks it wants to hear at precisely that moment, counting on national amnesia to preserve him from the embarrassment of having to redeem his promises with acts.[11]

10. In his State of the Union address in 1987, President Reagan said, "The calendar can't measure America because we were meant to be an endless experiment in freedom, with no limit to our reaches, no boundaries to what we can do, no end point to our hopes." Some months earlier a New York City schoolteacher, explaining why it was pointless to teach history, said, "Our children don't think they have anything to learn from dead people."
11. President Reagan was elected on the promise to balance the budget. Within six years his administration had run up the national debt to $2 trillion.

It is the desire to escape the indignities of time that gives to the settings of American wealth an oddly tropical character. Not that the weather is always warm, or the buildings invariably made of stucco, but somehow the atmosphere is suffused with the torpor of the tropics. Having served a fair amount of time within the gardens of the American Eden, I notice that the nominal geography doesn't make much difference to the character of the place. Whether in Coconut Grove or Beverly Hills or Winnetka, or Bar Harbor or Locust Valley or Newport, the settings conform to the standardized images of the fashion and decorating magazines. I think of a summer sea and windmills behind topiary hedges; I hear the sound of tennis balls and dance music, and I can smell the scent of jasmine and honeysuckle and cut grass; I think of rooms with silk wallpaper in which the guests play ceaseless games of bridge or piquet or backgammon; of photographs in silver frames and flowers on a marble table in the hall; of music in twelve speakers and somebody famous standing under one of Andy Warhol's soup cans; of a midnight supper served on a terrace and a young girl saying of a lost college roommate, "She lives down on the Lower East Side somewhere, with a lot of Negroes and things."

The impressionist view of the sea doesn't necessarily preclude the hope of consciousness; nor do the flowers from Marla or the wine that costs $275 the bottle. At least one of the people present owns something thought to be worth owning—a newspaper, a politician, a football team, an island in the Bahamas. Most of the guests have eaten dinner at Le Cirque or the Four Seasons, danced at Castel's, stayed at Claridge's and attended a party given by Swifty Lazar.

Why then is the furnishing of the resident mind as bare as the floor in the maid's room? Why is the talk so relentlessly trivial—a soporific murmuring of platitudes as steady as the sound of water running through the filters in a pool?

The disparity between wealth and intellect troubled me until, reading carefully the advertisement for the Trump Tower, I understood what should have been the obvious analogy to the nursery. The rich, like well-brought-up children, are meant to be seen, not heard. Enameled figures embodying the abstractions of beauty and power, their status as precious objects forecloses any further hope of discovery. What could they possibly learn from one another? How could they afford the risk of evolving into somebody else? Too much has been invested in their clothes, or, if celebrities, in the expensive fabrication of their public personae. Like characters in an Arcadian fairy tale, the rich inhabit a realm of being rather than a world of becoming. They have no use for the ambiguities of existential development.

Money has so little competition in the American scheme of things that in social gatherings of the rich it is impossible to come across somebody who is not rich. The guests belong to one of only two dispensations—other people as wealthy as the hostess, or celebrities prominent enough to have become as collectible as the furniture. Maybe I exaggerate the point, or maybe my memory has become conveniently selective, but never once in my encounters with the troupe of brilliantly lit personalities in the New York repertory company do I remember meeting a writer who was not well known, a scientist unaffiliated with a well-endowed institution, a politician out of favor or a businessman who didn't employ as many people as could be found on the Yucatán Peninsula.

On any given night at one of several addresses on the Upper East Side of Manhattan, I could expect to meet people renowned for their brilliance, whose photographs currently were decorating the pages of *Newsweek* or *Time*. They had seen everything at least once (in the manner of children sent to Europe and the opera), but lacked the capacity to combine the fragments of their observation into the structures of thought or meaning.[12] They talked about hotels and the view

12. *Habits of the Heart*, published in 1985 by the University of California Press, presents interviews with two hundred people who, despite their material comforts, professed themselves as mute as stones, utterly lacking a language in which they could express their longings, their moral purposes, the point of their lives.

of the Arno at sunset, about servants and games and their clothes. At least a few of the guests could turn these topics into charming little stories, but the bulk of their talk approached the exemplary norm set by President John F. Kennedy who, as portrayed by his nominal friend Ben Bradlee in *Conversations with Kennedy*, remained consistently petty, spiteful and vain.

Eventually I understood that the talk was irrelevant. The point of the evening's entertainment had to do with determining one's value in the social equivalent of a stock market. What was important was one's appearance in the room. Everyone marked present could safely assume that his or her name and reputation continued to hold a decent price. All those marked absent could be sold short. A truly fashionable party ended the moment it began, once everybody had been seen or not seen. The rest of the evening was superfluous. The guests might as well be spun sugar blown into the shapes of Venetian glass and filled with lemon mousse.

The photographs of the party appearing in the next day's paper, or the next week's issue of *W*, belong to the iconography of wealth. The dinner guests might as well be standing in the foreground of a Renaissance religious painting. Like the Medicis disguised as angels or shepherds, they have paid for the space, and expect to be introduced to the best people in Heaven. With an anxiety born of the fear of oblivion, they stare into the cameras with the same strained expression of a fourteenth-century Florentine moneylender peering at the Madonna. Understood in its metaphysical dimensions, Oscar de la Renta's drawing room exists within the same sphere of unrecorded time as a painted balcony in one of Sandro Botticelli's altarpieces.[13]

Of the most famous people in the room, it was not only presumptuous but also naïve to expect any correlation between the

13. Remarking on the stasis of celebrity, Whoopi Goldberg told *Playboy* magazine in 1987, "Stars don't get to *do* anything. Stars only *are*. They're a state of mind."

inward and outward surfaces of their personae. They went to so many meetings, attended so many conferences or parties, gave so many interviews, that they no longer had time to study or think. Although well-briefed by assistants bearing portfolios of data, they seldom knew how to translate numbers into social or political reality. Occasionally they read books written by their friends or looked at newspapers in which they could see the comforting reflection of their own name. Any further effort imposed an all but intolerable burden on their function as ceremonial effigies. It was enough that they had consented to appear; they couldn't also be expected to have something to say.

The emphasis on the trivial meets the specifications of White House protocol. Guests invited to small dinners for President Reagan received a telephone call on the afternoon prior to the event in which it was explained, by one of Reagan's social advisers, that the president preferred the conversation "light" and preferably confined to three permissible topics—sports, gossip and movies. At the very best parties among the very richest people in New York City in the middle 1980s it had become fashionable to throw food. The diversion was thought to be frightfully amusing and eliminated the tiresome business of having to feign an interest in the conversation.

Within the houses of the rich, the better decorators strive for the ambience of a well-appointed nursery—the walls painted pastel, the sofas and chairs covered in chintz, the rooms filled with expensive toys and sporting equipment. The consultants employed to furnish suites of corporate offices (i.e., to provide a homelike motif to the abattoir in which the resident management goes about the business of cutting the hearts out of its competitors) say that the executives choose, almost without exception, paintings of horses, ducks and boats. The same topics of illustration adorn the walls of an expensive kindergarten and the cabins of company airplanes.

The larger American corporations grant their executives the privileges of infants. The company provides expense allowances, medical treatment, trips and entertainments, planes, picnics and outings, cars, club memberships and, above all else, a ferociously protective secretary, who, like a good English nanny, arranges the daily schedule, pays the bills, remembers to send flowers for anniversaries and birthdays, makes dinner reservations and invents excuses that the nice gentleman's creditors or mistress might find plausible. The comforts and conveniences supposedly permit the executives to do a better job; in fact, they encourage the habits of infantilism prevalent at the higher altitudes of corporate privilege. Remarking on the condition to *The New York Times* in November 1982, a chief executive officer (name withheld on instruction of public relations counsel) said, "They sort of handle you like a precious egg."

If I look back over a period of thirty years' acquaintance with presidents of companies and directors of corporations, I see a succession of amiable gentlemen posed around the square of a card table, chatting pleasantly on a thirteenth green, rolling dice from a leather cup in a country club bar. They could talk intelligently enough about the specific instances of a specific deal (i.e., shoptalk narrowly defined); once the conversation ranged beyond the vicinity of their immediate financial interest, I can remember none of them making other than pleasantly vacant references to their comfort and their travel plans.[14] The phrase, "I got it in Palm Beach," could as easily refer to a new putter as to a suntan, an electronics company, a third wife or a venereal disease. If pressed by the need to sound important—to themselves if to nobody else—the more ponderous executives mentioned the current outrage in the newspapers and exchanged the tokens of received wisdom about the gold and credit markets, the loss of taste and standards,

---

14. Charles Francis Adams, reflecting in his autobiography on his life in the railroad business and his long acquaintance with such men as E.H. Harriman and J.P. Morgan, wrote: "A less interesting crowd I do not care to encounter. Not one that I have ever known would I care to meet again, either in this world or the next; nor is one of them associated in my mind with the idea of humor, thought or refinement."

the untrustworthiness of politicians and the malevolence of the Soviet Union. In January 1986 the monthly magazine *M* (a journal wholeheartedly devoted to the adoration of wealth) published an article entitled "Those Privileged CEO's and Their Princely Ways" in which the gentlemen in question were described as "the aristocrats of the age." The article accurately and admiringly reflected the vacuity of the presiding sensibility, noting the favorite topics of conversation (cars, corporate jets, golf, exercise, one's own salary and the wickedness of the press), the cherished aspirations (the perfect putt, a Cabinet post, a first-name relationship with Henry Kissinger, having an article published in the *Harvard Business Review*) and necessary luxuries (good-looking golf shoes, bodyguards, Mont Blanc pens, quiet wives and retinues of executive assistants). Elsewhere in the article it was explained that CEOs sometimes have trouble learning "to relate down" to the lesser folk in their employ and that families can be better understood as "executive support systems."[15]

Although pointing out that corporate executives often take inordinate pride in their airplanes, the article neglected to mention the fits of possessiveness that sometimes seize the owners of these shiny and expensive toys. Some years ago on a rainy night at LaGuardia Airport in New York two gentlemen from Pittsburgh, each in his own plane, found themselves delayed on the same runway. Both belonged to proper families—Richard Mellon Scaife,

---

15. Ralph Nader encountered the preferred sensibility when, in the course of questioning corporate magnates for his book *The Big Boys*, he attempted to interview John Welch, chairman of General Electric: "I was making a final entreaty for an interview when suddenly Welch's voice changed to a mixture of rapid pleading and a 'lemme outta here' tone. 'I don't need this,' he cried. 'I'm just a boy with knickers and a lollipop. I don't want to be part of a book. I'm just a grungy, lousy manager . . . . You can have access to the company on any other basis . . . . I don't want a high profile . . . . I'm just a grunt . . . . I'm just a man in a room.' No combination of written words could capture the wonderfully off-the-cuff, ingenuous voice of this supercharged general of GE."

heir to banking fortune, and the late Henry J. Heinz, heir to soup and ketchup fortune—and both were returning to Pittsburgh to attend the same charity ball. Heinz's plane, three or four planes behind Scaife's, developed mechanical trouble. Heinz climbed down into the rain and hurried forward to beg a ride home. Scaife appeared in the door and looked at Heinz with suspicion. Heinz explained the predicament, observing also that they were going to the same dance. But Scaife wasn't about to share his toy with any of the other children at the party. "No room," he said. "Go commercial."

The wish to be cared for, more prevalent among the rich than among the poor, is also characteristic of most journalists with pretensions to rank. During the decimations of CBS News in the winter of 1987, quite a few correspondents observed that because they were engaged in the upholding of a "public trust," they deserved to "be protected from the harsh realities of the world." Within what is undoubtedly the richest of the American compounds—the residential quarter on Manhattan's Upper East Side between Sixty-first and Eightieth streets—the local oligarchs (resting on a collective income of $4.4 billion a year) never stand in line and seldom feel the rain.

The infantilism of the American equestrian classes has an unhappy effect on the children born within the walls of the precarious Eden. The parents compete with the children for the available time, toys and attention. The weight of money, like the mass of an object within a gravitational field, imparts a corresponding velocity to the gratification of desire, and the speed with which one's wish can be made flesh constitutes a barrier to self-denial. People might want to love their children, but they don't have the time to notice, much less feel, their children's need. Given their wish to make time stand still, the future appears as an ominous looming on the horizon, a dreadful shadow falling across the pools of Narcissus. Children stand in the doorways like ghosts at a banquet—*memento mori* reminding a man of his own mortality and prompting him to ask, with increasing bitterness and resentment, why the world should become older.[16]

Assigned at an early age to the care of servants, surrounded through most of their lives by enemies whom they mistake for friends, the children of the rich tend to become orphans. They become as badly crippled as George Amory, their talent and sexual desire inhibited by what they instinctively and correctly recognize as the hatred of their progenitors.

Expressed at the level of public policy, the rage against the future results in the foreclosures of "zero growth," the steadily higher prices paid for objects that represent an investment in the past (gold, real estate, paintings, etc.), the pyramid of the national debt, the subtraction of funds from the purposes of research in the sciences or almost anything else that raises the grotesque possibility that the next generation might enjoy a range of pleasures unavailable to the senior partners.[17] How else is it possible to account for the fecklessness of a society that invests so little in the health and education of its children and seeks to buy off its citizens with toys, network television and drugs instead of demanding, in the way of a wise parent, that they rise to the aspirations of which they are capable? A politician's campaign promise is like the revision of a rich man's will, the holding out of an illusory benefit in return for a vote or a

16. Cornelia Guest, proclaimed deb of the year in 1983, informed a representative of *The Washington Post*, "Everything is going to stay exactly the same in New York. Nothing is going to change. The people aren't going to change. The parties aren't going to change."

17. In most environmental tracts, as well as in a good many popular movies, the future is barely recognizable as human; it appears in the guise of something dark and unclean, as if it were a monstrous womb likely to give birth to mutant and crawling things. On seeing the first ascent of Montgolfier's balloon from the palace of the Tuileries in 1783, the Maréchale de Villeroi, an ancient noblewoman of the *ancien* régime, fell back among the cushions of her carriage and sobbed, "Oh yes, now it's certain! One day they'll learn how to keep people alive forever, but 1 shall already be dead."

becoming show of respect. Sooner or later, however, the selfishness of the fathers provokes anger in the sons, which in turn incites, in Wall Street brokerage houses as well as on Harlem streets, bitter distrust of law, custom and anything else that stinks of institutional authority.

The work of sustaining the American equestrian classes in the illusion of a magical present falls to the lot of their servants. When not worrying about their health and safety, the ladies and gentlemen of quality complain about the difficulty of finding "decent help." The amenities provided by the Trump Tower ("maid service, valet, stenographers," etc.) speak to only the preliminary sets of expectation. For forty years I have listened to people complain about the service. On first joining the conversation among the well-dressed guests around a pool it is hard to know whether they are talking about a cook, a hairdresser or a secretary of state. The murmuring of the rich and their intellectual factota—in the drawing rooms of Washington and Southampton as well as in the journals of polite literary and political opinion—has a disappointed sound. English professors avowedly leftist and dowager aunts unashamedly fascist make the same observations about the decay of craftsmanship and the frightful expense of maintaining an adequate domestic or military establishment.

The boom in the "service industries" testifies to the immense wealth of a society that can afford to hire an increasing number and variety of upper servants—swamis, consultants, stock analysts, quack doctors, tennis instructors, dieticians, tax lawyers, accountants, agents, caterers, speechwriters, oracles, pedicurists, futurists, plastic surgeons, psychiatrists, gossipmongers, metaphysicians wearing the livery of the Ford Foundation or the American Enterprise Institute. The services can become fairly sophisticated. In New York it is possible to hire, for $500, a decorator who knows how to place pillows in a drawing room by tossing them casually about with just the right feeling of insouciance. A brochure distributed in 1986 by a Los Angeles company offered "the ultimate parking service." The second paragraph read as follows: "Valet parking is no longer a luxury for home entertaining. It has become an expected and welcome service, as it sets the tone of the party and sends the guests away at the end of the evening feeling very special and nurtured." At a dinner in New York in December 1986 I ran across an acquaintance who had been in San Francisco that autumn and reported meeting a consultant in sadomasochism. The consultant offered counseling and instruction to clients interested in those forms of degradation that offered the best chances of sexual, psychological and social success. His business had fallen off as a result of the AIDS epidemic, but on occasion he still provided the coroner's office with an opinion as to what might have killed an enthusiast who neglected to master one of the more complicated techniques.

Transposed into the sectors of public and civic behavior, the desire for decent help results in a bureaucracy of miraculous size and refinement. The country asks of its government what the rich ask of their servants. Accordingly, American democracy maintains an opulent domestic staff in Washington, employing a vast retinue of functionaries, orators, regulatory officials, aides-de-camp, secretaries, weapons analysts, deputies and augurs who perform the chores and ceremonies of government. Many of these services belong to the category of the superfluous, and the rules of etiquette can become as elaborate as those operative at Versailles during the reign of Louis XV.

When the American president travels outside the precincts of Washington he is accompanied by a crowd of 400 retainers (valet, barber, food-taster, speechwriters, communications specialists) as well as by another 400 representatives of the national media. Mrs. Reagan was in the habit of forwarding a replica of her own bed to the palaces or embassies in which she expected to stay the night. Occasionally she ordered the walls of the guest rooms painted her favorite shade of red in anticipation of her arrival.

Under a republican form of government the citizenry supposedly accepts the responsibility for managing its own affairs, but over the last quarter of a century the heirs to the American fortune have lost interest in the tiresome business of self-government. Rather than vote or read the Constitution—a document as tedious as the trust agreements that the family lawyers occasionally ask them to sign—the heirs prefer to go to Acapulco or Aspen to practice macrobiotic breathing.[18] They have better things to do with their lives than be bothered with the details of preserving their freedom. They spend their time making themselves beautiful, holding themselves in perpetual readiness for the incarnations promised by dealers in cosmetics and religion. The country still flatters itself that it enjoys the self-government of a sovereign people, but for at least a generation the conduct of its business has been left in the hands of the servants, both public and domestic.[19]

Much of the same sort of languid fantasy seized the last generation of Southern aristocrats in the years preceding the Civil War. Within the sanctuaries of their plantations they could play with the toys of courtly romance. The management of their affairs were assigned to their estate agents and to their factors in Savannah, Charleston or Richmond. These gentleman bought and sold their cotton, taffetas and slaves.

In 1987 the United States as a whole bears an unsettling resemblance to the antebellum South. We import luxurious manufactures and imperfectly redress our trade balance with the export of agriculture and raw materials. The well-to-do gentry affect an aristocratic disdain for commerce and trade, and their gossip about politics betrays the infantile contradictions of people who want lower taxes and better public services, less child molesting and more pornography, no military draft and stronger armies, less

18. Jonathan Kozol estimates that as many as 70 million Americans don't have the skill to read the Bill of Rights.

19. When testifying before Congress, Robert F. Kennedy read cue cards held up by his assistants, laboriously mouthing the words that he hadn't previously seen and barely understood.

crime and more profit. The business magazines that publish worried articles about the decline of American productivity—the editorialist bemoaning trade imbalances or the extent of consumer debt—also publish, often in an adjoining column, four-color advertisements for gold-headed golf clubs and matched pairs of Rolls-Royce town cars.

By abdicating their authority and responsibility, the sovereign people also relinquish their courage. Like rich old women in Palm Beach or a committee of dithering lawyers, the American electorate listens to the wisdom of its public servants as if to voices of minor oracles. Politicians and cabinet ministers appear in the role of the omniscient butler who finds phrases of art with which to conceal the embarrassments of the young master's profligacy and reduced circumstances. If the young master no longer belongs to the hunt club, it is not because the young master cannot pay his bill but because the hunt club has been admitting Koreans. If the chauffeur has to be let go, it is not because the young master cannot afford to buy gas for his Düsenberg but because the chauffeur took to drink and Marxism.

Just as a conscientious governess hurries her well-dressed charges past unpleasant sights sometimes met with in the park—an old man mumbling obscenities, a derelict lying in a drunken stupor on a bench—the custodians of the rich hold at bay the world of death and time. The rich learn not to notice what isn't nice. On passing through a slum or an underdeveloped country lost in the mud of the Third World, they ask one another how it is possible for people to live in such dreadful places, as if, gazing into the Caribbean Sea through a glass-bottomed boat, they were to exclaim, in sympathetic but startled voices, "How is it possible for fish to breathe in water?" They forget that people also inhabit a landscape of the mind, and they assume that happiness cannot be separated from a clean and well-lighted address.

At college I knew several boys whose mothers discouraged their sons' acquaintance with anybody who lived in towns not adequately represented in the Social Register. If a boy didn't come from Grosse Pointe or Burlingame or Fairfield County, then his place of origin was listed under the heading *terra incognita*, a probably savage heath where beasts and minority groups tore at one another for bones.

Some years ago, during a brief absence from *Harper's Magazine*, I was asked by the president of a New York bank to provide him with a monthly review of events in what he called "the outer world." He lived in a large house in Westchester County, on well-kept grounds behind a privet hedge. Every morning he was driven to Manhattan in a limousine fitted with tinted windows, and he ascended to the seventeenth floor of his headquarters building in a private elevator. Most days he talked to people almost identical to himself—other bankers dressed in the same suits, sharing the same barbers and opinions, belonging to the same clubs and forming their impressions of the world from the same sets of statistics. The banker knew that he lived within a cocoon of abstraction and that he lacked what he called "peripheral vision."

"About the economy," he said, "I know as much as anybody else, which isn't much, but at least it's something. But about the kinds of political ideas that might be out there snuffling around the perimeter, I don't know anything at all. I can't guess where the next blow is likely to come from."

The credulity of the rich subjects them to the petty tyrannies of their servants—lawyers who inflict small humiliations on their patrons, denying them a second house or third marriage; doctors who recommend monstrous cures; social critics who, in mincing voices and with moistened lips, preach the virtues of reaction.

Never before in its history has the United States been so heavily armed or spent so much money on its health. Yet the newspapers and literary gazettes bring unending reports of helplessness and alienation, of malignancies in the body politic and the encroaching shadow of the Soviet empire. The prompters of public alarm announce a "missile gap" or news of American rivers boiling with nuclear waste. They speak of cancer in the rain and Nicaraguan ogres in the woods beyond the tennis courts. Every now and then the consensus of alarmed opinion declares a "year of maximum danger."[20]

On their own initiative, and as a result of their own efforts, the rich acquire little else in their lives except illness. Their collection of infirmities, mental as well as physical, constitutes their principal accomplishment and, second only to the servant question, their principal topic of conversation. Who has not spent long afternoons listening to the interminable chronicles of disease—hospital tales, accounts of heart attacks and nervous breakdowns, reports of mysterious symptoms, urgent bulletins describing the advance of age spots or the subversive appearance of a faint wrinkle on the cheek? Certainly it is fair to say that as a people Americans suffer from acute hypochondria, an expensive and delicate condition of the soul available only to the rich. So virulent are the symptoms of our uneasiness that we can become inordinately frightened of the nations likely to do us the least harm. Who can imagine the British empire in the nineteenth century, or the Russian empire in the twentieth, being so terrified of states as weak as Libya, Nicaragua, Grenada and Vietnam?

The feeling of being vulnerable increases with the feeling of self-importance, and pretty soon the heirs to American fortune come to imagine themselves as fragile as antique porcelain. Their counselors observe that with enough effort it is possible to avoid a specific risk (death by asbestos poisoning, say, or lung cancer caused by cigarette smoke), and so they go on to assume that with even greater and more costly efforts ("Star Wars," say, or machines that scrub particles of dirt from the air) they can escape all risks. The fear of death sponsors the need for more regulation, more bureaucracy, more weapons, more places in the federal household for the cook's impoverished cousins—anything and everything the butler wants if only he will consent not to abandon them.

20. I have heard this moment in time variously given as 1954, 1962, 1974, 1977, 1980, 1984.

Every now and then the heirs make self-pitying remarks about their own weakness, but they have become too frightened, and, at the same time, too comfortable, to regain their independence of mind. The familiar lamentations ("failure of nerve," "crisis of confidence," "loss of will") are phrases of flattery. Self-blame constitutes an exquisite form of self-praise. No matter how severe the adjectives, the conversation remains fixed on oneself. For the last forty years all the best people have complained of neurotic disorders. The doctrines of modernism substitute art and shopping for religion, and the lives of the saints (James Joyce, Virginia Woolf, Yves Saint Laurent) demonstrate the relation between neurosis and genius. The neurosis distinguishes its host from the anonymous crowd of stolid and capable citizens who endure their lives with a minimum of self-dramatization. Who pays attention to people who don't make piteous cries? Who wants to pay $100,000 for the movie rights to their chronicles of marriage and divorce? Who bothers to publish their photographs in *Vogue*? The acknowledgment of illness becomes proof of spiritual innocence, something akin to a house on the beach at East Hampton or a feather boa bought at an auction on behalf of public television.

The higher servants exploit the fear and trembling in the drawing room in order to magnify their influence and promote the cause of their own self-aggrandizement. The learned doctors of foreign policy, like society physicians who prey upon the anxieties of aging heiresses, remind the trembling patient of the trouble that can befall the unwary traveler in the Third World who strays too far from the Hilton Hotel and supplies of safe drinking water. The career of Henry Kissinger offers an especially instructive example of the rewards available to the artful pander. Being a good deal more erudite than his employers, he persuaded them that no matter what misfortune overtook his statecraft, he continued to know what he was talking about. Partly it was his accent and his actor's sense of dramatic pause; largely it was the ignorance of his audience.

Late in the spring of 1978 I had occasion to watch Kissinger at dinner at the Council of Foreign Relations. No more than twenty-five people had gathered in the library to listen to the professor's learned exegesis of the current crisis. With Dr. Kissinger, as with any other Dr. Cagliostro, the crisis is always current. Dr. Kissinger at the time languished in the shadow of a temporary eclipse. He was out of office in Washington, and a number of critics were writing hostile commentaries about his policy in Iran and Cambodia; although he was desperately trying to open lines to the next Republican candidate for presidency (whether George Bush, Gerald Ford or John Connally), he had failed to gain the confidence of people in Ronald Reagan's entourage. Even so, with an aplomb expressive of his contempt for the decorous company seated among volumes of old news, Dr. Kissinger delivered an urbane and witty discourse on the bipolar dilemma. He made references to Russia in 1905, to Metternich and Castlereagh, to the Treaties of Brest-Litovsk and Versailles, to the demography of Africa and Kaiser Wilhelm's passion for uniforms. It was the kind of monologue that would have been accepted as ordinary conversation around a college high table at Cambridge University or across a café table in Paris. But to the gentlemen assembled in the library, most of whom hadn't read anything other than best-sellers recommended by the Book of the Month Club, Dr. Kissinger's erudition seemed to fill the room with a magician's brightly colored silks. They listened with their mouths open, as if they were children at a birthday party. When Dr. Kissinger concluded with a joke and a bow, the audience responded with grateful applause.[21]

21. That anybody continues to take seriously Henry Kissinger's opinions, much less his comic opera visions of nineteenth-century realpolitik, strikes me as a wonderful testimony to the credulity of the age. Kissinger has been wrong, utterly and consistently, about every important realignment of international affairs over the last quarter of a century—wrong about the Russians, the Vietnamese, the American Congress, Nicaragua and the Shah of Iran; wrong about strategic bombing, oil prices, inflation, terrorism and the international currency markets.

I don't remember whether George Shultz was in the room, but several years later, having become secretary of state, Shultz gave a public demonstration of "the management style" appropriate to not very well-informed corporate oligarchs. Like President Reagan, Shultz didn't know how or why the United States had gotten into the dreary business of shipping weapons to Iranian terrorists. Testifying before the Senate Foreign Relations Committee in December 1986, the secretary looked somehow like a baby who had lost its rattle. Nobody had told him that the American ambassador in Beirut was conducting back-channel diplomacy with the Israelis, and he was pretty damned mad about that. "I am, to put it mildly," he said, "shocked." In response to a series of questions about the particulars of the arms deals in Iran, Nicaragua and Washington, Shultz confessed his all but complete ignorance. "I don't know the ins and outs of that . . . I don't have the facts . . . I do not know in detail, in fact, I don't know much at all."

Among all their enclaves and retreats, the bourgeois masters of the universe place their fondest trust in their games and their clubs. Within the interstices of a game time ceases to exist. For as long as the light holds or their money lasts, the players inhabit the realm of fairy tale known to the myriad captives of a thousand and one obsessions, to bridge and backgammon addicts, to alcoholics and the guests at an orgy. At clubs dedicated to playing games members can also take comfort in being that much further inside the American womb, that much closer to the wellsprings of money and privilege. Not only do they see the chairman of the board in his office, but they also see him at his ease under a redwood tree or at a picnic table. The sense of intimacy enlarges the sense of security. The effect is further magnified by the clubs within clubs, little groups of ten or twelve or twenty that meet for lunch or dinner at regular intervals to congratulate themselves on their arrival at the center of the maze.

The Bohemian Club in San Francisco, arguably the most prestigious of the clubs frequented by the corporate elite, convenes a three-week encampment every summer in a redwood grove about a hundred miles north of the city on the Russian River. Each of the club's six hundred members (all male) invites a prominent guest (also male) to spend a weekend or a week, or as many days as the gentleman's calendar will permit, in one of the fifty-odd cabins artfully disposed among the old and patient trees. The guest list reads like a Who's Who of American commerce; limousines come and go bearing personages of inestimable importance, and for three weeks in July the Sonoma County airport extends its meager services to the squadron of jet aircraft owned by the nation's leading corporations.

On the first day of its encampment the club conducts a ceremony known as "the cremation of care." On a small pond near the entrance to the Grove the member designated as "the master of the revels" sets afloat a tiny replica of a Viking ship burdened with a tiny figure of a corpse in a shroud. When the toy ship reaches the center of the pond it bursts into flame. The members and their guests, sprawled at their ease on the grassy shore, raise the subdued echo of a college cheer. The miniature fire releases them from the prison of time. The wax corpse embodies all the worst of home and office— the nagging claims of wife and children, the insolence of rendered bills, the intractability of markets that defy the laws of physics and monopoly. To my grandfather, who loved the Bohemian Grove as much as life itself, this symbolic consummation so devoutly to be wished meant that for the next twenty-one days, until the club stewards swept up the floors on that terrible morning in early August, he was free to pursue his longing for the ineffable, free to gamble without restraint, free to wander through the saturnalia staged in the tourist cabins along the Russian River.[22]

22. The rules of the encampment prohibit the admission of women to the precincts of the Grove. Members seeking sexual diversion could go "over the wall" to one or another of the temporary bawdy houses in Guerneyville. During the encampment the San Francisco Police Department took over the management of these cabins to make sure that none of the young ladies, perhaps too much impressed by the wealth and celebrity of their clients, should give way to the extortionist temptations of higher capitalism.

I didn't attend one of the summer encampments until 1967, the year after my grandfather died, and I remember being alarmed by the musical shows. Founded in San Francisco in the late nine-teenth century by a group of ne'er-do-well writers, among them Jack London and Ambrose Bierce, the club retained a tenuous con-nection with the arts. Bierce and his friends soon went bankrupt and sold the premises and the club motto, "Weaving spiders come not here," to some of the city's more prosperous citizens. The new members kept up the pretense of an opposition to social conven-tions of the day, and by the middle 1960s their dissent took the form of elaborately staged musical entertainments written and directed by those members who once had been active in university dramatic societies. Because no women are allowed within the sanctuary of the Grove, the female parts were played by men, and I remember being sadly and frighteningly reminded of prep school and the lost boys in Peter Pan. Even the costumes were green.

Clubs also establish the proofs of belonging and the touchstones of legitimacy. People on the inside recognize one another by the associations of emblem and place, by virtue of their attendance at the same schools, because of their familiarity with the same resorts, golf courses and wine stewards.[23] Those clubs that accept their members for reasons of social or professional worth replicate, on a more intimate scale, the ethos of the dominant American insti-tutions. They serve as staging areas for the opinions that become the received wisdom and for the businessmen who become Cabinet

23. The U.S. Army expects its officers to have heard "the sound of the guns," which means that for an officer to receive promotion to the rank of general he must have commanded, at least once in his career, troops under fire. It doesn't matter so much whether the officer lost half his men in a poorly calculated assault. What matters is that he was there, that he acquired the distinction of being present. When I first went to work in the newspaper business it was useful to have served, at least for a few months, as a police reporter; later it became important to have covered, no matter how inaccurately, the war in Vietnam.

members. Perceived as metaphors, clubs approximate the fantastic dream of a plutocracy aspiring to the condition of Hugh Hefner—safe in bed and dressed in one's pajamas, supported by a staff of thirty-five servants, preserved by the artifices of interior light in a world out of time, surrounded by girlfriends who seem, increasingly, to resemble governesses.

The American republic was founded on the proposition that the boundaries between the nation of the rich and the nation of the poor were easily passed. The country's history abounds with exemplary tales about men who went west and found a fortune, who made the proverbial journey from rags to riches. To some extent the passage is still possible; certainly it is more possible in the United States than in any other country in the world. But within the last two generations, as the balance of wealth has shifted heavily from labor to capital, the frontiers have come to be more heavily defended and more closely watched. Candidates for membership in the Bohemian Club have applications submitted on their behalf at birth and count themselves lucky if they gain admission by the age of forty-five. The doorman at the Area nightclub consults a list—a computer printout redrafted every afternoon—bearing the names of the happy few allowed to pass the rope. Given the latitude to choose a few uninvited faces from the crowd clamoring at the entrance—among them women wearing clear plastic dresses and feathered earrings—the doorman, loyal to the tradition of American success, favors, in the words of the *Times*, "the distractingly attractive and the obviously rich."

Despite the ceaseless murmuring of applause, the equestrian classes never feel entirely content. They worry that they might be at the wrong party, that somebody else, wealthier or more current than they, might have been invited to a more important address. Only once during the social spectacle of the last twenty years do I remember a room in which, at least for a few hours, a pervasive feeling of gratified desire sustained a crowd of at least four hundred people in a bubble chamber of collective euphoria. The effect, as obvious as a demonstration in particle physics, took place in the vacuum of the late Truman Capote's Black and White Masked Ball in the autumn of 1966—an entertainment in honor of Katharine Graham, chairman of *The Washington Post*, and of Capote's newly published book *In Cold Blood*. *The New York Times* conferred upon the party the patents of significance by publishing the guest list. Police barricades surrounded the Plaza Hotel, and as the guests—the brightest names from the spheres of show business, society, finance and the media—passed through the gantlet of cameras, the crowd in the street remarked on the costliness of the women's clothes. Directly behind Capote in the receiving line, Suzy Knickerbocker, then the dominant gossip columnist in New York, stood listening to the recitation of names, the expression in her eyes as cold as glass. The guests had been required to wear masks, at least until midnight; some of the women looked like cats, others like Venetian ladies of the eighteenth century; the men wore whatever amused their wives or their boyfriends. No table was better than any other table; nobody needed to jostle for a place nearer Frank Sinatra or Marianne Moore. Neither did people feel compelled to betray one another with envious gossip. It was enough to be present, to be counted among the company of the elect. Because everybody was famous, everybody was safe.

While watching the dancers among the black and white balloons it occurred to me that at the point where images encounter one another the moral dimension disappears. Any image was as good as any other, no matter how it had been acquired or sustained. A White House adviser responsible for murdering 40,000 peasants in Indochina could chatter to the author of a best-selling tract denouncing the atrocity of the Vietnam War. Norman Mailer could talk to William F. Buckley about the mechanics of a mayoral campaign in New York, and Sargent Shriver, then the director of the Peace Corps, could dance with an international demimondaine wearing an emerald worth $500,000. For the time being, time had become circular. The dancers moved in a circle of stillness, where, for as long as the music played, nothing had happened that could not be altered or revised, where everything remained possible and an infinite number of transformations hovered just out of reach, where the glow of limitless promise lighted the faces of the guests with a flush as soft as candles, where history was a tale told not by an idiot but by a headwaiter.

7. DESCENT INTO THE MIRROR

To suppose, as we all suppose, that we could be rich and not behave the way the rich behave, is like saying that we could drink all
day and stay sober.

—L.P. SMITH

AT ONE OF THE LAST PARIS REVIEW REVELS THAT George Plimpton
staged in the fading din of the 1960s, huge balloons had been
affixed to the ceiling of a West Side discotheque; on the surface of the balloons, slide projectors flashed photographs of
many of the well-known personalities present in the strobe
light. The managers of the revel had also set up a closed-circuit television system within the little world of the party,
thus allowing the guests to look at themselves as well as at one
another as they passed from the dance floor to one of several bars
and anterooms that defined the universe of celebrity. The technical
effects evoked an oddly cubist combination of images. While talking
to Joan Baez, it was possible to see her appearing in concert on the
surface of a balloon as well as on the television screen in conversation with oneself. At the same time, the loudspeakers might be
amplifying the sound of Joan Baez's voice, the lyrics of her desolate

song running on a parallel track with the fragments of her desolate talk.

Toward the end of the evening I overheard a brief but oracular colloquy between two extraordinarily pretty girls seated on a circular banquette. Both were blondes in their early twenties, and both were wearing the miniskirts of metallic sheen then considered emblematic of women's emancipation. Maybe they were also wearing cartridge belts thought to convey sympathy for Bob Dylan and Che Guevara. The pulsing of lights caused them to appear and disappear at four-second intervals in the midst of the enveloping sound:

First Girl: "You're working for Givenchy?"
Second Girl: "No, McCarthy."
First Girl: "Yes, well, it's the same thing, isn't it?"

The riposte sums up not only the moral dandyism of the 1960s, a style of feeling to which Tom Wolfe gave the name "radical chic," but also the dreaming narcissism of the 1980s. People who wish to make time stand still can think of nowhere else to go except into the depths of the mirror. The golden horde sets off on expeditions into worlds out of time, and the transforming power of money pays the cost of summoning the images that flatter the vanity of the sponsor. Once having turned inward into the magical present, people come to believe that words stand as substitutes for things—that the phrase "supply-side economics" actually means something, that "Star Wars" is a real weapons system, that the military pageants staged over the coast of Libya or on the island of Grenada demonstrate the existence of a coherent foreign policy, that the Ayatollah Khomeini could be bound to the American cause with the gift of a Bible and a cake.

Prior to the burgeoning of the newly rich American society at the end of the Second World War, the descent into the mirror was a privilege available to the relatively few people who had both time and money to hire the props and pay for costumes. Edith Wharton, writing about the twilight of the Gilded Age, set Lily Bart "drifting on a tide of opulent diversion." In Newport at the turn of the century the ladies and gentlemen possessed of conspicuous leisure staged fashion shows for their dogs; the so-called lost generation of the 1920s went to Paris to play at being artists.

In California as a child I first became acquainted with the more elaborate journeys into the looking glass through the example of a friend whose mother, granddaughter of a nineteenth-century railroad baron, liked to dress him up in costumes she had seen in famous paintings. On his first day at a public elementary school in the early 1940s the boy, dressed as Thomas Gainsborough's "Blue Boy," emerged from the safety of a chauffeured town car into the sunlight and jeering scorn of his new classmates. At the Hotchkiss School I knew a boy who chose to imagine himself a gun-fighter on the old Oklahoma frontier. He carried out this charade with immense solemnity, and never once do I remember being so gauche as to make a joke. From a tailor in New York he ordered several suits in the style of the 1870s; at Abercrombie and Fitch he bought an authentic Colt revolver that had once belonged to a cavalry officer stationed at Fort Leavenworth during the Indian Wars. He also acquired a hat, a string tie and boots. During school vacation he fought gun duels with the western heroes prominent in the early days of television. The butler would roll the television set into the drawing room and the boy, whose parents were invariably attending a charity or masquerade ball, would dress himself up in the nostalgia of the Old West. Standing at what he thought was a sporting distance from the screen he would wait, his right hand held slightly above his holster, for the moment when the good guy faced the bad guy in a deserted, dusty street. The boy fired at whichever of the two figures drew his gun against the camera.

Afterward he poured himself a drink in the library while the butler cleared away the broken glass.[1]

The wealthier students at Yale took a good deal of trouble to be seen wearing torn cashmere sweaters and white shoes so badly scuffed that they had achieved a patina of anonymity. They wished to convey an impression of simplicity and very old money. The better clothing stores in New Haven sold white shoes already worn into a becoming shade of dirty gray. These shoes cost more than a new pair, but they relieved the wearer of the embarrassment of having to risk being thought, if only for a few days, a parvenu. (A variation on this same charade is now being sold to the mass market by Ralph Lauren in the form of clothes meant to suggest the understated elegance of the 1930s: Lauren's emblem of a man on a horse and his use of the name "Polo" testify to his astute understanding of the social rank implicit in the distinction of an equestrian class.)

For young men accustomed to money, the prospect of its absence seemed romantic. Feeling themselves deprived of the capacity to act, they imagined that if they could feel the goad of necessity they might become somehow "creative." More than once at Yale I listened to young men say that if they were poor, they could write novels. Sometimes they said they wished they had been born either Jewish or black—if Jewish they could belong to a group with a common and recognizable enemy; if black, they could become musicians, untrammeled by conventions of family and social class, free of inhibitions that prevented them from becoming "real people" capable of leading "real lives." The girls at Vassar and Smith lamented the absence of

---

1. At the age of thirty, still undecided as to what part he wished to play in the world, the retired gunfighter was still fool enough to think he had a choice. He once showed me passages from a journal he kept in the summer of 1965. In June he was considering a career as a poet. In July he remembered that his mother owned a large interest in Lehman Brothers, and it occurred to him to become an investment banker and accept his fate as an enemy of the common man. In September, remembering the example of his uncle, he was considering the vagabond life of a professional gambler.

meaning in Oyster Bay and wondered if the sky was a different color of blue in Paris or Barcelona. They took French lessons or studied the piano, in the meantime complaining about the stuffiness of their parents and believing, with Jane Fonda and Patricia Hearst, the world well lost for love or art or revolution.

During the 1960s in New York, possibly because of my occupation as a journalist, I began to notice that society as a whole was acquiring an extraordinary talent for playing charades. Given the large number of people in the United States who had become rich, or, more to the point, who had become converted to the faith in money, narcissism traded at discount prices. Their boredom, which an earlier century would have called "ennui," set in motion the frantic round of amusement meant to convey the illusions of meaning, and their money filled the spaces left by the subtraction of purpose and feeling. The counterculture exaggerated the passion for dressing up. Tour groups left on Wednesdays and Saturdays for wherever it was that somebody reported finding the Islands of the Blessed, and everybody who was anybody could afford an exercise consultant, a guru or a cause.

My great-aunt Evelyn, at the age of sixty-three, took up a career as an opera singer. Every afternoon between the hours of three and six, wandering through the halls of a house in which the servants fled the sound of her approach, she sang, loudly and in a false soprano voice, selected arias from the works of Richard Wagner and Giacomo Puccini. When her teacher pronounced her the equal of Renata Tebaldi she hired Town Hall for her debut. The performance was well attended. My great-aunt had taken the precaution of informing her many friends, relatives and dependents that anybody marked absent from the occasion would be deemed ineligible for a place in her will.

The concert lasted for nearly three hours, without intermission. Holding herself firmly erect in front of the grand piano (she was a large woman, not given to frivolity or theatrical expression), my great-aunt sang her entire repertoire. Every now and then she made an inexplicably sudden and imperious gesture with the palm frond that served as her only prop. On the dying of the last unhappy note the audience rose to its feet in a storm of tumultuous applause. Cries of "Brava!" echoed through the hall. The accompanist bowed deeply and kissed the diva's hand. A destitute nephew came forward bearing roses for which he had pawned his watch. A daughter in law was heard to remark that never before had she understood the importance of Gluck.

Under the Reagan cultural dispensation in the 1980s, these sorts of spectacles aspired to the pretensions of the baroque. Gilbert Kaplan, publisher of *Institutional Investor*, fancies himself a musician, and in the winter of 1982 he rented the American Symphony Orchestra in order that he might conduct, at Carnegie Hall, Gustav Mahler's Second Symphony in C minor. Although unable to play an instrument, Kaplan had learned the score by listening to records. The violin section smiled obediently, as if playing requests at a debutante dance, and the several hundred invited guests applauded loudly and tried to think of adjectives with which to flatter the maestro in return for his champagne.[2]

Also in 1982, albeit in a slightly different genre, David Rockefeller entertained at Sunday luncheon at his estate in Pocantico Hills the entourage of the late Sékou Touré, the African despot who seized the government of Guinea in 1958 and transformed a backward colony of the French empire into a reasonably efficient police state. Rockefeller provides most of the subsidy for the Council on Foreign Relations in New York and takes a keen but amateur interest in the destiny of nations. Despite the large sums of money bestowéd on Touré by his would be patrons in the United States and the Soviet Union, the standards of living in Guinea showed a steady decline. Touré found it prudent to eliminate at least 100,000 political

2. Delighted with his success. Kaplan has since repeated his performance with symphony orchestras in Budapest, Tokyo and Rio de Janeiro. Presumably the maestro was thoughtful enough to bestow on the orchestras some sort of gratuity expressive of his sympathy and appreciation.

enemies. Because the killing was done in the name of progress and freedom, the American commercial banks could continue to invest in the moral beauty of dialogue between north and south.

At the luncheon with the Rockefellers, Touré's wife was dressed in white mink hat and white mink coat which dragged becomingly along the floor. Rockefeller welcomed Touré with an elaborate toast, saying that when he was last in Conakry, Touré had met him at the airport in a Mercedes limousine and that on their subsequent drive through the streets of the city Touré dispensed with the services of a chauffeur. Miracle of miracles, Touré had driven the car himself. To Rockefeller this proved that Touré was a great African leader, a man of the people who had taken to heart the immortal lessons of democracy. Touré responded by saying that in the hall of Rockefeller's house he had noticed a portrait of Abraham Lincoln; he was reminded that both Abraham Lincoln and Rockefeller were great leaders because they were great revolutionaries. After luncheon Rockefeller ordered one of his nineteenth-century carriages brought around to the front door, and set jauntily off, driving the horses himself, with Mrs. Touré beside him on the box and Touré seated in back with Mrs. Rockefeller. Being an American, and therefore innately modest, Rockefeller omitted the ceremony of posting long lines of cheering supporters along the roads of his estate.

Within the spheres of literary interest, excursions into the mirror account not only for the writing of a good many books but also for the rise and fall of countless journals of political and literary opinion. A certain kind of rich man afflicted with symptoms of moral dandyism sooner or later comes to the conclusion that it isn't enough merely to make money. He feels obliged to hold views, to espouse causes and elect presidents, to explain to a trembling world how and why the world went wrong. The spectacle is nearly always comic, but in the spring of 1985 Mortimer Zuckerman, a Boston real estate developer, carried humor to the heights of parody. Most newly arrived publishers at least have the wit to regard their property as a kind of very expensive rubber duck. They content themselves with giving lunches for wandering dignitaries and deciding the broad questions of editorial policy. Zuckerman had it in mind to make a grander entrance into the intellectual limelight. Not only did he buy *U.S. News & World Report* for $185 million, but he appointed himself editor in chief and resident sage. It was in the writing of his biweekly column that he achieved his most wonderful effects. As if striving for what one admirer (Andrew Ferguson in the Washington *City Paper*) described as "profound inanity," Zuckerman discovered an editorial voice magnificently and uniquely false. Week after week, traveling to Moscow before the Geneva summit conference or to Manila just before the revolution, he returned with breathless announcements. "Readiness for war is part of the problem as well as part of the solution," or, "Preemptive surrender is not good negotiating doctrine." Not even the editors at *Newsweek* aspire to such discoveries.

Equally picturesque examples of the delusions to which the American equestrian classes fall victim no doubt will come readily to the reader's mind, and I don't think it necessary to supply voluminous documentation from the front pages of the *New York Post*. The dreams of self projected on the nursery walls can take forms as various as Michael Cimino's production of *Heaven's Gate* (a film that bankrupted United Artists) or Lieutenant Colonel Oliver North's fanciful reconstruction of the political realities of the Middle East and Central America.[3] Within the corridors of large

3. The 1986 variation on Cimino's theme of egoism was the production of *Ishtar*, directed by Elaine May and starring both Warren Beatty and Dustin Hoffman. Columbia bought the names without seeing the script. Five months late and priced at $51 million ($28 million over budget), the film was pronounced dead on arrival at the box office.

Before traveling to the Venice summit conference in the spring of 1987, Nancy Reagan sent an equerry to adjust all the mirrors in the villa in which she would be spending three days. She wanted to be sure that the mirrors were hung to the height at which she was accustomed to seeing the most flattering reflection of herself.

American institutions, corporate as well as governmental, the narcissistic turn of mind appears to have become norm rather than exception. Any institution rich enough to sustain its own definition of reality becomes a palace of mirrors. When a corporate grandee in New York or Washington says to his secretary, "Get me London," he means an office in London in which he can talk to a man who shares his own assumptions and views of the world. The resident hierarchs recognize themselves as ornamental figures dependent upon the whim of the institution, and the aspirants to privilege know how easily they can be replaced. The language of flattery isn't difficult to master, and most executive duties can be as impressively performed by another group vice president, another deputy secretary for Middle Eastern affairs, another assistant managing editor. At least half, perhaps 90 percent, of the discussion within any large institution turns on questions of status and appearance—who has the bigger office; who rides in which limousine; who accompanies the secretary of state to Geneva or goes with the CEO to Los Angeles or Peru; who carries the candidate's shoes; who travels first class and who goes coach; who sits in the green room or the owner's box.[4]

As the business of administering a large institution becomes mainly a matter of ritual, the interoffice propaganda becomes more necessary than statements released to the public. The people working for the organization must believe their own press notices. It isn't enough merely to do one's job; one must actively imagine that the questions important to the institution are those on which the country, perhaps the free world, depends for survival. Having listened to a good many self-congratulatory speeches at annual conventions,

4. While serving as secretary of state during the early years of the Reagan administration, General Alexander Haig refused to travel to Europe in an Air Force plane that lacked proper windows. Most journalists of any reputation insist on first-class airline accommodations when invited to make speeches about the inequities of the American distributions of wealth.

I have been struck by how often the objectives announced as the institution's primary reasons for being prove to be precisely those promises on which it cannot make good. Universities claim to inculcate in their students the love of learning, and yet, three or four years after graduation, most of the students abandon the habit of reading books. The legal profession preens itself on its concern for justice, and yet most lawyers devote their lives to preserving whatever interest, just or unjust, pays the highest fee. The military believes that it preserves the nation from harm, that without it nothing is safe, and yet it poisons the American atmosphere with nuclear radiation and, by its deranged stockpiling of weapons, it constitutes a constant threat to the world's peace. Prisons supposedly protect society; in fact they serve as spawning grounds for accomplished criminals. The media assume that they unite society, binding it together with lines of communication and understanding, and yet most of their efforts result in suspicion and rancor.

Within the walls of the institution the accomplishments of one or two legendary figures justify more general claims to significance. Among New York bankers, it is still said that Walter Wriston, the former chairman of Citibank, is a man of large vision and humane purpose, the sort of fellow who would never foreclose on widow or orphan; George Marshall supposedly embodied the spirit of the Army, Learned Hand the spirit of the laws. Everybody neglects to mention that such men, always extremely rare, probably achieved their success despite the weight of institutional intrigue and bias. As with *The Washington Post*, which first tried to discourage Bob Woodward and Carl Bernstein from looking too closely into the Watergate affair, most institutions worthy of the name rid themselves of people who display too much energy and talent. It is only after the truants have discovered penicillin, or won the Nobel Prize, or captured a Vietnamese hillside against heavy odds, that our institutions claim them as their own and reward them—preferably posthumously—with a medal or an honorary degree.

Once our American corporations attain a certain size and complexity, the chief executive officer loses touch with the mechanics of the business; except in a general way he no longer understands the commercial sequences that provide him with stock options and a secretary. Like the heirs to American fortunes, stewards of our more prominent institutions might as well be guests seated on the afterdeck of somebody else's yacht. The bankers among them find it hard to explain the fluctuations of the bond and stock markets; the publishers seldom know one typeface from another; the statesmen have trouble remembering the names of the countries with which the United States has signed treaties. Nobody knows how to navigate the vessel or repair the machinery in the event of an accident.

Nor can they acquire the necessary knowledge. Their dilemma is the same as that of a journalist who knows he cannot possibly verify the facts that need to be checked. Who can foresee the consequences of another war in the Middle East or the result of populist legislation enacted by a bewildered Congress? Who can predict the movement of interest rates or the possibility of revolution in Brazil? Who knows what the media will do, or the tax reformers, or the Russians?[5] If the institution is large enough, the answers to any of these questions impinge upon its profits or continued existence. And yet nobody, least of all a committee of experts, can come up with the answers. The questions have become too many, the details too complex. The technologies change so fast that a physicist or engineer finds much of his knowledge obsolete within six or seven years of leaving graduate school.

Knowing they inhabit a hall of mirrors in which appearances take precedence over facts, our more philosophical corporate

5. In early October 1986 the wisest counselors in the mass media believed (together with almost everybody else in the country) that what they called "the Reagan Era" would last until the end of the century. By Christmas, poking around in the wreckage of the Iranian arms scandal, they wondered if President Reagan could survive another week in office.

hierarchs accept their ignorance with equanimity. The chairman of a New York bank once explained the operative dynamic over lunch at "21," nodding across the room to presidents of other corporations to which he had made several disastrous loans. "Think of it in terms of baseball," he said. "If only one out of every two decisions goes bad, that's a damn good batting average. If most of my guys at the bank hit .500 for the season, I'd say we were ahead of the game."

If the facts no longer matter as much as the images, it's important that somebody make the decisions with the appearance of resolve, which is why the same kinds of people can succeed as managers of oil companies or foundations or universities or television networks—that is, within any institution large enough to depend on the observance of ritual. They combine a political instinct with a priestly function, and as soon as they begin to aspire to a high place within the organization they abandon the empirical habit of mind.

Within lower tiers of the hierarchy, of course, facts still matter, and it is possible to encounter minor executives who retain a degree of humility as well as a grasp of relevant information. They share the experience of the project foreman or the parish priest. But once ascended to the higher ranks, these same individuals incline to forget faces and names, and at the highest levels of decision the members of corporate boards of directors perform what they recognize as an elaborate ceremony. Knowing they cannot know what they are expected to know, they become adept in the art of asking ritual questions.

"What are the tax consequences?" "Have we heard from everybody with an interest in this acquisition?" "Will the sponsor object?" "How many more names must we add to the list?" "What will be the implications in Europe, in Bolivia, on the price of the Swiss franc?"

The people who ask such questions, many of whom serve on six or seven boards, want to be reassured. Few of them can afford the time to study the subject at hand, but they wish to feel they have done what is expected of them. Even if they understood the answers to be wrong, they couldn't make the necessary corrections. They listen for the soothing voice of the factotum.

"Yes, Mr. Chairman, all that has been looked into."

"No, General, we checked on that, and there's nothing to worry about in C Company."

"I am informed, Mr. President, that we have a man in Vienna."

Precisely this habit of mind lost the war in Vietnam, destroyed the *Challenger* and wrecked the credibility of the Reagan administration. The hierophants at NASA heard only what they wished to hear about the readiness of the space shuttle. President Reagan accepted the soothing lies offered by his subordinates on the National Security Council.[6]

Remarking on the weightlessness of American politics, Senator Daniel P. Moynihan, echoing the observation of the New York banker, long ago conceded the primacy of appearances. About a week before the election of President Jimmy Carter we were sitting in a restaurant on West Fifty-seventh Street, and Moynihan, waving his arms in the air, laughed uproariously at the absurdity of his predicament. As a senator, he said, he was expected to hold informed opinions under as many headings as were listed in the Federal Directory—on weapons and civil rights as well as on nuclear energy, education, Indians (American and Meskito), communications theory, military intelligence, Arizona groundwater and the volume of barge traffic on the Mississippi River.

"It's a joke, of course," he said. "A dangerous joke, maybe, but still a joke."

Government, he said, had become representative in the theatrical instead of the constitutional sense of the word. Because nobody

---

6. The media, of course, discovered that something was amiss only after the catastrophes had been made explicit. Intent upon preserving the illusions of America the Beautiful, the media cannot bring themselves to question the pomp and majesty of apparent success. They conduct inquests, not investigations.

could know what he or she was expected to know, somebody had to perform the rituals of wisdom. Somebody—the actor, newsman, publicist, politician—had to pretend to be wearing a robe and crown of stars and go before the assembled cameras to say that he was the north wind.[7]

Incompetent armies deify the commander, and in Washington what is important is the appearance of a thing and the reflection in the glass (i.e., the editorial pages of *The Washington Post*), not the eventual playing out of policy in some distant and muddy swamp in Indochina. Officials make their reputations on decorous theories as well as on the patronage of ministers more highly placed. Whether the theories bear any relation to reality matters less than their appearance in handsomely printed portfolios. To the American commanders in Vietnam, both military and civilian, what was real was the image of war that appeared on their flowcharts and computer screens. What was not real was the experience of pain, suffering, mutilation and death.

To the extent that the complexities of twentieth-century politics (like the complexities of twentieth-century biology and accounting) multiply at an exponential rate, the concerns of government become as small and stylized as the performances on Marie Antoinette's stage at the Petit Trianon. Authority attaches to personality because a governing class founded on anything else—on ability, say, or knowledge—would be too quickly superseded. Even if a politician knew something about particle physics or credit markets, within two or three years his information would be as old as reports from the battlefields of Antietam or Little Big Horn.

The emphasis on appearance results in a corresponding loss of the sense of specific gravity. It is a peculiar but defining characteristic of the social classes afflicted with the infirmities of wealth that

7. Moynihan's remark also echoed the even earlier observation of David Burnham who, recognizing the ritual nature of modern government, described the president as "the Pontifex Maximus of the American civil religion."

they often complain of a feeling of weightlessness.[8] For at least ten years I have listened to corporate hierarchs of various denominations try to account for what they vaguely describe as a drifting in the void. They preside over multinational fiefs richer than Venezuela and employ more people than lived in Florence at the zenith of the Renaissance, and yet they feel no palpable or fleshly sense of power. Nor do they feel the consequences of their actions. Appearances pass muster as reality, words stand surrogate for things, "junk bonds" count as honest money and yet nothing happens. The world goes on as before, and it turns out that nobody else seems to notice the unbearable lightness of being.

If the corporation is large enough or important enough to the nation's defense, the government will provide it with a subsidy. Citibank can make disastrous loans to Argentina and Brazil, but the gentlemen responsible for those loans continue to receive comfortable salaries and generous pensions. General Motors can manufacture a poorly designed car, but the automotive gentry in Detroit suffer no loss of ease. Ogilvy & Mather can launch, at a cost of $40 million, an advertising campaign that fails to move the product, but nothing happens to the most highly placed people in New York. Yes, a few hundred or a few thousand lesser subordinates might have to leave on short notice, but the sad events in question might as well have occurred among anonymous tribes on the upper reaches of the Zambesi River.

---

8. Weightlessness was reflected in the marketing strategies of the last few years: lightness of things—beer, cars, diet, relations between people, shampoos, images, music, lack of attachment. There have been 352 lite or light products in supermarkets since 1982.

Stendhal noticed the peculiar gravitational effects as long ago as 1840. "When I lack money," he said, "I'm bashful wherever I go. I must absolutely get over this. The best way would be to carry a hundred gold louis in my pocket every day for a year. The constant weight of the gold would destroy the root of evil."

The business magazines do their best to provide flattering portraits and adoring odes to entrepreneurial success, but still the subjects of the hired praise fret about their lack of visibility. Their decisions bear upon the well-being of entire states and industries, but when they walk into restaurants, nobody knows their names. They look at ballplayers selling hairspray, or actors hustling jogging shoes and American Express cards, and they wonder at the injustice of a world that casts so much light on persons of so little substance.

A fair percentage of the mergers, takeovers and leveraged buyouts of the middle 1980s accomplished nothing other than shoring up the vanity of the principal traders. The deals consumed many millions of dollars in superfluous fees, failed to improve the efficiency of the companies engaged in the *coups de théâtre* and cost many thousands of people their livelihoods. But for the few men whose names appeared in the papers the deals offered proof of their own magnificence.[9]

The feelings of inferiority and deprivation have prompted a fair number of corporations to supply the pomp and ceremony once provided by Louis XIV to the nobility resident at Versailles. Possibly this is because corporations have learned that if they neglect to provide these dignities, then their executives, anxious to catch a glimpse of themselves in the shop windows of the media, might betray stockholders to hostile takeover or leveraged buyout. At the very least the corporations stage a ceaseless round of spectacles, conferences and

9. Possibly the stupidest of these spectacles pitted the Bendix Corporation against the Martin Marietta Corporation. Before the comedy was finished, Allied Corporation and United Technologies appeared onstage, with the result that four primary American defense contractors holding combined assets of several hundred billion dollars recruited a small army of lawyers and investment bankers to assuage the vanity of a few overpriced plutocrats worried about their place in the sun. It was never clear what Bendix wanted, just as it was never clear why Mobil acquired, at ruinous expense, Montgomery Ward, or why Carl Icahn, proclaiming he knew nothing of airlines, felt compelled to buy TWA and force the company to the edge of bankruptcy.

entertainments. Individuals can no longer afford to keep up appearances at the levels of opulence maintained by a bank, oil company or movie studio. The more discerning organizations employ a staff to consider the distinctions between museum shows and theater benefits, to order the wine and hire the music, to decide between the underwriting of a tennis or a golf tournament, to drum up invitations for the chairman to address a congressional committee or a meeting at some distant and prestigious institute.[10]

The most precocious business executives demand principal roles in their own corporate advertising campaigns. The settings vary according to taste and the measurements of the executive's self-esteem. Sometimes we see the gentleman in an impressive office imparting a sense of wealth, efficiency and calm to a world too often disfigured by bankrupts and louts. Sometimes we see him in a helicopter or at a construction site, demonstrating a sense of entrepreneurial energy and movement. Sometimes he merely stands in front of the camera with a chicken or a rack of suits.

These performances apparently have become the subject of negotiation at the point of signing corporate magnates to employment contracts. It is no longer enough to offer salaries in excess of $1 million as well as country club memberships, chauffeured automobiles, free medical care, stock options, clothes allowances and annual vacations on the Riviera. These benefits might satisfy less ambitious executives, but the gentlemen with the wide grins and the glad hands demand the most precious of modern commodities—a publicly licensed personality. They seek to enter the sacred grove of celebrity, and a leading role in the company's advertising campaigns provides them a ticket of admission.

10. Of the 10,000 parties arranged by Ridgewell's Caterers in Washington in 1986, at least 80 percent were paid for by a corporate patron. Similar ratios undoubtedly prevail in New York and Los Angeles. If the chairman wishes to say something important about trade or literature or geopolitics, learned public relations counsel provide a text suitably embossed with ancient quotations.

The corporation choosing to bestow this sublime favor sends its executives to the equivalent of what used to be called "finishing schools" for young ladies of gentle birth and polite intellectual attainment. The executives sit in a studio and learn to talk to a television camera, which is the modern analogue of learning to talk to the Duc d'Orléans. They learn to refrain from fidgeting in their chairs, to wear their hair at modish length, to walk gracefully through an assembly line or accounting department, to keep their fingers from drumming on the lectern, to speak forcefully, and, above all, to avoid raising their voices when exchanging civilities with the ladies and gentlemen of the press. These latter personages open and close the doors to the lighted drawing rooms of celebrity, and they must never, never be made to look foolish. But no matter how lavish the expense, almost every one of these would-be grandees somehow manages to look and sound as wooden as Walter Mondale. The humor of their predicament rests on the paradox that they apply for the license of personality only after they have renounced all claim to identity other than the one permitted by company rules.

The weightlessness of the world in the mirror gives rise to the vogue for androgyny because people drifting in the suspensions of reality find it difficult to establish sexual identity or definition. Within the frame of the mirror the pilgrims in search of a plausible face can try on the thousand and one masks to which Freud gave the name of the polymorphous perverse and to which the trendier dress designers affix the labels of high fashion.

For some years now, it has been no simple matter in New York to tell the boys from the girls. Girls dress like boys and wear their hair short; boys wear their hair long and spend a lot of time comparing foreign and domestic after-shave lotions. The fashion magazines promote "the androgynous look" and illustrate it with high-tech photographs in which both boys and girls appear to be dressed as parachutists.

The androgynous image is further amplified by rock musicians (among whom it is mandatory) as well as in the style known as "punk," in the advertisements for hairspray and silk shirts, in the jargons of health and physical fitness. In the dramas mounted on prime-time television, men play the parts of happy homemakers, women play police detectives. At the more sophisticated discotheques, men and women wear each other's clothes and can choose, on alternate evenings, if they have both the money and talent for it, to give either a masculine or feminine performance of their character.

In keeping with the sexual ambiguity of the age, Dior in 1982 published a series of advertisements conceived and photographed by Richard Avedon in which two male characters ("Oliver" and "Wizard") appeared in various phases of suggestive undress with a woman named "The Mouth." Avedon explained that he invented the three "Diors" because "three is never boring." A copywriter supplied cute captions for the pictures—"When the Diors got away from it all, they brought with them nothing except *The Decline of the West* and the butler"; "when they were good, they were very, very good, and when they were bad, they were gorgeous." The clothes, of course, were suitably precious, and so were the three people posing in attitudes meant to express their frightfully witty escapes from ennui.

Money in sufficient quantity sustains the illusion of infinite possibility, and the liquidity of gender, like the liquidity of cash, holds out the ceaselessly renewable promise of buying into a better deal. In the world of the mirror it is always permissible to seduce or betray almost anybody else in the dream.[11] Not at that particular moment, of course, not in front of the lady's husband or the gentleman's wife, but on some convenient occasion when a coincidence of schedules happens to place the concerned parties in the same town or on the same beach at the same unencumbered moment.

11. Among both men and women the incidence of marital infidelity rises in conjunction with increase in income. Of the married men earning $20,000 a year, only 31 percent conduct extracurricular love affairs; of the men earning more than $60,000, 70 percent.

The androgynous states of mind sustain the divorce rates and make it possible to postpone the tiresome business of growing up. To the extent that both sexes tailor their feelings to fit the measure of status and money, the structures of gender, like the obligations to family or loyalty to principle, come to be seen as so much troublesome baggage impeding one's movement into F. Scott Fitzgerald's "orgiastic future."

In the rarefied atmospheres of wealth and celebrity the liquidity of gender counts as an asset, and the idea of money becomes as confused as the idea of sex. Understood not as a commodity, not as something that must be earned and has the value of the labor of getting it, money becomes, a mystery, a shower of fairy gold. The liquidity of gender and the delight in masquerades were much in vogue at Rome in the Age of Empire, in England during the reigns of the early Stuarts, at the court of Versailles under Louis XVI, in Nazi Germany. The preferred aesthetic shows itself in an emphasis on surface and gesture, as well as in the reverence for images.

The successful Broadway shows of the last decade take the form of revues, dependent for their effect on the energy of the music and dance numbers, utterly lacking in character and plot. The same weakness distinguishes movies and literature of the last generation. The movie cameras glide over sensuous surfaces, dwelling on the texture of a gun barrel or the shape of a woman's head, but the principal characters seldom achieve clear definition. Always it is hard to know who is doing what to whom, or why anybody says one thing instead of another. The television dramas rely on automobile chases (thus conveying the impression of movement if not of development) and on situations explained by set decoration (richly appointed house signifies rich man, etc.) rather than the architecture of thought.

The contemporary belief in the magical properties of images resembles the pantheist worship of rivers and trees. The pagan invests everything in the universe with an aura of personality. A river god sulks and the child drowns; a sky god smiles and the corn ripens.

One of the most luminous instances of the modern dispensation occurred some years ago in New York, when the weather correspondent for WABC's *Eyewitness News* caught a cold. The producers of the show hit upon the notion of broadcasting the evening's dispatches from the young woman's bedside. At the appointed moment in the script, the scene shifted to an apartment somewhere in Queens. The ailing dryad was seen sitting up in bed with a quilt drawn around her shoulders, smiling bravely through her symptoms, bringing her audience reports on the next day's chances of rain. Setting up an intimate location shot meets the prevailing definition of news as an aspect of personality, and maybe I do the producers of *Eyewitness News* an injustice by assuming that they sent their cameras into darkest Queens merely to amaze and astound their rival impresarios at WCBS and WNBC. It is conceivable that they believed that if their weather correspondent failed to make her evening propitiation to the storm gods, it would rain for forty days and forty nights.

Because in the United States there is no such thing as a poor celebrity, the aura of klieg lights confers the same sense of ease and protection that attaches itself to manifestations of great wealth. When the Metropolitan Museum in New York sponsored the exhibition of Tutankhamen's gold, I used to wonder why so many people shuffled so reverently past the relics of the pharaoh's golden funeral. Why did they come, and what did they hope to see? The museum's Egyptian galleries, crowded with objects no less beautiful than those accompanying the pharaoh on his voyage into eternity, ordinarily remained as empty as the upper reaches of the Nile. On most Sunday afternoons the stone figures looked down on a lost child, a boy and girl holding hands on a bench, a bearded gentleman making notes for an eccentric theory of civilization. Why then the fascination with the same objects made in gold? Because the gold itself, dormant and inanimate, attained the rank of a rock star. How much more satisfying if the gold could speak and move. When Pavarotti sings, Mailer writes and Minnelli dances, it is as if King Tut's gold had come to life, singing, writing and dancing.

With any luck and the right sort of promotion, an individual can become a commodity as precious as an ounce of rhinoceros horn or a designer label pasted on T-shirts, perfume and boxes of chocolate. Celebrities of all magnitudes bestow the gifts of immortality, awakening with their "personal touch" inanimate throw pillows, automobiles, blue jeans and chairs. Athletes show up on television breathing the gift of life into whatever products can be carried into a locker room. Actors pronounce ritual incantations over the otherwise lifeless forms of cameras, tires and brokerage firms. The popular worship of images thought to be divine has become so habitual that people find it easy to imagine celebrities enthroned in a broadcasting studio on Mount Olympus, conversing with one another in an eternal talk show. By granting the primacy of names over things, the media sustain the illusion of a universe inhabited by gods and heroes as well as by satyrs, nymphs and fauns. Barbara Walters struck the appropriate note when, in the midst of interviewing newly elected President Carter in the autumn of 1976, she said, in the hushed whisper of a suppliant at a woodland shrine, "Be kind to us, Mr. President. Be good to us."[12]

The belief in the transfiguring power of personality derives its egalitarian bona fides from Jean-Jacques Rousseau's romantic pastoral of man as a noble savage at play in the fields of the id, of man set free from laws and schools and institutions, free to constitute himself his own government, free to declare himself a god. In a spirit that would be well understood by editors of *People* magazine, Rousseau's writings dwell on his desire to walk into a room and seize the instant

12. The pagan instinct runs counter to the idea of civilization, which defines itself as an advance toward impersonality—toward a system of justice that doesn't depend on the whim of a judge, toward a conception of art that rests on something other than applause for the signing of the emperor's concubine. Albert Einstein once remarked that the beauty as well as the utility of science consists precisely in its impersonality. Of Sir Isaac Newton's art it is impossible for critics to say that because they really don't care much for Newton, the laws of motion deserve a bad review.

and universal approbation of everyone present, to focus on himself all eyes, all praise, all sexual feeling. Precisely the same desire animates the life and work of individuals as sympathetic to the spirit of the age as Lee Iacocca, Ronald Reagan and Shirley MacLaine.

But in a society that delights in movement and change, not even immortality lasts forever. What has been given also can be taken away. Because the public image comes to stand as the only valid certification of being, the celebrity clings to his image as the rich man clings to his money—that is, as if to life itself. Continual publicity becomes as necessary as the oxygen that sustains the artificial environment of a space capsule, which is why even the most luminous of celebrities so often can be persuaded to show up for the opening of a shopping mall. Once dependent upon their reflections in the media they will go almost anywhere to meet a camera or gossip columnist.

The figures in the mirror fear the media in the same way that some aboriginal tribes fear the anthropologist with a camera. The aborigine believes the photograph will steal his soul. The man who genuinely shuns publicity (cf. Thomas Pynchon, Evan Connell, William Gaddis) knows he would be imprisoned within an image from which he would be hard put to escape. The media cannot adjust to the development of character. Despite its seeming fluidity, television is a remarkably rigid medium that makes use of personae as immutable as the masks in an African ritual or the commedia dell'arte.

During the last advance of the Ice Age the temperature dropped so suddenly that some mammoths under the Siberian snow have been found with flowers in their mouths. The making of television images happens as quickly, and a man must be careful about the face he wears on his first appearance in the media. He seldom gets a chance to put on a different one. Most actors and politicians remain forever fixed in the role that first placed them in a producer's Rolodex. Mailer begins and ends as the *enfant terrible* of American letters, Richard Nixon as the Machiavelli of American politics. W.H. Auden once observed that only in America do so many writers produce, in their youth, one interesting or important book and then, over periods as long as forty years, nothing else except timid imitations of themselves. He attributed their sterility to their wish to make a sublime product that would eliminate all competition.

Mindful of the media's rigidity the promoters of political and literary images know that once they have shaped the public mask (e.g., Jimmy Carter as the pure-hearted country boy embodying the belief in rural virtue) their client will have to commit a felony at high noon in Times Square before the media will change their collective mind. This same principle governs the making and selling of opinions. Only after an idea has been frozen into the solidity of cliché can a politician use it as a slogan or the producers of Hollywood movies shape it into the molds of fantasy and romance.

A society overwhelmed by complexity places a correspondingly high value on simplification. It is no surprise that Americans bestow their highest honors and rewards on those individuals who perform their rituals. The media seldom deign to notice those people or professions on whom society utterly and uncomprehendingly depends. It is probably fair to say that the more visible the personality, the less likely he or she performs an essential task. If the water engineers went on strike, cities would become uninhabitable within a matter of hours; equally extreme consequences would attend a strike by a fire department or by the few doctors still not engaged in psychoanalysis or cosmetic surgery. But who would miss Dan Rather? The keeping of celebrities might also be compared to the keeping of pets, and it is a mark of the society's affluence that it can indulge its passion for exotic breeds. The cost of maintaining ornamental figures on the order of Sam Donaldson or Alexander Haig exceeds what even John Jacob Astor stood willing to pay for a racing stable. Before the advent of the postindustrial society the labor strike was a form of expression popular among the working classes. Ruffians in ragged clothes committed unspeakable acts of sedition, and the press obligingly portrayed the labor union as a mob. But now the strike has become an upper-class occupation—a last resort of actors and big-time ballplayers. Who can recommend the use of fire hoses against members of the Screenwriters' Guild who receive $50,000 for a script? Who marches at the side of third basemen who earn $350,000 for a season in the sun? Clearly the fellows suffer terrible deprivation, but what do they want? If it isn't a question of wages or hours on the job sites, then presumably their grievances have to do with a fear they have become superfluous. The strikers ask to be appreciated, and the strike becomes a demand not for a commodity as vulgar as money but for recognition of their value as precious ornaments.

The officials who succeed at the pantomime of government understand the theatrical nature of their offices. The people who criticize President Reagan for his moral and intellectual emptiness, like the people who still cast Henry Kissinger in the role of villain, apply the wrong sets of criteria. Charlatans, they say, scoundrels and liars who dress themselves in as many policies as Johnny Carson puts on funny hats. Possibly so, but beside the point. Given fewer opportunities, Kissinger would have done well as a talk show host. Fortunately for him, although not so fortunately for the United States, he found his patron in Nelson Rockefeller instead of William Paley.

The necessity of keeping up appearances, of course, is nothing new or unique to businessmen, journalists or politicians. Unemployed actors in Los Angeles feel obliged to drive a rented Rolls-Royce or Ferrari to establish an aura of success. Hollywood producers trying to make an impression in New York stay at the Pierre Hotel and spend $400 a day on room service, $350 a day on phones and $375 a day to keep the limousine waiting in case somebody wants to go to Nell's or send for pizza.

But to the extent that appearances become primary to the governing of an institution—and to the degree that men define themselves by their titles, dress, speech and manner—the American equestrian classes take on characteristics of an eighteenth-century court society. It isn't an especially elegant society, not yet as refined in its tastes as the aristocracy assembled at Versailles, but it has begun to show some of the same weaknesses that eventually wrecked the French nobility on the shoals of revolution.

Kissinger Associates charges its clients $250,000 per annum for "geopolitical strategic consulting" and for arranging introductions to some of the world's more highly placed tyrants and arms dealers. A duchess employed in Marie Antoinette's household received an equivalent stipend for combing the queen's hair or holding the queen's glove.

Washington lobbyists earn substantial fees for the favor of taking their clients to lunch in the Senate dining room or the White House Mess. The Goncourt brothers, in their journal of Louis Napoleon's Second Empire in France, noted an entry in a lawyer's ledger of bribes: "To Monsieur X, government minister, the sum of 40,000 francs for having taken my arm in the foyer of the opera."

Given the wealth and power of the American supremacy over the last forty years, it is no wonder that Americans have come to imagine the rest of the world as nothing more than a series of images gliding in and out of the mirror of the news. Like actors in a Japanese Noh theater, the diplomats speak a stylized language of threat and counterthreat, their tropes echoed by a media long since accustomed to the part of a docile chorus. The familiar troupe of diplomats and anchormen travels to Tokyo, Mexico City or Geneva to discuss the law of the sea, terrorism, the international monetary system, the chance of World War III. Always it is difficult to remember that the abstractions bear any relation to a specific instance, that some-where beyond the compound—three blocks from the hotel or across the street from the conference center—the "cultural dysfunction" or "social disenfranchisement" has been made manifest by a man with a knife in his hand.

The narcissistic habit of mind confirms the assumption that the world is a movie theater and diplomacy a higher form of screen-writing. President Reagan's amiable improvisations on the themes of geopolitical romance, or American statesmen explaining such things as "the domino theory" and "the arc of crisis," bring to mind a remark attributed to Lloyd George, the British Prime Minister at the Versailles Peace Conference in 1919. In the midst of redrafting the map of Europe, Lloyd George turned to an aide and said, "Refresh my memory. Is it Upper or Lower Silesia that we are giving away?"

I first encountered the governing temperament in the fall of 1957, when, having studied history for a year in England, I returned to the United States with the notion of working for either the *Washington Post* or the CIA. My interest in foreign affairs had been awakened by the Suez and Hungarian incidents of 1956 and by my inability to understand, much less explain to a crowd of indignant Englishmen, the policy of John Foster Dulles. In 1957 the *Washington Post* and the CIA could be mistaken for different departments of the same corporation. Newspapermen traded rumors with intelligence agents, and although the gilding on the Pax Americana was beginning to wear a little thin, anybody who had been to Yale in the early 1950s couldn't help thinking that the totalitarian hordes had to be prevented from sacking the holy cities of Christendom. Failing to find a job with the *Post*, I took the examinations for the CIA. These lasted a week, and afterward I was summoned to a preliminary interview with four or five young men introduced to me as "some of the junior guys." The interview took place in one of the temporary buildings put up during the Second World War in the vicinity of the Lincoln Memorial. The feeling of understated grandeur, of a building hastily assembled for an urgent, imperial purpose, was further exaggerated by the studied carelessness of the young men who asked the questions. All of them seemed to have graduated from Yale, and so they questioned me about whom I had known at New Haven and where I went in the summer. I had expected to discuss military history and the risings of the Danube; instead I found myself being asked to remember the names of the girls who sailed boats off Fishers Island, or who had won the summer tennis tournaments in Southampton and Bedford Hills. As the conversation drifted through the ritual of polite inanity (about "personal goals" and "one's sense of achievement in life"), the young men every now and then exchanged an enigmatic reference to "that damn thing in Laos." Trying very hard not to be too obvious about it, they gave me to understand that they were playing the big varsity game of the Cold War. Before I got up to leave, apologizing for having applied to the wrong office, I understood that I had been invited to drop around to the common room of the best fraternity in the world so that the admissions committee could find out if I was "the right sort."

From that day forward I have never been surprised by news of the CIA's vindictiveness and inattention. Good, clean-cut American boys, with the best intentions in the world, and convinced of their moral and social primogeniture, must be expected to make a few good-natured mistakes. If their innocent enthusiasm sometimes degenerates into sadism, well, that also must be expected. Nobody becomes more spiteful than the boy next door jilted by the beautiful Asian girl, especially after he has given her the beach house at Cam Ranh Bay, $100 million in helicopters, and God knows how much in ideological support. It is a bitter thing to lose to Princeton and to find out that not even Dink Stover can make the world safe from Communism.

This same undergraduate insouciance has remained char-acteristic of American foreign policy for the past thirty years. Administrations have come and gone, and so have enemies and allies, but the attitude of mind remains constant, as does the tone of voice. It is the voice of Henry Kissinger explaining to a lady at dinner that a nation, like an ambitious Georgetown hostess, cannot afford to invite unsuccessful people to its parties. It is the voice of McGeorge Bundy, who told an audience of scholars in the early 1960s that he was getting out of Latin American studies because Latin America was such a second-rate place. It is the voice of James Reston finding something pleasant to say about this year's congenial dictator, or the State Department announcing its solidarity with Cambodia and expressing only mild regret about the regime's program of genocide.

After 1968 the inflection of the voice became slightly more irri-table and petulant. During the early years of the decade the heir to the estate flattered himself with gestures and exuberant rhetoric appropriate to an opulent idealism. He had access to unlimited resources (of moral authority as well as cash), and he stood willing to invest in anybody's scheme of political liberty. Nothing was too difficult or too expensive; no war or rural electrification too small or inconsequential. The young heir undertook to invade Asia and to provide guns and wheat and computer technology to any beggar who stopped him in the street and asked for a coin. After 1968, when the bills came due and things turned a little sour, the heir began muttering about scarcity and debts, about the damage done to the environment and the lack of first-class accommodation on spaceship earth. Nobody becomes more obsessive on the subject of money than the rich man who has suffered a financial loss. The fellow feels himself impoverished because he has to sell the yacht. President Nixon closed the gold window, and associate professors of social criticism dutifully taught their students that sometimes money weighs more heavily in the balance of human affairs than the romance of the zeitgeist.

Even so, the assumptions of entitlement remain intact. Although feeling himself somewhat diminished (as witness the success of the philosopher-merchants on the neoconservative Right) and somewhat older (as witness the dependence on sexual and spiritual rubber goods), the still-prodigal son continues to believe himself possessed of unlimited credit. He is still heir to the fortune, no matter what anybody says about his horses and dogs, and he can damn well play his game of policy in any way he damn well chooses.

In American military circles, it is considered poor form to discuss fortification and the strategies of attrition and civil defense. The whole notion of fortification is seen as stodgy, corrupting, somehow un-American. It brings to mind the depressing memory of stuffy French generals on the Maginot Line in the early weeks of the Second World War. The United States owes it to itself to cut a more dashing figure in the world. Where is the fun in fighting dreary rearguard actions? The young men in the Pentagon and the military academies speak of forward thrusts, of broad-gauged advances, of assaults and landings and insertions.

All the fine talk conceals a not too subtle irony. When it comes to a question of how to go about these romantic maneuvers, the United States relies less on the daring and intelligence of its commanders than on the superiority of its expensive equipment. It is assumed that wars will be won by the avalanche of American resources, materiel, production, logistics and assembly lines—i.e., by bureaucrats who need be neither impetuous nor brave. The faith in gadgetry and the "tech fix" accounts for the incalculable investment in missiles, bombs, airplanes, and anything else that can be bought in the finest sporting-goods stores. Nobody has the bad manners to insist that strategic bombing has yet to be a decisive factor in any of the century's wars. The rich man depends on his technology in the same way he depends on his trust fund. Even if he makes no effort to think about the great bulk of his capital, it goes about the business of gathering its daily ransom of interest and dividends. The miraculous nature of this contrivance persuades the heir to believe in the divinity of machines.

One proof of a great power is its belief that it can afford to be forgetful. A rich nation's collection of treaties bears resemblance to a rich man's stock portfolio. The lawyers and secretaries gather so many pieces of paper that the heir to the fortune no longer knows what any document means. Agreements signed by his forefathers— NATO, SEATO, CENTO, etc.—might as well be Mexican railroad bonds. As careless of its allies as a rich man is careless of his friends (on the ground that he can always buy new ones), America cannot quite manage to perceive the reality of the world elsewhere.[13]

God knows we try hard enough. We send camera crews to the uttermost ends of the earth, decorate the front pages of our

---

13. When one of the members fails to show up on the first tee of a truly exclusive golf club, his companions seldom bother to ask more than a perfunctory question as to his whereabouts. Walking down the fairway to the first green somebody might say, "I wonder what happened to Harry Brooks" in just about the same tone of voice that he might say, while walking down the second fairway, "I wonder what happened in Vietnam." Neither question is serious because neither answer is important.

newspapers with foreign names and datelines, endow learned journals and research institutions, dispatch our corporate executives to the Aspen Institute for weeks of earnest briefings—mostly to no avail. The American correspondents don't get sent to the important posts in Moscow, Tel Aviv or London unless their editors already know their agents will confirm the presuppositions already in place.

On a Sunday afternoon during my first summer as a reporter for the *New York Herald-Tribune* in the early 1960s I was sent to a meeting of Black Muslims in Harlem. The editors expected a story of violent black men threatening revolution. Malcolm X made what seemed like an interminable speech, rambling and demagogic, condemning the white establishment and all its works, demanding that the federal government cede to blacks the states of Georgia and Mississippi. At appropriate intervals the crowd chanted, "Oh yes!" or "You tell 'em, brother!" or "That's right!"

But none of the threats were threatening. Everybody present was dressed in his or her best clothes, the little girls in starched dresses and patent leather shoes, the little boys as well-behaved as the choir in church. Although I was one of only two white men in a crowded auditorium, I never once felt frightened. Malcolm X was conducting a political variation on a revival meeting, speaking the language of ritual catharsis. Nothing in his performance, or the response of the crowd, suggested the least hint of violence. The words were terrifying, but the spirit in which they were said contradicted their apparent meaning.

On my return to the newspaper office, the editors wanted a story that could justify a headline foretelling riot and bloodshed. I explained that so literal-minded an interpretation was utterly false. Disgusted with my lack of journalistic acumen, the editors assigned another reporter, who hadn't been present, to write the story conforming to their own wishes and fears.

In one of his books of memoirs, Harrison Salisbury, foreign correspondent of *The New York Times*, describes a comparable incident during his tour of duty in Moscow. The editors in New York somehow had become convinced—possibly because of an important rumor overheard at an important dinner party—that the Soviet Union was about to invade Western Europe. They told Salisbury to count the number of tanks and infantry divisions massed on the East German frontier. Salisbury, of course, found neither tanks nor infantry divisions for the simple reason that none were present. Still the editors in New York preferred the truth of their own revelation. It took Salisbury the better part of a month, filing voluminous cables, telegrams and dispatches, to persuade them to abandon their hope of war.

The provincialism of our media reflects the insouciance of its audiences, almost none of whom expect the president of the United States to possess a working knowledge of history and geography. Ronald Reagan and Jimmy Carter arrived in Washington with only the sketchiest knowledge of diplomatic affairs, but so did presidents Kennedy and Johnson. So do most senators and congressmen, remarkably few of whom bother to travel to the Soviet Union to look upon the "Evil Empire" against whose implacable enmity they dedicate so much of the nation's income. Reagan's ignorance of history is by now the stuff of nightclub jokes. When asked questions of a historical character he responds in the language of myths and dreams, attributing to Lincoln or the Roosevelts sentiments they never expressed, assigning the causes of the Second World War to whatever circumstances might agree with the bias of the voters in the room or with a half-forgotten scene in an old and patriotic movie. Just as it was a matter of some doubt as to whether Jimmy Carter could have located Czechoslovakia on a map, so it is unlikely that Reagan can remember whether Colombia is in South or Central America.

The failing is characteristic of a nation in which the standard of geographical literacy is traditionally low. The Association of American Geographers discovered in 1982 that only 40 percent of American college students could point to the United States on a map of the world; 40 percent of American high school seniors thought Israel was an Arab state. The national belief that the rest of the world isn't real coincides with the conviction that the past is irrelevant. The contemptuous phrase "you're history" signifies nothingness.

During the inquest that takes place in the American media after a particularly embarrassing failure abroad, it inevitably turns out that nobody knew very much about the culture of the country in which the failed policy was destined to bring about a happy result. Certainly this was true of Vietnam, where, many years later, the Washington mandarinate discovered that the task of "preserving democracy" might not have been so easy for people to whom the idea of democracy was as foreign as the taste of a McDonald's cheeseburger. The war vanished almost as suddenly as it had come, as if it were a guilty secret nobody wanted to discuss with a Park Avenue psychiatrist. In the middle 1970s, during the aftermath of the war, the recriminations subsided into a distant muttering in the academic quarterlies, and the much touted national debate about "the lessons of Vietnam" never took place. The novels about the war all had the oddly surreal character of a dream. The authors didn't know how or why they got to Vietnam, and none could fix the experience within historical or political coordinates that might have explained their sudden arrival in what turned out to be a very badly managed summer camp.

The press and the politicians sometimes blame the CIA for being so poorly informed, but the accusations seem to me unfair. The inattention of the CIA reflects and embodies the carelessness of the society for which it acts as agent. On leaving his club the rich man never looks behind him to see if the waiter is holding his coat; in much the same way the United States doesn't take the trouble to notice much of what goes on in the world's servants' quarters. The American press reports news from Africa that deals with disputes between whites and blacks; between armies of blacks only large-scale civil wars deserve mention in the dispatches, and then only if the Russians agree to sponsor one of the contenders. The rich man never knows why other people do what they do because it never occurs to him that they have obligations to anybody other than himself. Few among the nation's more prominent journalists speak or read French. It would exceed the bounds of all decent patriotism to expect more than two or three of them to read or speak Russian, Chinese or Arabic.

Although promoting the illusion of happier results, almost all American magazine and television advertisements take place within the enchanted gardens outside the world of time. One in particular stands out as an exact but ironic analogue of the American experience in Vietnam. Expressed as a two-page photograph selling Mark Cross luggage, it showed a beautiful woman wearing silk pajamas being carried from a Rolls-Royce by her chauffeur at Newport, Rhode Island; against a background of light rain and fog, followed by a maid holding an umbrella over her head, the woman clutches a precious rose. The accompanying text explains that the luggage summers in the south of France and winters in St. Bart's. Of the woman it is said, "She lived as if in a dream." She reminded me, both in her attitude and pose, of General William C. Westmoreland.

By 1986 the war had been reprocessed into the trite melodrama of a Sylvester Stallone movie, and the media carefully ignored any evidence (cf. William Gibson's *The Perfect War*) that discounted the myth of a triumphant American army cheated of its victory by a timorous civilian authority and a lying press. As late as 1970, seven years after Americans accepted the burden of the war and two years after the Tet offensive, no scholar in the United States was devoting his or her full time to the study of Vietnam; no American university offered a tenured professorship in Vietnamese studies, and fewer than thirty students in American schools were engaged in learning the Vietnamese language.[14]

The makers of American foreign policy, most of them trained in abstractions of investment banking or the law, seldom question the great truth that all the important events of the last fifty years

14. The repeated failures of American policy in Iran (in the Nixon, Carter and Reagan administrations) proceeded from the same sort of profound ignorance. Few of the intelligence agents sent to Iran bothered to learn the Persian language; Nixon and Kissinger understood nothing of the economics of oil; Carter thought the Shah invincible, and Reagan's roadshow Machiavellians (Robert McFarlane, John Poindexter and Oliver North) couldn't tell the difference between a terrorist, an arms merchant and a mullah.

have centered upon the United States. Other nations come and go in supporting and character roles. Because their stories get written for them in Washington or New York, their national identities retain the character of picturesque backgrounds for a trendy movie complete with social statement.

To the rich almost everything in the world is make-believe, and they cannot understand how other people take seriously what they regard as diversions and toys. The dreaming narcissism of America's overlords suggests that Louis XV didn't get the axiom quite right, that instead of *"après moi, le déluge,"* the dictum should read, "after me, nothing." The egoist cannot conceive of the world without his presence in it.

8. HOLY DREAD

Thus much of this will make
Black white, foul fair, wrong right,
Base noble, old young, coward valiant.
. . . Why, this
Will lug your priests and servants from your sides,
Pluck sick men's pillows from below their heads.
This yellow slave
Will knit and break religions, bless the accursed,
Make the hoar leprosy adored, place thieves
And give them title, knee and approbation
With senators on the bench. This is it
That makes the wappened widow wed again;
She whom the spital-house and ulcerous sores
Would cast the gorge at, this embalms and spices
To the April day again.
— WILLIAM SHAKESPEARE, *Timon of Athens*, IV, iii

THE COMPLEX MECHANISMS OF THE MODERN WORLD DEPEND as certainly on the faith in money as the structures of the medieval world depended on faith in God. The gold, grain and credit markets are always open—if not in New York or London, then in Geneva, Bombay or Hong Kong. Money circles the globe literally at the speed of light, shifting with the aplomb of angels through the time zones, simultaneously tracing its intricate figures in a thousand computer terminals. It takes an enormous act of faith to assign meaning—much less health, happiness, life itself—to an abstraction seen fleetingly on a screen. As opposed to an object that can be firmly grasped—jewels, furs, paintings, gold coins—credit consists of nothing more substantial than a promise to pay. The flesh becomes word, and the numbers turn into poetic metaphors.

Since the eighteenth century the immense expansion of the world's wealth has come about as a result of a correspondingly immense expansion of credit, which in turn has demanded increasingly stupendous suspensions of disbelief. To the extent that a society employs an intrinsically worthless medium of exchange—paper, numbers on a screen—its wealth becomes greater, but so also does its credulity. Make the numbers big enough, and then make them immanent, like God, in all the world's phenomena, and people will believe almost anything.[1]

During the 1960s I spent a good deal of time traveling around the country in one or another of the press entourages that attend the comings in and goings out of the nation's more prominent citizens. Assigned for a period of months in 1965 to the White House press corps, I occasionally went with President Johnson to his ranch in Texas. Attached to the late Nelson Rockefeller's presidential campaign in the spring of 1968, I listened to him make airport speeches in half the states in the Union. At random intervals, I accompanied the presidents of oil and automobile companies in their stately

---

1. Salvador Dali, at the age of eighty-two and embarked on the promotion of a new perfume, gave a press interview in 1986 in which he discussed his lifelong study of alchemy. "Liking money like I like it," he said, "is nothing less than mysticism. Money is a glory."

A year later Suzy Knickerbocker confided to the readers of her gossip column in the *New York Post*, "Perhaps it's dreadful that money is God, but that's the story."

progress through the provinces of their corporate holdings. It always surprised me to discover that most of the other reporters on these journeys, sometimes as many as forty or fifty print and television correspondents, were afraid of airplanes. Because they were so often in the air, frequently in bad weather en route to obscure destinations, they figured that sooner or later the odds were bound to catch up with them and that somebody other than the managing editor would punish them for their presumption.

I remember a correspondent for *The Washington Post* once confiding that his habitual feeling of dread left him in only two circumstances—when he was aboard Air Force One with the president of the United States, and when he was on a corporate aircraft in the presence of an individual who either owned or controlled assets in excess of $500 million. I asked him why this was so, and he said he hadn't thought much about it, but he enjoyed a similar peace of mind when riding in stretch limousines. We had boarded a commercial flight for New York after leaving the season's candidate to the comforts of a weekend in California. Somewhere over Missouri, the gentleman from the *Post* ordered his fourth Scotch and said that not even God would dare strike down the president of the United States or the chief executive officer of Mobil Oil.[2]

Several years later I heard a variant of the same superstition attributed to Robert Vesco, the swindler and friend of Richard Nixon who, in the early 1970s, stole $750 million from the Fund of Funds. The story might be exaggerated or apocryphal, but it was told to me by a man who represented himself as a witness to the incident. As follows:

2. Precisely this superstition accounts for the continuing preoccupation with the sinking of the *Titanic*. Like the ship of which they were representative, the wealthy personages on board, among them an Astor and a Widener, were supposed to be invincible, gods of Henry Adams's "bankers' Olympus." Two days later, on April 1912, the *Empress of Ireland* sunk in the Gulf of St. Lawrence, drowning 1,000 passengers. Nobody remembers the incident because the deceased belonged to an invisible and nonequestrian social class.

Some months before Vesco fled the country in 1975 (taking up residence in Costa Rica to escape federal prosecution for criminal fraud) he was riding in a plane that encountered rough weather on its approach to LaGuardia Airport. Vesco owned the plane, and as it circled over New Jersey in a delayed holding pattern, he dissolved into gibbering terror. Pushing through the door to the cockpit, Vesco told the pilot to get the managers of the airport on the radio.

"Tell them I'll buy it," he said. "Tell them that if they let me land, I'll pay whatever they ask. You understand? I want to buy the fucking place."

As befitting even a crooked financier, Vesco's faith in money was perhaps excessive but certainly not atypical. The power of money is so obvious that its acolytes come to think of it as omnipotent. Wherever they look they can point to its victory: well-known criminals ride through the streets in limousines, dishonest politicians hold offices of public trust, whores inspire the love of princes and the adoration of gossip columnists. From these meager observations the faithful make a child's religion. Holding himself in low esteem, uncomfortably aware of his precarious grasp on other people's attention, the man besotted by a faith in money believes that if it can buy everything worth having, that if it can prolong life, win elections, relieve suffering, make hydrogen bombs, declare war, hire assassins and go south in the winter, then surely it can grant him the patents of respect and triumph over so small a trifle as death. Just as the aborigine imagines himself safe from harm within the sanctuary of his idol, or a child believes he controls the world by magical wish, so the plutocrat deems himself immortal within the precincts of his money.[3]

---

3. Within the not too distant future the wonders of biotechnology undoubtedly will allow the very rich to buy not only new hearts, lungs and kidneys but also new brain tissue exempting them from the sorrows of senility. As likely as not the market in human organs will be supplied by donors in the impoverished regions of the Third World, proving the truth of the Yiddish proverb: "If the rich could hire other people to die for them, the poor could make a wonderful living."

Like most superstitions, the religious faith in money has some basis in fact. When Andy Warhol was shot twice by one of his deranged film stars in June 1968 the ambulance drivers didn't recognize him for a celebrity. They picked him up at his New York "Factory," on a poor but trendy street, and on the way to the hospital, thinking him as worthless as everything else in the neighborhood, they didn't feel compelled to hurry. Warhol noticed that the ambulance was stopping for red lights and mumbled something about the urgency of his wound. For an extra $15, the drivers said, they would turn on the siren.

The chapter on death in the artist's book *The Philosophy of Andy Warhol* consists, almost in its entirety, of these words: "I'm so sorry to hear about it. I just thought that things were magic and that it would never happen."

We live among the miracles of scientific invention, making common use of lasers, penicillin, computers, nuclear energy and genetic engineering. But none of these wonders stirs the poetic imagination. We feel the glory of revelation only when presented to the embodiment of unutterable wealth. Some years ago at El Morocco, a New York nightclub known for the profligacy of its wastrel clientele, I was sitting with a group of people who kept staring at a dough-faced man dozing at a table near the band. Not recognizing the gentleman, I asked why he was the object of such intense veneration. I was told he was the grandson of a Chicago grain merchant who had received, in the summer of 1887, a tip on the commodity exchange and so founded a great fortune. Nobody knew what else to say about him. Apparently he had accomplished nothing in his life other than to spend the income from a substantial trust fund. A woman said he was known to be rude; another woman said she had seen him once before, at a party with circus motif in Southampton, offering his drink to an elephant. The gentleman in question might as well have been carved in wood. Obviously he had been anointed by God; his fortune had come to him from the divine cloud of unknowing that also had descended upon the Rockefellers, the Harrimans, the

Mellons and last week's winner of the New Jersey lottery. In the United States fortunes have their own histories. It is the money, not the achievement, that echoes down the halls of the generations. Point out a lineal descendant of Thomas Jefferson or Ralph Waldo Emerson and the fellow will scarcely merit a glance.

Our American assumption that money rules the world is as fundamental among its titular enemies as among its devoted friends. The socialist believes that money is malign, that only the power of the state can hold it safely in check; the capitalist believes that money must be set free, that only in the hands of enlightened individuals will it bestow the gifts of property and production. Neither the socialist nor the capitalist believes that money can be safely left in the custody of ordinary, probably heathen and unwashed, human beings.

If money were not perceived as somehow divine, then why should it rouse the passions of the people who blame the world's suffering on "the rich," "the interests," "the monopolists," "the oil companies," "the Jews," "the robber barons," "the nabobs," or "the banks"? The zealots who rage against the evils of wealth bear witness to their faith by the fervor of their blasphemy. Nothing so damages a socialist's faith as the experience of meeting a rich man. He cannot bear the disappointment. Expecting to come face-to-face with Satan, he finds himself introduced to a small and frightened clerk worried about his stomach or his will.[4]

---

4. Observing the timidity of the plutocracy in nineteenth century France, Jules and Edmond Goncourt composed for their cousin on the Bourse a rich man's prayer: "Oh Lord, may my urine be less cloudy and my hemorrhoids less annoying. May I live long enough to make another 100,000 francs. May the Emperor stay in power so that my income will increase, and may Anzin coal continue to rise on the stock market." The text and tone of the prayer admirably expresses the spirit not only of Ivan Boesky and Carl Icahn but also that of the presidents of most American banks and business corporations.

As further testimony to the American faith in money a poll conducted in 1985 discovered that more of the respondents were afraid of evil consequences implicit in a credit card than in a nuclear bomb.

Despite our ceaseless murmuring about money, we prefer not to know too much about its nature or mechanics. We would rather believe in mysteries—in stock prices that rise from $10 to $100 in the space of a week, in the making of instantaneous stars out of salesgirls found by a film producer in a drugstore—and we suspect that if we inquire too closely our questions might be construed as acts of impiety. People absorbed with their own money worries can count to the penny the sums of their unhappiness, but about the larger movements of money they remain as innocent as squirrels.

This is fortunate for the army of stockbrokers, tipsters, loan officers and insurance salesmen that feeds on the national religion in the manner of locusts feeding on an orange grove. Year after year the country's most eminent economists make predictions consistently ridiculed by events; year after year the brokerage firms sell hundreds of millions of shares in companies that go nowhere but down; year after year the editors of investment newsletters charge handsome fees for advice that is as worthless as the geopolitical advice published in the academic quarterlies. Nobody minds very much because it is understood that learned gentlemen speak and write an unintelligible language not unlike church Latin. It doesn't matter if they prove to be wrong because it is understood that they are in the business of mumbling prayers. Their function is ceremonial, and to the extent that the worship of money becomes more extensive among larger sectors of the population their presence becomes increasingly imperative—as directors of corporations, as counselors in the White House, as holy men publishing sermons in the newspapers.[5]

5. We have almost as many transcendental definitions of money—"store of value," "means of measurement," "instrument of power," "symbol economy," "universal commodity," etc.—as Muslims have names for Allah. The banking community in New York revered Paul Volcker, former chairman of the Federal Reserve, as the great shaman who rescued everybody from the flood and fire apt to accompany a repudiation of the Third World debt. The bankers clung to this belief despite the fact that the FDIC in 1987 possessed a fund of only $13 billion with which to pay depositors of failed banks.

Never were these gentlemen more urgently or more pointlessly consulted than during the stock market panic in the autumn of 1987. On Monday, October 19, the Dow Jones industrial average lost 508 points, and before nightfall the newspapers had proclaimed the end of the world. The calamity descended upon the multitude in Wall Street with the force of biblical revelation. It was as if the Antichrist had worked an anti-miracle, which, within a matter of hours, converted the nation's most devout capitalists into faithful socialists.

Before the markets opened on Monday, the financial operatives employed in the money trades believed themselves to be standing on safe and hallowed ground when reciting the catechism of their belief in unfettered free enterprise. If asked to make after-dinner speeches they would have said (unhesitatingly and with unctuous rectitude) that it was the government's duty to mind its own business, lower taxes, stay off the backs of the people and leave the markets—the free and life-giving markets—well enough alone.

For seven years they had embraced the claptrap economic theory of the Reagan administration and born witness to the moral beauty of capitalism unbound. By noon Monday, nobody was singing any more hymns to Mammon. Before the awful day ended roughly $1 trillion of net worth had vanished as mysteriously as the last unicorn, and the lamps of faith had been extinguished in the electronic twinkling of ten thousand computer terminals.

Nobody, of course, knew where or why the money had gone, but clearly somebody had to say something. For the rest of the week oracles of all denominations—learned economists, alarmed portfolio managers, former Treasury officials—hurried in and out of the media issuing statements of solemn reassurance.

The effect was comic. Swindling financiers who had stolen fortunes behind the screens of insider trading were seen preaching the virtues of fiscal integrity. Chairmen of brokerage firms bloated with the fees skimmed off merger and takeover deals hastened to assure their audiences (i.e., the customers they had so smilingly gulled) that the economy was "fundamentally sound," that the banks were as safe as South African gold and that their salesmen were still "bullish on America."

The princes of Wall Street distributed the blame for their misfortunes far more generously and evenhandedly than they were accustomed to distributing profits. Giving voice to rumors drifting through the news, they assigned the fault to the trade and budget deficits, the Germans, Washington, government spending, national debt, lack of leadership, the Japanese, the arbitrageurs, mindless greed (somebody else's, not their own), programmed trades, the futures index and the Ayatollah Khomeini.

Together with the recriminations, the apostasy continued throughout the week. The speeches and excuses became increasingly preposterous as stock prices—heedless of even the most responsible advice—drifted further downward into the abyss. Without notable exception, the *ci-devant* believers in the blessed wonder of Reaganomics recanted their faith in the free market. Capitalism, it turned out, wasn't the fairy godmother or magic wand it had been made out to be in the songs and legends of the Reagan administration. No, capitalism wasn't like that at all. As a matter of fact, capitalism on a bad day could be downright mean. Bust was as much a part of its nature as boom. What markets could give, markets could take away.

By Friday afternoon nearly everybody with access to a microphone or an editorial page had forsworn his or her allegiance to what, only a month before, had been advertised as "the entrepreneurial spirit." By terrified and nonpartisan consent the authorities agreed it was time for the government to regulate debt, manage the economy, fix the international monetary system, raise taxes and do whatever was necessary (even if it meant getting back on the backs of the people) to restore the confidence of the American public. So fervent was the hope of rescue, and so rapid was the conversion to the new socioeconomic faith, that over the course of the week the only speculations that improved in value were those in government bonds.

The October panic in the stock markets proved the nonideological character of the American faith in money. No economic theory, no political conviction, no wall of rhetoric or line of thought can survive a loss of 500 points on the Dow. Against manifestations of such divine magnitude, any secular wisdom is a faint and paltry thing, as light as apple blossoms and as thin as straw.

The devastation brought about by the mere flickering procession of numbers through the world's computer screens—first in Tokyo and then in London and New York—also proved how precariously the world's credit is balanced on the scale of superstition. What is true is what enough people believe to be true, and facts often matter less than rumors.

To a large extent the stock markets depend on the willingness of all involved—seller as well as buyer—to suspend the faculty of thought. Consider the modus operandi of the Wall Street tout. Invariably he has acquired his information from a secondary source, from a man who heard it from a friend who knows the president of the company. He never has the word from the primary source (from the mergers and acquisitions department of Merrill Lynch, say, or a dishonest arbitrageur), because if he had that kind of news he would not need to sell it in the pages of a newsletter. Instead he would make a discreet fortune and retire to a villa on the Côte d'Azur. What would be the point of whispering in corners? Why concern oneself with a dog-eared map on which a drowned ship captain once marked a faint cross?

The buyers neglect to ask themselves such questions; if they did, they wouldn't be buyers, and the tout wouldn't find it worth his time to trouble them with dreams. The distance of the primary source gives the tout a theatrical space in which to set up his lights and scenery. The buyer never meets the man who knows, and so he remains free to imagine a figure of his own invention. If he met the authority in question, he might become frightened; he might recognize him as an accountant in a shabby suit or as an old politician sick with drink and half-remembered lies.

The tout needs only to judge the precise distance at which the buyer begins to see visions not unlike those vouchsafed to early Christian saints. The distances vary according to the buyer's temperament and the kind of information being offered for sale. Some buyers prefer to know nothing; others need to equip themselves with the complexity of childish detail—the performance of the horse in the mud, the price earnings ratio, the rumors in Japan, the Javanese theory known only to the intimates of George Bush.

None of these things matter very much. All of them can be rearranged as the occasion demands. They don't matter because the transaction always takes place in the realm of magic—in the dark grove of the imagination where all things remain possible, where death and time never intrude upon the idiot dancing. The most convincing touts succumb to their own seductions. They come to believe in the divine origins of their information, and they forget that they overheard the conversation in a men's room, or that the senator was talking about something else, or that yesterday's horse finished seventh.[6]

The credulity of the rich accounts for the ease with which they can be persuaded to invest in nonexistent oil wells and fraudulent tax shelters. Following a rhythm as regular as the reports of holiday traffic, newspapers every few weeks publish stories that begin with questions such as the one asked by *The Wall Street Journal* in October 1982: "SAN DIEGO—Why did hundreds of affluent, well-educated and successful investors turn over millions of dollars to J. David Dominelli?" Or with statements such as the one in *The New York Times* of May 15, 1981: "For

---

6. Sir Walter Raleigh, promoter of the first American colony in Virginia, perfectly embodied the spirit of the new country. At the age of sixty-four, convinced he was going to find "The City of the Golden Man" on the upper reaches of the Orinoco River, he sold all of his own and his wife's property to outfit the expedition. He envisioned a trail over a mountain of crystal to a high, cold city, its walls and roofs decorated with golden jackals and encrusted with precious stones. To a doubting investor he said he was as sure of finding the place as of "not missing the way from my dining room to my bedchamber."

28 years, the police and prosecutors in eight countries have been compiling dossiers on a man who now calls himself Eduardo Rabi—while he was living in penthouses in New York, riding antique Rolls-Royces in South America, gambling in the casinos of Monte Carlo, mixing with the best society in Paraguay and Uruguay, and allegedly getting away with $60 million in swindles."

The stories never lack for humor, and almost always the sting turns on the same conjuror's trick. The swindler poses as a man of immense wealth, and the mark, no matter how well off, imagines that the man richer than himself stands that much nearer the godhead. Among the well-known people gulled by various swindlers over the last two or three years I can remember Alexander Haig, Norman Lear, Giscard d'Estaing, Woody Allen, Dick Cavett and Erica Jong. The aforementioned J. David Dominelli, otherwise known as "Captain Money," set up his Ponzi scheme with no more than a few hundred dollars in the basement of a Mexican restaurant in La Jolla. Within five years the scheme attracted $200 million, and Captain Money, like the sorcerer's apprentice, didn't know how to shut down the flow of cash. He bought everything he could think of—three jet aircraft, dozens of $100,000 sports cars, racehorses worth $650,000, ski condos in Colorado and beach property in Del Mar—but still the customers kept coming. The richer the captain seemed, the more desperately the suckers wanted to deal themselves into the catastrophe. The current passion for mergers and acquisitions, many of them financed with instruments of debt known as junk bonds, rests on what a literary critic might call the finance of the absurd. The collapse of the Penn Square Bank in Oklahoma City in 1982 followed from the credulity of bankers in the habit of making $20 million loans while drinking champagne from cowboy boots.[7]

---

7. Asked to comment on the loss of jobs likely to result from the collapse of that bank, an impatient bank examiner, looking for trace elements of liquidity in the desert of the balance sheet, said, in an irritated tone of voice, "Excuse me, I only represent banks, not people."

Among the public demonstrations of the credulous state of mind, none of which I am aware proved as convincing or as humorous as the Senate's confirmation of the late Nelson Rockefeller as vice president of the United States. Rockefeller had been appointed to that office by Gerald Ford, and in November 1974, on television and in full view of a nation still alarmed by Richard Nixon's plundering of the public trust, the Senate Rules Committee had to decide whether the candidate deserved the confidence of his countrymen.

The committee couldn't get beyond the miracle of Rockefeller's fortune. The senators learned that he possessed $218 million, which was still a lot of money in 1974, and even the skeptics among them prostrated themselves like slaves staring into pharaoh's golden face.

Not a single senator could bring himself to ask a hard question. So great is the American belief in money that when such a man as Rockefeller reveals his net worth even the blasphemous feel moved to worship. They forget what they know about themselves and what they have observed in others; their reason fails them, and they retreat to the limits of consciousness prevailing in 3000 B.C.

The presence of money in large sums impresses the feeling of holy dread even on people supposedly indifferent to its radiance. In New York in the late 1970s I knew a banker who at least had the wit to understand that when the numbers passed six figures he lost touch with his critical intelligence. He was employed as a vice president in the uptown office of the Chase Manhattan Bank, and every day at 10 a.m. the clerks in the Wall Street office displayed on a closed-circuit television system the bank's outstanding debt, foreign exchange positions and current cash balance. The numbers appeared on a screen, but my friend, drinking coffee with the senior management and trying very hard to seem wise, hadn't the faintest conception of what they meant. He might as well have been looking at Druidic runes or Linear B.

Although expressed in a different mode, the same unspoken regard for the mystery of cash characterizes the technique of the successful borrower of bank funds. He knows he must pretend he doesn't need the loan. Even if he is destitute, even if he stands in imminent peril of losing wife, children, house and reputation, he must affect a well-bred indifference to the petty details of the deal under discussion. He has a better chance of borrowing $10 million than $10,000 (the latter sum being so small as to raise the specter of need), but only if he keeps his composure and preserves a manner bordering on contempt.

It is no accident that banks resemble temples, preferably Greek, and that the supplicants who come to perform the rites of deposit and withdrawal instinctively lower their voices into the registers of awe. Even the most junior tellers acquire within weeks of their employment the officiousness of hierophants tending an eternal flame. I don't know how they become so quickly inducted into the presiding mysteries, or who instructs them in the finely articulated inflections of contempt for the laity, but somehow they learn to think of themselves as suppliers of the monetized DNA that is the breath of life.

The senior bank management, of course, looks upon borrowers as pilgrims come to make confession. The ceaseless signing of documents and forms reminds people of their existence as functions of a divine arithmetic and integers derived from an economic first cause. One of my uncles, a man of firm New England upbringing, liked to say that he chose the profession of banking "because, goddamnit, people have to tell you the goddamn truth." He expected his customers to make an honest disclosure—not only of their financial assets but also of their conduct.[8] Over the years I have known a good

---

8. Toward the end of what had been a mercifully placid career, my uncle retired in some haste when his bank was driven to the ledge of bankruptcy by a convergence of bad loans Several unscrupulous debtors had falsified their credit statements, and my uncle went to Weston, Connecticut, believing that the country was doomed. He joined right-wing political organizations and devoted the last fifteen years of his life to writing sermons in the form of letters to newspaper editors.

many people too abashed to ask impious questions about the condition of their own holdings and accounts. They imagine that the trust officer will reproach them for their wastefulness and folly, chastising them for having committed the unpardonable sin of placing a higher value on life than on property. The society knows of no ritual so solemn as the opening of a safety deposit box after the death of one of its wealthier citizens. Men in dark suits—executor, lawyer, accountant, auditor, heir—enter the vault in attitudes of profound reverence. Nobody speaks as the sacred box is withdrawn from its crypt in the wall and borne, silently and slowly, to the lighted table on which, as if at an altar, the attending clergy examine its entrails. If the estate is believed to be large enough to warrant the analogue of a high mass, the state taxing authority sends an agent (i.e., a papal nuncio) to duly note the presence of every bond, deed, certificate and jewel. The naming of the objects, in voices hushed with wonder, is equivalent to the singing of the Magnificat. The society knows no more exalted an anthem of praise.[9]

Conversely, I once knew a man who, when feeling intimidated by the trustees of his estate, pictured them in goatskins shaking feathered rattles and wearing crowns of reindeer horns. The image relieved him of his anxiety. Instead of a reproving conscience he saw before him bookkeepers so terrified of the god in the vault that they dared not speak in the vernacular.

If even a secular religion can be defined as those sets of attitudes people take for granted, then it is by their unquestioning adherence to the rule of money that Americans make good the proofs of their

---

9. Within the last two or three years all the admiring journalistic accounts about the "new breed of traders" on Wall Street (i.e., the young men earning upwards of $1 million a year at the First Boston Corporation or Goldman Sachs) mention the monkish habits of the brotherhood. Everybody rises at 5 a.m., to charter a Lear jet or make a call to London; hardly anybody sleeps more than a few hours a night or eats anything except bologna sandwiches. Speaking of their devotion to money, a psychiatrist quoted in *The Wall Street Journal* observed, "To these people business is God."

faith. The people of medieval Europe didn't think of Christianity as one of several theologies among which they could pick and choose as if doctrines were scarves on sale at Bloomingdale's. The evidence of faith was simply what one did and said, the way one lived one's life. People might not always act in accordance with the tenets of the faith—murder, lechery and avarice being as popular in the twelfth century as in the twentieth—but the presiding superstitions seemed as immutable as the seasons. Similarly, modern Americans find it impossible to conceive of a world in which money doesn't have the last word. The bottom line is synonymous with the judgment of God, and the contemporary businessman who fails to earn $1 million a year can feel as riven with guilt as the medieval knight-at-arms denied the rites of absolution. When they don't know what to do about any of the thousand and one evils that plague mankind, Americans scatter incense or rose petals—that is, they "throw money at the problem." The money almost always fails to work the expected miracle because it is intended not as a specific remedy but as a votive offering.

The feeling of pious awe that obtains within the sanctuaries of the nation's banks also permeates its better department stores. The sumptuousness of the ornament in Bergdorf Goodman or the Trump Tower is meant to inspire in the congregation the attitude of reverence once prompted by stained glass windows and the music of a brass choir. The faithful go shopping in much the spirit that Christians once stopped to pray at wayside shrines. Mothers tell their daughters that if they feel depressed, the best thing to do is buy a new dress. No matter how small or frivolous the object, the buying of something new lifts the spirit and bears witness to the miracle of cash. The transaction comforts people with a presentiment of salvation and with a sense of having acknowledged the perfection of a supernatural design.

The feasts of consumption thus become rituals of communion. The faithful consume goods and services as if they were partaking of the body and blood of Christ. The more costly the substance consumed—a dress by Valentino, an ounce of cocaine, a cruise around the world priced at $265,000 for three months— the more perfectly the communicant enters into a union with God. An advertisement published in 1986 in *Time* magazine by Pioneer Electronics (manufacturers of the Pioneer SX-V500 Audio/Video Quartz-Synthesizer Non-Switching Receiver) displayed the photograph of an obviously rich and self-satisfied young man standing in front of a priceless painting and apparently listening, on the Pioneer SX-V500, to a Mozart piano concerto. Echoing the words of the Eucharist, the copy read: "Mozart died to bring me pleasure."

Perceived as sacraments, the acts of consumption acquire a spiritual meaning not always apparent to a European, a moralist or a bookkeeper. Nothing is superfluous and everything counts. Because it is a matter of eating God, the consumption of gossip or Vuitton suitcases is as devout a proof of piety as the consumption of toilet water, tofu, tennis balls and trips to Florida. The products contain symbolic properties not dissimilar to those the Catholic Church assigns to wafer and wine. Taken in appropriate quantity and with a decent regard for ruinous expense, the products bestow health, long life, status, sexual prowess, intelligence, national security, happiness and peace of mind—all the blessings that devout Christians expect from the gift of God.

The mystical nature of American consumption accounts for its joylessness. We spend a great deal of time in stores, but if we don't seem to take much pleasure in our buying, it's because we're engaged in the acts of sacrifice and self-definition. Abashed in the presence of expensive merchandise, we recognize ourselves (in Tiffany's, Bergdorf Goodman or Rallye Motors) as suppliants admitted to a shrine.

Just as the rat in the behaviorist's maze comes to love not the cheese at the end of his labor but the lever that works the mechanics of his reward, so also the people who come to prefer the touch of money to any object or experience for which money can be exchanged. Money itself embodies all the pleasurable states of feeling into which it can be transferred. The substitution of meaning accounts for the grasping of misers as well as the extravagance of spendthrifts. Karl Marx well understood this peculiar transformation of flesh into coin. He appreciated the damage done to people who allowed their faith in money to outbid all other claims on their humanity, which is why, one hundred years later and despite the absurdity of much of his political writing, revolutions continue to be mounted in his name.

"Money," Marx said, "is the visible deity, the transformation of all human and natural qualities into their opposite, the universal confusion and inversion of things." He also said that "the divine power of money resides in its essence as the alienated and exteriorized species-life of men. It is the alienated power of humanity." These somewhat cryptic remarks describe the same sleight of hand to which Shakespeare alludes in *Timon of Athens*. Because the workings of the international economy require that all forms of wealth and property become subordinate to the rule of money, they must also become alienated from any other measurement of value.

The relation between people is given over to an object, to something external to human feeling, need or expression. People no longer act as intermediaries between themselves; they rely on the intervention of a power outside and above themselves—that is, on money. Objects (or individuals) retain their value only insofar as they represent money. Once separated from the intermediary of money (i.e., once divorced from God), objects and individuals lose their value. Money becomes the divine Other precisely because it can transform all human and natural qualities into their opposites, because, in Shakespeare's language, it can make "foul fair, wrong right, base noble, old young, coward valiant." By assigning the right of definition to a power other than ourselves, we abdicate our human offices in favor of "this yellow slave," that "will knit and break religions, bless the accursed, make the hoar leprosy adored, place thieves and give them title, knee and approbation."

Prior to the age of big-time capitalism money had value because it represented objects. Invert the equation and the objects, like the people, retain their value only to the extent they represent money. By assigning to money the powers that properly belong to human intellect and imagination, the devotees thwart or suppress their attempts at love, compassion, art and thought. They revolve like marionettes around the embodiment of great wealth made manifest in persons or institutions. Whether employed as authors, call girls or presidents of corporations, they learn to value themselves in proportion to the money others will pay for their labors. The subsequent dissolutions of self remove, as if by surgery, the faculties of intellect and will. The moment of astonishment, which has something in common with the ecstasy of religious self-abasement, reduces people to a sense of their futility and worthlessness. The paralysis of thought can last for a few hours or several days; among people in the more advanced phases of the disorder it can last for many years, sometimes for an entire life.

It is, of course, nothing new to say that an inordinate love of money results in predictably high yields of stupidity and despair. The Bible is explicit on the point; so are any number of secular writers, among them Juvenal, Dante, Shakespeare, Balzac, Dickens and Freud. If it could be seen as architecture or heard as music, mankind's worship of money might invite comparison with Chartres Cathedral or the Mass in B minor. No other labor of the human imagination embraces so many talents and behaviors, not a few of them psychotic. The offerings placed on the altars of wealth display so bewildering an infinity of forms that a true and diligent expounder of the faith would need to account not only for the price of a matched set of ICBMs but also for the cost of the orange trees at Versailles, Anne of Austria's black pearls, the diplomacy of George III and the diamond in the ear of the last Krupp.

Even so, I think it fair to say that the current ardor of the American faith in money easily surpasses the degrees of intensity achieved by other societies in other times and places. Money means so many things to us—spiritual as well as temporal—that we are at a loss to know how to hold its majesty at bay.

The arriviste theologians in Massachusetts assumed they had been granted what they called a "special appointment," and knew they would suffer the punishment of ecclesiastical foreclosure if they failed to make good on the deal and bungled the subdivision of New Jerusalem. If America failed, the cosmos failed. Not only would Americans have nowhere to go, but the whole scheme of salvation—laws of nature, history and science; the ground of being; the rigging of human thought—would all come loose and blow away in the wind.

Henry Adams in his autobiography remarks that although the Americans weren't much good as materialists they had been so "deflected by the pursuit of money" that they could turn "in no other direction." The national distrust of the contemplative temperament arises less from an innate Philistinism than from a suspicion of anything that cannot be counted, stuffed, framed or mounted over the fireplace. Men remain free to rise or fall in the world, and if they fail it must be because they willed it so. Visible signs of wealth testify to an inward state of grace, and without at least some of these talismans posted in one's house or on one's person an American loses all hope of demonstrating to himself the theorem of his happiness. Seeing is believing, and if an American success is to count for anything in the world it must be clothed in the raiment of property. As often as not it isn't the money itself that means anything; it is the use of money as the currency of the soul.

Against the faith in money, other men in other times and places have raised up countervailing faiths in family, honor, religion, intellect and social class. The merchant princes of medieval Europe would have looked upon the American devotion as sterile cupidity; the ancient Greeks would have regarded it as a form of insanity. Even now, in the last decades of a century commonly defined as American, a good many societies both in Europe and Asia manage to balance the desire for wealth against the other claims of the human spirit. An Englishman of modest means can remain more or less content with the distinction of an aristocratic name or the consolation of a flourishing garden; the Germans show obscure university professors the deference accorded by Americans only to celebrity; the Soviets honor the holding of political power; in France a rich man is a rich man, to whom everybody grants the substantial powers that his riches command but to whom nobody grants the respect due to a member of the National Academy. But in the United States a rich man is perceived as being necessarily both good and wise, which is an absurdity that would be seen as such not only by a Frenchman but also by a Russian.[10] Not that Americans are greedier than the French, or less intellectual than Germans, or more venal than Russians, but to what other tribunal can an anxious and supposedly egalitarian people submit their definitions of the good, the true and the beautiful if not to the judgment of the bottom line?

W.H. Auden thought the most striking difference between Americans and Europeans was to be found in their different attitudes toward money. No European associates wealth with personal merit or poverty with personal failure. But to the American what is important is not so much the possession of money but the power to earn it "as a proof of one's manhood." Having proved he can earn money an American can safely throw it away—scattering it like confetti on chorus girls or like holy water on the founts of charity.[11]

No matter how bitter the lessons of their experience, people stunted by the faith in money insist on believing that it is something more than an utterly colorless abstraction or convenient arithmetic cipher. They imagine that it possesses an inherent spirit or substance.

10. Also by anybody who has had to listen to an after-dinner speech by Donald Trump or George Steinbrenner's exposition of a baseball season.
11. By now, of course, Auden would have had to amend his observation to account for the descent of women into the pits of trade. Not only the proof of manhood but also the proof of womanhood rests on the capacity to make a fortune. "A poor American," Auden said, "feels guilty at being poor, but less guilty than an American rentier who has inherited wealth but is doing nothing to increase it. What can the latter do but take to drink and psychoanalysis?"

Wishing to assign to money a moral value, they resist the notion that money is neither good nor evil, the symbol, not the substance, of wealth. The devotees on the radical left attribute to it the sum of the world's evil; believers on the reactionary right conceive of it as the store of the world's virtue. Enthralled by the Dionysian beauty of cash, the faithful of all sects and denominations blur the distinction between money as a commodity and money as sacrament.

It is the blurring of this distinction, the unwillingness to recognize money as an arbitrary system of measurement, that inflicts so much suffering on people taught to accept price as a synonym for meaning. Money is like fire, an element as little troubled by moralizing as earth, air and water. Men can employ it as a tool or they can dance around it as if it were the incarnation of a god. Money votes socialist or monarchist, finds a profit in pornography or translations from the Bible, commissions Rembrandt and underwrites the technology of Auschwitz. It acquires its meaning from the uses to which it is put.

Deployed as a tool and understood as a secular product (comparable to wheat, coal or intelligence), money ranks as one of the primary materials with which mankind builds the architecture of civilization. Large numbers of people, many of them Americans, continue to use money in this manner, and the success of the American economy testifies both to their energy and their clarity of mind. Although a constant motif in American history and metaphysics, the dream of money never provided the impetus from which the country drew its greatest strengths. George Washington was obliged to borrow money to pay his travel to his first inauguration. Abraham Lincoln had little use for riches, and Thomas Jefferson died bankrupt. A genuine indifference to the radiance of money has been characteristic not only of the nation's principal artists and scientists but also of the founders of its largest fortunes. Even the most humorless of the late nineteenth-century plutocrats seem to have taken money less seriously than their heirs and publicists. They understood that laissez-faire capitalism, like all economic systems, was amoral, a mechanism providing greater chances of liberty and prosperity to greater numbers of people than had been possible within feudal or mercantile systems. But for money itself they often expressed a gambler's contempt. By and large they were interested in something else—in an idea, a contraption, a theory of combination or a geometry of markets. Money was something that followed with the luggage, a secondary proof of grace accumulating in the hall with the invitations to dinner and the requests for press interviews, with the flowers, the catering bills and the art collection. Neither John D. Rockefeller nor Henry Ford were impressed by the magical aspects of money.[12] A similar indifference shows up in conversation with latter-day millionaires who have made their own fortunes; like highly paid athletes, the inventors of computer systems seem surprised that they should earn so much money for playing what they often describe as a game. Andrew Carnegie acknowledged the same primacy of mind over matter when he observed that the mere "amassing of wealth is one of the worst species of idolatry."

Perceived as divinity—seeming to transform day into night, old into young, crime into philanthropy—money serves the totalitarian or oligarchic interest and urges men to embrace their longings for the demonic. Gouverneur Morris, brother to a signer of the Declaration of Independence and a friend to both Talleyrand and Marie Antoinette, looked at the extravagance in France under the *ancien régime* and recognized the result implicit in too fond a love of money. "Wealth," he said, "tends to corrupt the mind and to nourish its love of power and to stimulate it to oppression. History proves this to be the spirit of opulence."[13]

---

12. To a biographer Rockefeller once said: "I know of nothing more despicable and pathetic than a man who devotes all the hours of the waking day to the making of money for money's sake."

13. Ivan Boesky attributed his crimes to his own too passionate love of money, "a sickness I have in the face of which I am helpless."

These two images of money—secular and divine—exist simultaneously in the minds of most men in most times and most places. The implacable enmity between the two factions gives rise to the argument that is the American dialectic. It is a question of emotional algebra, and on the balance of the fractions depends not only the happiness of individuals but also the destiny of nations. If the incumbent majority speaks the language of mutual faith and credit, it will form voluntary associations, endow universities, consign its capital not simply to the bond market but to the advance of human reason as well as the expansion of the public good. But if too many people hear in the whisper of bank notes the voice of God, then sooner or later (usually sooner) they lose so much of their humanity that the language of mutual faith breaks down into sullen chant. The believers in fairy gold, no matter how well-intentioned their tax-deductible gifts to the Metropolitan Opera, join the circle of an old and pagan dance.

9. COINED SOULS

To stay rich, people must be nearer to the dead than the living.
　　　　　　　—STEPHEN VIZINCZEY, *An Innocent Millionaire*

Money is mourned with deeper sorrow than friends or kindred.
　　　　　　　—JUVENAL, *Satires*

EVERY FEW DAYS ONE OR ANOTHER OF THE COUNTRY'S eminent prophets wonders what has gone wrong with the once prosperous American enterprise. Why has the nation's productivity declined? Why is the debt so heavy and the balance of international trade so skewed in favor of Germany or Japan? What has become of the moral commonwealth, and why are so many politicians under indictment or in jail?

Perhaps I have been corrupted by my upbringing in the precincts of wealth, or possibly I have lived too long in the city of New York, but I suspect the answers have to do with ascribing authority to something as abstract and as inherently meaningless as money. The crippling effects of the general stupefaction account for phenomena as diverse as the passion for mergers and acquisitions, for the trade deficit and the absence of vigorous political debate among either Democrats or Republicans, for the emptiness of spirit that stares out of the face of national television. The ratings accorded to

Dynasty define the ethos of an age that thinks it possible to buy the future as if it were an oyster or a dress.

That the obsession with money dulls the capacity for feeling and thought I think can be accepted as an axiom requiring no further argument. The paralysis can be seen in statistical tables as well as in the expressions of art and politics. The economy weakens, and so do the indices of perception. Immobilized by fears of various denominations, too many people begin to look like animals standing perfectly still in attitudes of trembling defense. The attitude of mind leads not to safety, not to the "steady state" so lovingly promoted in the early 1970s as the rich man's dream of heaven, but, by the degrees made apparent during the late 1970s and early 1980s, into paralysis and debt.

From the beginning of the American argument the creditor classes have done their best to prevent the introduction of new ideas and new products as well as to forestall any seditious shifts in the balance of capital. During the years of the Reagan ascendancy the defense of property became a radical cause. Given the cost of bringing to market a newly designed car, weapons system or situation comedy, the ladies and gentlemen charged with making the necessary commitments find it hard to take chances with anything that isn't as safe as it is banal. The money looms so large (roughly $400 billion, for instance, in the nation's pension funds) that the people responsible for its deployment become easily frightened and prefer to leave the decisions to a computer program. Of the trades taking place on the New York Stock Exchange, 80 percent involve institutions—banks, mutual and pension funds, insurance companies. The individual investor has all but disappeared from the market, and the notion of the exchange as a reflection of "the people's capitalism" (a slogan popular in the early 1960s) has been reduced to absurdity.

The tax "reforms" passed by the Congress in the autumn of 1986 amidst almost universal applause clearly favor the safest and most sterile investments and work to the advantage of the least creative of the country's professions (i.e., lawyers, accountants, retailers, broadcasters, suppliers of franchised hamburgers). Labor allies itself with management in the effort to make time stand still, and their agents jointly lobby Congress for protective tariffs against the foreign manufactures with which they no longer can compete.[1] The frenzied speculation in the stock market adds nothing to the sum of the nation's well-being or common store of value. A few people become very, very rich, usually at the cost of destroying one or more companies that prior to their dismemberment had been providing employment, tax revenues and the hope of innovation. People who can think of nothing else to do resort to the law courts as a means of transferring wealth from one account to another.[2] Again, their efforts add nothing to the commonwealth. The shuffling of paper (a macroeconomic variation on the game of three-card monte) consumes more and more of the nation's energy and intellect. The litigiousness of the society aids and abets the shriveling of national enterprise. People wonder, with T.S. Eliot's Prufrock, whether they dare to eat a peach or move across the street. Relatively few people under the age of thirty-five can afford to buy a house—or even entertain the hope of ever buying a house.[3] Business can do nothing without consulting

1. American business cannot compete because it hasn't been trained to compete, at least not in arenas that bear anything other than a metaphorical resemblance to a free market. At least one quarter, and perhaps one third, of the American economy provides goods and services to a federal government (a.k.a. "Uncle Sugar") notorious for its corrupt purchasing practices. The larger American industries depend on the convenience of rigged prices and the protection of monopoly.

2. In the spring of 1986 a gentleman's mistress sued his wife for "alienation of affection," and a number of children in several states sued their parents for "wrongful upbringing."

3. In Manhattan modest one-bedroom apartments sell for $250,000; larger apartments sell for as much as $5 million. Rents priced at $1,500 a month are considered cheap. Elsewhere in the country approximately 10 million people give up more than 35 percent of their income to the cost of housing. At those rates a lot of people cannot afford to move around much anymore, and they become, quite literally, immobile.

lawyers. Newspaper editors worried about libel suits speak of a "chilling effect" and interpret the First Amendment as a license temporarily on loan from a sullen prince. Too many people, often against their will and better judgment, feel they have little choice except to join the legion of speculators. Their houses turn into real estate deals, and their assets ebb and flow like the tide, in and out of the stock market, the money funds, the gambling casinos.

To the extent that the desire for profit exceeds the desire for life, the translations of human beings into body counts or paying customers supersedes their uses as people. They become objects that can be sold at auction in celebrity raffles. Flesh has been transformed into property, which, in a commercial society, is akin to salvation. The rich achieve in life the apotheosis that lesser men achieve only in death. They become their own masterpieces, rare jewels for which the world offers more or less satisfactory settings, precious ornaments infinitely more beautiful than anything else in their art collections. At an expensive dinner party in Dallas I once sat next to a woman wearing a dress made of such heavy metallic fabric that she couldn't bend from the waist and could barely lift her arms. Taking into account her immaculate silence it occurred to me that she might as well have sent the dress on a hanger.[4]

At Yale University in the autumn of 1984 a drama student satisfied the requirement for his senior theater project by declaring himself a work of art. He walked around the campus for several weeks in the company of a friend whom he had appointed as his curator. He construed his mere presence (walking to class, shaving, doing his laundry, etc.) as an exhibition. The same aesthetic governs the lives of people stunted by their faith in money. Remarking on the impoverishment of coined souls, the British journalist Henry Fairlie once said: "The rich—in their own eyes, one fears, as well as

4. On being asked about his life in society, the husband of one of New York's most well-known and often-photographed guests said, "I follow my wife's dresses."

ours—are toys. The longer one gazes at them, the less enviable they seem. They only go through the motions of being themselves. They run down if they're not wound up during the day."

The translation of human beings into objects of art entails certain disadvantages. Most of these were revealed to the Lydian King Midas, who, being owed a wish by a satyr, asked that everything he touched be turned to gold. The wish was granted, and Midas, who was a fool as well as a poor judge of music, discovered that his meat and drink were made of gold. He would have starved to death had not the gods taken pity on his condition and released him from the paralysis of his golden wish.

The heirs to his stupidity lack his connections on Olympus. The substitution of money for all other value becomes so complete as to change them, if not into gold, at least into stone. To describe the rich as people is often to make a mistake with the language. Rich nouns or pronouns, perhaps, but not people. The rich tend to identify themselves with a sum of money, and by so doing they relinquish most of their claims to their own humanity. Their money becomes a synthetic fabrication of heart and mind, an artificial circulatory system. This is why it is so difficult to borrow from the rich, why they forget to pay their bills. To ask them for money is to ask them, literally, for blood. Having lost the capacity to distinguish between money as necessity and money as luxury, they imagine that the loss of the third car or the second sailboat will cause them to vanish. When preoccupied with the existential question of their net worth, the expression in their eyes narrows into a lizard's stare.

It is an expression I have seen often enough in the eyes of stockbrokers, gamblers and petty thieves. Maxime Du Camp noticed it in Gustave Flaubert's eyes when the novelist abandoned himself to the dream of riches. Assuming an income of 1 million francs a year, Flaubert liked to imagine himself possessed of coach horses that would be the envy of England, of servants who eased his feet into diamond-studded shoes, of a dining room decorated with espaliers of flowering jasmine and the fluttering of brightly-feathered finches.

"When these dreams took possession of him," Du Camp noted in his diary, "he became almost rigid and reminded one of an opium eater in a state of trance. He seemed to have his head in the clouds, to be living in a dream of gold. This habit was one reason why he found steady work difficult."[5]

The transformation of men into stone can take place within the instant of a single misplaced phrase. The abrupt change of manner often has been remarked upon by people who raise funds for charitable causes. For weeks or months they stalk their quarries of wealth, but if they make a careless movement, mention a specific sum at anything other than the precise moment, the prospective patron takes alarm and lumbers off into the library like a startled wildebeest. Whenever possible, of course, the rich prefer to endow monuments and tombs, and I never can pass by the Metropolitan Museum of Art in New York without thinking of it not as a gallery of living portraits but as a cemetery of tax-deductible wealth.

The coldness and indifference of the rich follow from their inability to take seriously other people's desires, and they constantly ask themselves the peevish questions, "Who *are* all those other people out there, and what in heaven's name do they *want*?" The self becomes so inextricably identified with money that the rich man imagines that only his attachment to it gives it meaning, substance and virtue. Money has no discernible reality in the hands of lesser mortals because lesser mortals have no use for it. When seized by occasional bouts of romantic sympathy for the poor, the rich construe the lower classes as a kind of clay in which to mold the images of reform. They get easily annoyed if the little marionettes begin to speak and think and move of their own volition. Nelson Rockefeller's son, Rodman, struck the right tone when, during the moral excitements of the 1960s, he decided to sponsor the cause of human rights. He made arrangements for a grand

5. The comparable states of mind habitual to the American plutocracy of the Gilded Age aroused Teddy Roosevelt's lifelong loathing for "the kind of money-maker whose soul has grown hard while his body has grown soft."

fete at the family estate in Pocantico Hills, offering to raise several million dollars for the NAACP if Martin Luther King, Jr., would issue a statement endorsing Rodman's father's candidacy for governor of New York. King refused to do so, and Rodman canceled the fete. His aides pointed out that King's political endorsement hadn't been previously discussed, that the invitations already had been sent, and that it would be exceedingly embarrassing, not to say humiliating, to rescind one's humanitarian concern on such short notice.

"I don't care," Rodman said. "It's my house and my money, and I can do what I want."[6]

In order to preserve the condition of soul appropriate to an object, the rich man learns to alienate himself from anything so subversive as thought, passion, intellect or imagination. He can buy a place in the midst of events (a box at the tennis matches, say, or an ambassador's post in London), but if he knows what's good for him and heeds the advice of the family lawyers, he will avoid the stronger and more dangerous sentiments. Among all the emotions, the rich have the least talent for love. It is possible to love one's dog, dress or duck-shooting hat, but a human being presents a more difficult problem. The rich might wish to experience feelings of affection, but it is almost impossible to chip away the enamel of their narcissism. They take up all the space in all the mirrors in the house. Their children, who represent the most present and therefore the most annoying claim on their attention, usually receive the brunt of their irritation.

Writing in *Ms.* magazine in the spring of 1986, Sallie Bingham, the estranged heiress to the Louisville newspaper fortune, noted the consequences of what could be called "the Midas effect":

Rich families shed, in each generation, their most passionate and outspoken members. In the shedding the family loses

6. Precisely the same tone of voice characterized the American announcement, by Secretaries Shultz and Weinberger, of the bombing raid on Libya in the spring of 1986.

the possibility of renewal, of change. Safety is gained, but a safety that is rigid and judgmental.

Of all the stories I have heard on this point, the saddest was one told to me by an acquaintance named Mills, who reached the age of thirty-five before he found the courage to ask his father why his father had never loved him. Mills had been born to the privileges of wealth, but he had chosen to make his career as a professor of political theories of which his father disapproved. Mills put the question at a time when his father was senior partner in a New York investment bank, a director of corporations and a faithful servant of the plutocracy. He had deeded his fortune to the Smithsonian Institution—on the ground that an institution would be more respectful of it than his errant son and unkempt grandchildren—and his answer to his son's question was as quick and instinctive as the movement of an alarmed wolf. Mills told me the story several years later, but he could remember the expression on his father's face as vividly as if the conversation had taken place that same afternoon.

"That's not true," his father had said. "I've always been utterly honest with you. I've always tried to deal with you exactly as I would deal with the Justice Department or the IRS."

Subject to the prejudices of his class, Mills's father over the years had been known to compare both the Justice Department and the IRS to marauding bands of the envious poor.

"I know that," Mills said, "but I am your eldest son, and I thought . . ."

He never succeeded in saying what it was he thought. Nor could he remember what he might have said. Before he could get to the end of his sentence, his father said:

"That's your mistake."

Mills never again mentioned the subject of his inheritance except in the presence of his own and his father's lawyer.

In cultural arenas the stupefaction induced by excessive faith in money results in an audible silence. The large publishing houses and Hollywood studios suffer the same inhibitions as General Motors and the Pentagon. The scripts must pass the judgment of commit-tees, and the committees, mindful of the enormous expense neces-sary to the manufacture and sale of the product ($40 million for a movie; $2 million as an advance against royalties for a celebrity's autobiography), seldom gamble on anything that hasn't been done before. The immense sums of money press down, like the weight of gravity, on the buoyancy of imaginative thought.

The debate that takes place in the nominally enlightened jour-nals of opinion betrays an equivalent lack of courage. The conversa-tion minces along like a dog on a leash, the arc of acceptable thought as narrow as the perimeters established by American troops in the wilderness of Vietnam. The writer who insults the wisdom in office risks losing his or her hope of patronage. Professors and sober-minded journalists who compose the American intelligentsia yield to nobody, not even to George Steinbrenner, in the keenness of their desire for money and preferment. Their writing reflects the calcu-lation of their advantage rather than their talent for expression. In the midst of the intellectual enthusiasms of the 1960s, I remember engaging in a heated argument with a Texas oil entrepreneur who held the New York literary crowd in open contempt. "How much do you think it would cost," he said, "to change them all into obedient hounds? Fifty thousand dollars a year? One hundred thousand a year? Seventy-five thousand dollars a year and guaranteed invi-tations to the White House?" At the time I thought the gentleman both a Philistine and a fool. Not many years later, having seen an impressive number of *soi-disant* liberals transform themselves into rabid conservatives for the sake of tenure, a foundation grant or their names in the literary press, I still thought the gentleman a Philistine, but not a stupid or unobservant Philistine.

Having been obliged to edit the kind of prose that A. Bartlett Giamatti once described as "the higher institutional," I suspect that its weakness and deadly earnestness reflects a fear of giving offense. Who can afford to say the wrong thing? Who knows what will happen next, or who will be appointed to what office, or what critic will be given one's book to review for *The New York Times*? Given the possible financial consequences, only very young writers or very old and famous writers can afford the risks of wit or plain speaking. Writers who still have reputations to protect have become successful by virtue of having become commodities, and they dare not take chances with the product. If William F. Buckley, Jr., allowed himself to endorse a liberal opinion, his readers might become restive and confused. They wouldn't be getting what they thought they had paid for, and they could complain that the label on the box of Buckley's conservatism falsely represented the merchandise within.

To the extent that the writers of the present generation feel themselves intimidated, impotent or enraged, their vision of the world tends to narrow and shrivel. In modern fiction, as in modern painting or television, the techniques of abstraction (i.e., of making the part a surrogate for the whole) reduce the scale of conception to an oblique fragment of talk between two or three characters on an empty stage. The writers produce miniatures, and the painters work within the limits of minimalist art. Their ambition becomes as small as the coteries that make up their audiences. In the less-crowded space of the nineteenth century, Tolstoi and Balzac could project their characters in rounded, rather than flat, dimensions, populating their scenes with human figures instead of with symbols. To the modern writer this would be too frightening. The world seems so huge and so full of terror that it becomes necessary to reduce it to a model or a toy. To concede too much reality to a character unlike oneself might result in a diminishing of self, and this alarms people—not only novelists but also evangelists and corporation presidents. Thus protagonists of both fiction and the higher forms of corporate advertisement resemble the authors of the play within the play, pitted against gigantic grotesques, no more believable than the balloons and floats dragged into the Rose Bowl on New Year's Day.

Remarking on the intellectual despotism characteristic of American discourse, Tocqueville said: "I know no country in which, speaking generally, there is less independence of mind and true freedom of expression than in America." Fortunately for the Reagan administration, Tocqueville's dictum is as appropriate to the 1980s as it was to the 1840s. The citizenry uncomplainingly submits to examinations of its blood, its urine and its speech. At the end of 1983 the General Accounting Office estimated that 225,000 current and former government employees with access to classified information had consented to the principle of censorship. The clerks in question signed an agreement stating that they would submit any text they might write (even unto the days of their death) to government review.

When highly placed government officials resign their office for reasons of principle or conscience, they go as quietly as thieves. By definition members of the equestrian class, usually lawyers or Wall Street bond salesmen, they preserve their silence out of respect for the protocols of wealth. If they were discovered to be "unsound" (i.e., the sort of people who make scenes and say what they think) their peers might pronounce them, by mutual and silent consent, ineligible for other places and titles within the honeycombs of privilege. An impressive number of functionaries quit the Johnson administration in disagreement with the president's self-defeating policies in Vietnam (among them Cyrus Vance, McGeorge Bundy, and Robert McNamara), but none raised even a whisper of a public objection. The criminal syndicates refer to the practice as the code of *omerta*.

The fear of change is as traditional among vicars of the American media as it is among the captains of American industry. Nothing so terrifies most reporters and editors as the arrival of a new idea. Hoping to extend indefinitely the perpetual present in which images pass for reality, the media deal in the semblance, not the substance, of change. Wars might come and go, but the seven o'clock news lives forever. When, in the winter of 1986-87, Premier Mikhail Gorbachev advocated radical changes in Soviet society and foreign policy, the American media insisted he was lying, that his much-advertised *glasnost* was nothing more than a ruse. The Washington columnists held as tightly to their inventories of stereotyped truth as a child to its nurse. To entertain, even briefly, the thought of genuine change was a possibility too painful to bear.

The performances in the national political theater might degenerate into farce or opéra bouffe, but only a licensed satirist can afford to say so.[7] Dependent on the gossip and good will of his patrons in office, no ambitious journalist dares risk giving offense to anybody important enough to provide him with a steady supply of news. Over dinner one night in a New York restaurant I remember both Tom Wicker and Edwin Newman explaining that while they were in service as White House correspondents it never occurred to them to ask a president a rude question. Katharine Graham, publisher of *The Washington Post*, continued to write coquettish little notes to President Nixon even while her paper was demanding his impeachment. In the few weeks before Nixon left the White House, Mrs. Graham was still assuring him they were the best of friends and would have dinner together once the unpleasantness had been put safely out of mind.

The balance of the current political argument favors the weight of objects, not the force of ideas, and the wisdom in office (both in government and media) interprets the word "conservative" to mean the safekeeping of property as opposed to the preservation of a habit of mind or a process of becoming.[8] The Department of Health and

---

7. As of the present writing only four journalists hold a proper license—Russell Baker, Art Buchwald, Dave Barry and Roy Blount—suggesting that one of the requirements for the office is a surname beginning with the letter B. Other journalists must be careful of their deportment. Above all, they must restrain the impulse to laugh. A best-selling tract, no matter what the burden of its improving text (cf. the works of Carl Sagan, George Gilder, Charles Reich, David Halberstam, Norman Cousins, Norman Podhoretz, etc.), is, by definition, humorless.

8. Under the prevailing set of superstitions, the big campaign money aligns itself with incumbents. For the senatorial election in the autumn of 1986 Senator Robert Dole (R.-Kan.) easily raised by September 15 a fund of $2,141,466. His opponent had found it hard to come up with $751.

Human Services needs fifty-five employees to respond to a letter from the secretary. Arms manufacturers applying for Pentagon contracts report having to fill out forms that sometimes number as many as 23,000 pages of small type. The Congress, intent on buying allies, insists that countries receiving American aid payments vote with the United States at the United Nations. The American armed services worry more about budgets than about military tactics. Only one soldier in every four can boast of a "combat specialty"; everybody else belongs to a headquarters' staff and ascribes to the belief that the orderly arrangement of documents takes precedence over the training of troops. When it comes time to appoint a secretary of state nobody can think of more than two or three ornamental gentlemen capable of performing the duties of so august and ceremonial an office. Within the purview of science the fear of litigation and the emphasis on profit (i.e., on applied rather than basic research) stifles the impulse toward experiment and innovation. The large amount of government money distributed through the institutes and the universities favors orthodox lines of reasoning. The venture capitalist money seeks out, especially in biotechnology, miraculous cures and transformations that can be sold at miraculous prices. The inertia of money and the presence of lawyers combine to yield a state of intellectual paralysis. Offering advice conforming to the wisdom of the age, a Washington attorney in the autumn of 1985 told his client, a research group supposedly on the frontier of the future, "Don't innovate; don't experiment; don't be venturesome; don't go out on a limb."

He might also have said, "don't think." Certainly this was the posture of the statesmen responsible for the American debacle in Vietnam. In *The March of Folly*, Barbara Tuchman attributes the stupidity of our military expedition in Southeast Asia to nonpartisan states of "self-hypnosis" that afflicted three successive presidents and their circles of sleep-walking advisers. Against all sense, and despite contradictions apparent in the facts, the American high command, both civilian and military, insisted on its cherished dream of power. Our reasons for fighting the war changed with the circumstances: first we were defending all of Asia against Communist subversion ("the domino theory"), then we were proving the credibility of American power (for fear that other nations on other continents might smile behind their hands), and lastly, after 50,000 Americans had been killed, to prove a point of honor. Tuchman cites the dictum of George Kennan, who said of the men in Washington (most notably Dean Rusk, Walt Rostow and Maxwell Taylor), "they were like men in a dream," incapable of "any realistic assessment of the effects of their own acts." Elsewhere in her book, Tuchman compares the stewards of American empire during the Vietnam War with the eighteenth-century British aristocrats who presided over the loss of American colonies. Both companies of fatuous gentlemen were distinguished by their ignorance and pride. Like the modern Americans, the British ministers and peers thought themselves invulnerable to the arrows of fortune. Being accustomed to the illusion of omnipotence (i.e., to the obedience of their domestic servants) they lacked a sense of political realism. Describing their qualities in a letter to Charles Fox, Edmund Burke attributed their foolishness to "plentiful fortunes, assured rank and quiet homes."[9]

The somnambulism characteristic of large corporations can be fairly well inferred from the number of companies lost over the past several years in the maelstrom of takeovers and leveraged buyouts. When denounced as upstarts, the acquisitors—gentlemen on the order of T. Boone Pickens, the Belzberg brothers and the once fortunate Ivan Boesky—invariably say the companies were too indolently

---

9. The fatuity of the British peerage prompted the lords to a flattering estimate of the nation's military prowess. Some months prior to the outbreak of the Revolutionary War, a British general and aide-de-camp to George III boasted, in the presence of Benjamin Franklin, that with 1,000 grenadiers he would undertake "to go from one end of America to the other and geld all the males, partly by force and partly by a little coaxing." The tone of voice brings to mind the American assumption of a Vietnamese rabble and Lyndon Johnson saying he was damned if he was going to be frightened of "a raggedy-ass little fourth-rate country."

managed, that the assets were dribbling through the fingers of corporate hirelings too soft and too frightened to command the respect of their accountants. The more sardonic of the speculators, notably Pickens, present themselves as blessings in disguise, agents of a divine financial ecology sent to thin the herds and winnow wheat from chaff. The argument is exaggerated, but it is true that the corporate executive, unlike the small businessman or free-booting entrepreneur, isn't paid to take chances.

Anybody who says this in public, of course, is likely to be thought un-American. In November 1986, Richard Darman, then deputy secretary of the Treasury, told an audience at the Japan Society in New York that the conventional American business establishment was "bloated, risk-averse, inefficient and unimaginative." Executives paid $1 million a year, he said, devote less time to research and development than "they spend reviewing their golf scores." He observed that most high-ranking members of "the corpocracy" owe their places not to character or intelligence but to "the strength of their demeanor and a failure to make observable mistakes." As can be well imagined, the publication of Darman's remarks provoked a flurry of outraged denials in the business magazines.

The corpocracy doesn't like to be reminded that an accomplished CEO bears comparison to a butler or gamekeeper—a dull but stouthearted and boyish fellow who can be counted on to look after the porcelain or the grouse; reliable enough to act as custodian of a large and valuable property, but not clever enough to steal anything important. In a word, he is precisely the sort of man prepared at Hotchkiss and Yale to fit the norm of mediocrity once defined by Paul D. Cravath, patriarch of the New York law firm of Cravath, Swaine and Moore, in terms of the qualities desirable in apprentice lawyers. "Brilliant intellectual powers are not essential. Too much imagination, too much wit, too great cleverness, too facile fluency, if not leavened by a sound sense of proportion, are quite as likely to impede success as to promote it. The best clients are apt to be afraid of those qualities."

The makers of mythologies about American business often mention "profit maximization" as the raison d'être of the corporate mechanism. Only seldom have I found this to be so. Maximization of profit would imply an operation run according to the arithmetic of performance, which would wreak havoc on everybody's comfortable arrangements. Let the rabbit of free enterprise out of its velveteen bag and too many people would have to be fired, too much idiocy exposed to judgment or ridicule, too much vanity sacrificed to the fires of efficiency. Such a catastrophe obviously would threaten the American way of life, to say nothing of the belief in free markets. As dependent as a child on the institution that suckles him, the devoted corporate manager seeks to build protective layers of bureaucracy, to expand and make stronger the shell of hierarchy, to keep the systems comfortably in place.[10] Once all the institutional needs have been met (i.e., tending the slowly revolving water wheel that yields jobs, money, income, taxes, benefits, insurance, stock options, picnics, limousines, pensions, dividends, etc.) then, if anybody has any surplus time or energy to invest, the institution might direct its attention to the making of a profit. The $190 billion spent on mergers and acquisitions in 1986 often resulted in institutions of elephantine size, but it has yet to be proved that the stately rearrangement of tables of organization resulted in better products or more intelligent management. Too much money was employed in the service of debt, which, like the money watering the sterile deserts of the weapons' industry, heavily depletes the funding available for thought.

The promoters of the American dream inevitably speak of the "rugged individual" who sets himself against the resident

10. The corporate grandees make a brave show of talking about risk and the maximization of profit. The set phrases appear in after-dinner speeches and annual reports, in memoranda circulated among junior management, in statements to the press. The drone of ceaseless repetition testifies to the importance of the phrases as ritual chant, such as Reagan's speech at St. John's and Peter Grace, "Business is tough . . . it's no kissing game." But, of course, it is.

establishment—cultural, political, scientific—and goes off into the appropriate wilderness to unearth beauty, truth or a fortune in California real estate. The hero is largely imaginary, apparently the invention of the literary East in the latter decades of the nineteenth century. Disenchanted with what they knew of crowded commerce in seaboard towns, the writers in Boston and New York comforted themselves with tales of the noble frontiersmen still at large on the Great Plains. In the 1920s and 1930s the romance was cut into strips of movie film by a generation of displaced Europeans who confused the history of the United States with their own reasons for leaving Odessa or Berlin. The image of the rugged individualist might sell automobiles and cigarettes, but as an exemplary model of a successful American life it is ruinous. Except in a few well-publicized instances (enough to lend credence to the iconography painted on the walls of the media), the rigorous practice of rugged individualism usually leads to poverty, ostracism and disgrace. The rugged individualist is too often mistaken for misfit, maverick, spoilsport, sore thumb.

No matter how effusive our rhetoric to the contrary, most Americans cannot bring themselves to trust the unaffiliated individual. We prefer to repose our confidence in institutions: a brand name, a corporation, a bank. It is the figure of Babbitt or Cyrus Vance, not Clint Eastwood, who represents the triumph of the American dream—the man who goes along to get along, who knows the right people and belongs to the right clubs, whose every opinion seconds the nomination of the chairman, who submits easily, and with a winning smile, to what Tocqueville called "the tyranny of the majority."

As often as not, corporate success depends upon the aspirant's willingness, over many years and under a bewildering variety of circumstances, to sacrifice whatever trace elements of personality might get him in trouble with the management or the police. The poor fellow learns to submerge his own being in the corporate being, to subvert his own voice to the institutional voice, to acquire the "plastic capability" President Nixon so much admired in General

Alexander Haig. Only when the candidate has enlisted in the ranks of Hollow Men does he become eligible for the reward of a tax-deductible personality; only when it is certain he will have nothing to say does the corporation set him up with a microphone and an audience.

Much the same process takes place within the withered groves of the American academy. The winning of tenure at a prominent university almost always obliges the candidate to give up his own voice and applaud, with possibly a few urbane and scholarly asides, opinions approved by the head of the department. The resulting stultification, described in some detail in Allan Bloom's *The Closing of the American Mind*, leads to an intellectual orthodoxy as narrow and humorless as the dogma espoused by the National Association of Manufacturers.

As Americans, we have a genius for organization, and we achieve our most impressive results when working together in groups. This appears to have been true of the national temperament since the first arriviste theologians formed a joint-stock company in Massachusetts Bay for the development of Puritan real estate. The pioneers moving west in the 1840s and 1850s gathered at Independence, Missouri, to join their wagon trains into corporate entities meant to last just long enough for the trek to California. Any man attempting to go it on his own would have been lucky to see Colorado. The hazards of the journey needed at least fifty wagons to set up a coherent defense against terrain, Indians and weather. The same talent for cooperation characterized the building of American barns and the settling of American towns. During the twentieth century the preference for large institutional combination increasingly has come to define American scientific and technological discovery as well as the method of American business and journalism. The distinctively American art forms—musical comedy, jazz, the movies—all rely on collaboration. So also the making of public personalities, which, contrary to the fables about stars born overnight in a shower of klieg light, requires a large supporting cast of technicians, distributors, agents, publicists, and beauticians, all harnessed together in the kind of team effort necessary to the construction of a shopping mall or an F-16. Big-time American journalism is group journalism, and the people who succeed at it learn to speak or write in the institutional voice of *The New Yorker, Newsweek* or *CBS Evening News*. Dan Rather's voice is the voice of a committee. More than illness or death, the American journalist fears standing alone against the whim of his owners or the prejudices of his audience. Deprive William Safire of the insignia of *The New York Times*, and he would have a hard time selling his truths to a weekly broadsheet in suburban Duluth.

When the chairman of a large corporation retires or finds it expedient to quit the premises in the custody of police, the event almost never affects the price of company stock. The investors know that the institution, not the individual, tends the engines of commerce. Nor is it ever just one publishing house or automobile company that stumbles into financial ruin; it is all publishing houses and all automobile companies. If the practice of free enterprise coincided with the theory, it would be reasonable to expect that an exceptionally gifted organization (more attuned to social change, more subtle in its technology, more aggressive in its marketing strategy) would defy the prevailing trends and so accumulate earnings worthy of the sainted J.P. Morgan. But except on the margins of the major industries, or among companies small enough to retain the character of free-booting partnerships, the miracle almost never occurs. The oligopolies behave in the manner of stately sheep, all tending in the same direction, all comforting themselves with the same bleating explanations borrowed from the same newsletters and trade association speeches.

Whether lawyer, politician or executive, the American who knows what's good for his career seeks an institutional rather than individual identity. He becomes the man from NBC or IBM. The institutional imprint furnishes him with pension, meaning, proofs of existence. A man without a company name is a man without a country. Strip him of his corporate rank and titles, and not only does he sink into obscurity, but he is also likely to vanish from the sight of the insurance companies—which means that his life, invisible and uninsured, is no longer worth the price of salvation.

In the faces of innumerable company functionaries (within the ateliers of the media as well as in the honeycombs of large corporations), I have seen precisely the same hunted look that I noticed in George Amory's eyes that winter afternoon at the Plaza Hotel. What would happen to them if they were to be abandoned by the organization that furnishes them with titles, degree, comfort and permission to exist? Where would they go, and who would hire them? Who would notice them? In what voices would they speak?

The loss of an institutional identity gives rise to the spectacle of the retired corporate hierarch revolving like a dead moon in the orbit of his extinct influence. If he retires on Monday, his telephones fall silent on Tuesday; on Wednesday his portrait disappears from the brightly lit galleries of the business press, and by Friday nobody is much interested in his observations about NATO or the rate of inflation. The effect is even worse in Washington. Government functionaries deprived of their function have nothing else on which to base their claims to self, which is why American officials so seldom resign on matters of principle.

Money always implies the promise of magic, but the effect is much magnified when, as now, people have lost faith in everything else. During the 1960s and early 1970s the political and cultural argument in the United States still reflected at least a residual belief in competing systems of value, in possibilities loosely associated with the talk of disarmament, social justice, environmentalism and human rights. By the time President Reagan arrived in the White House the aspirations of prior decades were seen as so much dreaming nonsense.

To the extent that we forget how to love or respect one another—preferring to regard each other as commodities or targets of opportunity—we settle for the emblems of status, abandon our hopes for what Schopenhauer meant by happiness *in concreto* and set our whole hearts on happiness *in abstracto*—that is, on money. The belief in what isn't there, in a fiction instead of a fact, accords with the transcendental bias of the American mind and our long-established preference for the impalpable and the unseen.

10. ENVOI

A city for sale, and doomed when it finds a buyer.
>—JUGURTHA, commentary on Rome, c. 104 B.C.

TWENTY YEARS AGO IT WAS STILL POSSIBLE TO BELIEVE that the rest of the world wished to become as much like the United States as time, money and circumstance would permit, that everybody's image of the future looked like an American postcard. Other countries might not wish to own quite so splendid a military establishment, and maybe they wouldn't have the resources to support three television networks and two divisions of the National Football League, but presumably they wanted all the toys in all the windows on Fifth Avenue. Surely they knew that the very idea of the future came in an American box—complete with instructions for assembling a Constitution, a McDonald's hamburger franchise, a row of Marriott hotels and a First Amendment.

The familiar assumptions no longer bear quite so comforting a relation to facts. During the last three or four years I have noticed that when traveling in Europe or Asia, or in conversation with foreign visitors in Washington and New York, I meet relatively few people who set much store by the example of the United States. Their indifference has nothing to do with ideology. They admire the precepts of freedom as well as the proofs of the American economic triumph. They watch reruns of *Dallas*, wear blue jeans, drink Coke, and go out of their way to praise American movies, American flags and American rock songs. They show little affection for Communist systems of government or belief. Nobody denounces the evils of American imperialism; nobody preaches Marxist sermons. Without prior consultation, and probably without meaning to do so, the travelers from abroad make a more subtle observation. They conceive of the United States as a market they can exploit rather than as an ideal to which they can safely aspire. They speak of America as if it were the Old World not the New—the past, not the future.

In the winter of 1987, at a quasi-diplomatic function coincident with yet another conference on the precarious American trade balance, I met a man from Turin who observed that although an Italian automobile worker earned less money than an American automobile worker, at least his countryman had a job (unlike the 13,000 workers let go by General Motors the previous autumn); certainly he retained more of his income as savings and held higher hopes for his children. On the same occasion a woman from Singapore expressed her doubts as a question. She had spent the afternoon shopping on Fifth Avenue and had been impressed by the prices of luxury—$4,000 for a watch at Tiffany's, $750 for a silk nightgown at Saks, $150 for a forty-five minute consultation with the exercise director at Elizabeth Arden.

"How can America stand on the side of the future," she asked, "when it sets the example of eating the future?"

She wondered why Americans didn't restrain their appetite for the world's cash. Why borrow so much—from the Japanese, from schoolchildren, from Europeans, from anybody and everybody willing to bankroll a third and fourth mortgage on the American dream—for no other reason than to finance the consumption of superfluous goods? At the end of 1986 the total consumer debt (mortgages, junk bonds, credit card balances) reached $7 trillion, as opposed to a total money supply within the United States (what the Federal Reserve denominates as M-1) of $700 billion. During the five or six years prior to 1986 consumer spending doubled ($300 billion to $600 billion), and the Americans sold to foreign buyers assets worth $1 trillion in land, corporate equity, buildings, bank debt and manufacturing capacity. By the spring of 1987, the rates of default on mortgages and personal credit card debt had arrived at an all-time high.

We stood near a high window of a new office building in midtown Manhattan, admiring the view to the south. Across the Hudson River we could see the glittering lights of a real-estate deal in the mud flats of New Jersey. I thought of the city's undeniable opulence, of the condominiums decorating the Atlantic coast from Hoboken to the Florida Keys; I thought of the thousand and one success stories smiling from the pages of the magazines on the nation's newsstands, of ballplayers earning $1 million a year and television commercials selling for $600,000 a minute, of the optimistic voices in Wall Street and Washington promising bigger and better and more. For a moment I could imagine a nation as rich, happy and prosperous as the America seen in the postcards.

But then I thought of the men and women asleep in the streets of the opulent city, of contracts canceled and farms foreclosed, of thousands of not-so-successful stories of people fired by AT&T, GM and CBS, of an economy geared to the mechanics of fraud and a permanent state of war. I thought of George Amory, and of the countless others like him, desperately trying to keep up appearances, glad to abandon the claims to their freedom for another twenty minutes on Park Avenue, willing to eat the future (or anything else presented to them) in order to deny, with John C. Calhoun and the doomed Confederacy, their fear of sinking in the world.

I have suggested in these notes that we have allowed money to become an end in itself and made of our mistake a child's religion.[1] A similar clutching at the straws of money was evident in Rome during the first century B.C. and in France just prior to the revolution of 1789. Observing the transformation of the Roman Republic into an empire, the historian Sallust attributed the wish for despotism to, among other causes, "unequal distribution of wealth, exorbitant veterans' demands, depopulation of the countryside, high unemployment of citizens, debt-ridden farmers, bread and circuses, costly military ventures, oppressive taxes for some, and a government controlled by wealth."

The summary stands as a fair description of some of our own circumstances, and as a reasonable approximation of some others, but as premonition it is surpassed by the remarks of the bookseller Ruault in Paris in 1786. His letter to his brother bears extended quotation:

> Money there must be, and there's an end to it; money for expenditure known and unknown; money for the ordinary and for the extraordinary; money for the five or six kings reigning in France who dip so generously into the public treasury; money for the king of Paris, the king of finance, the king of war, the king of the fleet, the king of foreign affairs, and the King of all these kings, who, they say, would be the thriftiest of them all if it weren't for his wife, his brothers, his cousins, and so forth . . .
>
> Finance has grown so powerful, so proud, so despotic that one must believe it can go no higher and must infallibly perish before many years have passed. When finance is

1. The emptiness of the faith in money reveals itself in the monthly best-seller lists, which, together with the instructor manuals for the making of new fortunes, contain so many tracts promising spiritual remedies for the despair associated with rabid consumerism.

honored, says Montesquieu, the state is lost. A fearful revolution is very imminent; we are very, very close to it, at any minute we are going to reach a violent crisis. Things cannot go on longer as they have been, that is self-evident. There is nothing but speculation, finance, banking, discount, borrowing, wagering, and payment. Every head is glued to money, crazy with speculation. A little patience, and we may see some pretty goings-on in 1800! In the meanwhile, though, we must live and contrive not to be carried away by the coming debacle.

Farewell, dear friends, do not take my prophesies too much to heart. Curl yourselves up tightly in your little den, let the madmen get on with their folly, and let us try to remain simple spectators when the hollow mountain, that groans beneath the weight of all these thousands of brainless fools who are crawling over it, finally comes crashing down.

Historical analogies deserve to be regarded with suspicion, but it is easy enough to imagine the American envoys in Paris in the evening hours of the eighteenth century reserving similar judgments about the perfection of the *ancien régime* and the loveliness of the court at Versailles. Not unlike the contemporary American plutocracy in New York, Washington and Los Angeles, the French aristocracy employed an army of hairdressers, upholsterers, cabinetmakers, cooks, fencing masters and tennis instructors. Marie Antoinette, known to the salon gossips as "Madame Deficit," was in the habit of paying her dress designers $1 million a year, a sum that the wives of important Hollywood movie producers might regard as a trifle low. The Americans had come to borrow money for their revolution, and I am sure they were polite. I can imagine Ben Franklin complimenting the queen for a pair of shoes that cost $16,000, or Thomas Jefferson saying to the Comte d'Artois that it was a pity the comte had lost $1.5 million the previous evening at cards. I also can imagine Franklin and Jefferson thinking that neither the shoes nor the card game would have made much sense in Philadelphia.[2]

A good many intelligent and well-meaning people have remarked on the pathologies of wealth that I have described in these notes, and quite a few of them have suggested possible methods of rousing the American enterprise from its stupefying dream. As yet, however, these voices have not rallied a constituency likely to accomplish the task at hand, probably because the exhortations rely too heavily on the chanting of the word, "leadership."

The statement that America lacks leadership has by now become so safe and meaningless that it appears in every speechwriter's lexicon of unassailable truth. No properly outfitted presidential candidate would think of showing up at a supermarket or press conference without a list of mournful remarks about the nation's loss of leadership. So also every corporate magnate, cab driver and newspaper columnist pressed for a few weighty words on the topic of the American destiny—all agree that only leadership can rescue the nation from folly and ruin.

Having made the announcement, the speaker usually mentions one of several stock examples thought to possess the correct sheen of significance. Depending on the mood and the occasion, he refers to the trade or the moral deficit, to illiteracy in the schools, to the

2. Franklin expressed his disgust with the customs of the Old World as early as 1774, in a letter from London to John Galloway of Pennsylvania. Arguing against the idea of American independence at the First Continental Congress, Galloway had proposed some sort of union or federation between the colonies and Britain. Franklin thought the British too degraded in their political habits of mind, and he asked Galloway to consider "the extreme corruption prevalent among all orders of men in this old rotten state," with its "numberless and needless places, enormous salaries, pensions, perquisites, bribes, groundless quarrels, foolish expeditions, false accounts or no accounts, contracts and jobs [that] devour all revenue." Writing from London in the same decade, John Adams compared the city to the old Roman Republic, "venal and ripe for destruction." Together with Franklin and Jugurtha, Adams could as easily have been writing about Washington in the 1980s.

mindless self-dealing characteristic not only of the credit markets but also of the media. All present nod their heads and know they have been made wise.

Of course, says the choir of alarmed voices gathered in ballroom or town square—leadership. By God, it's leadership that's missing. We can send a man to the moon but we can't balance the budget or clean up the wreckage in Detroit, and do you know why? For the same reason the country is being governed by a pack of fools. Because leadership has gone out of our lives.

This ceremonial repetition of the word has an ennobling effect because nobody knows what it means. Most ladies and gentlemen who mourn the passing of the nation's leaders wouldn't know a leader if they saw one. If they had the bad luck to come across a leader, they would find that he might demand something from them, and this impertinence would put an abrupt and indignant end to their wish for his return. When Christ showed up in Jerusalem saying the kind of thing leaders have an awkward habit of saying, the authorities nailed him to a cross.

It never occurs to editorial writers that leaders practicing leadership might insist on renunciations which—if carried beyond the elementary lessons of giving up cigarettes and the third whiskey before dinner—might seriously interfere with everybody's habitual round of pleasure and hypocrisy. The voices in the ballroom want the kind of leadership that makes a brave show in the world but doesn't cost much more than the annual fees charged by Home Box Office or the Council on Foreign Relations. This is another way of saying they would prefer, no matter how loud their protests to the contrary, as little leadership as possible.

The disingenuousness of the lament becomes apparent in the context of the supporting adjectives. The mourners speak of leadership as if it were an innate quality or skill, vaguely comparable to a talent for playing the piano or solving crossword puzzles. They think of it as a function of personality, a gift akin to a despot's cruelty or a saleman's winning smile. When casting around for exemplary proofs of leadership, they mention military commanders and foot-ball coaches. Probably it is safe to assume that the man most people have in mind for the job would bear a comforting resemblance to Muammar Qaddafi. A man of lighter color and broader education, of course, but still a handsome, authoritarian fellow who plays polo, commands the unswerving loyalty of his troops and brooks no seditious gabbling on the part of a liberal press.

The sporting and military analogies establish a false compar-ison. Leadership consists not in degrees of technique but in traits of character; it requires moral rather than athletic or intellectual effort, and it imposes on both leader and follower alike the burdens of self-restraint. Edmund Burke put the proposition as follows: "Society cannot exist unless a controlling power upon will and appetite be placed somewhere, and the less of it there is within, the more there must be without."

This is the news that the ladies and gentlemen in the ball-room prefer not to hear. For good reason. The United States was founded upon the egalitarian premise of boundlessly expanding will and appetite—for goods, land, experience, wealth, fame. Envisioning a romantic panorama of man at play in the meadows of paradise (of man set free from constraints of laws and schools, free to con-stitute himself as his own government, free to declare himself a god), Americans unloosed their restless energies in a direction precisely opposite to the one indicated by Burke. By holding to the maxim that "nice guys finish last," and choosing to look upon acts of self-denial as sure marks of "a loser," we make the most deep-rooted human conflict the stuff of musical comedy.

If the ceaseless murmuring about leadership has failed to pro-duce any demonstrable result, it is because the would-be saviors of the American enterprise address themselves to symptoms instead of causes.

Failing a war, revolution or economic collapse, too many inter-ests align themselves with the inertia of money. The difficulty does not lend itself to economic tinkering. Efforts at the redistribution of wealth invariably lead to the same injustices under different letter-heads, and except in times of war or illness, moral awakening is as hard to come by as a winning number in the New Jersey lottery. It is not a question of taxes, interest rates, tariffs, investment policy or monetary reform. It is the prior question of an attitude toward money that is synonymous with religious devotion.

The ancient writers referred to this superstition as the worship of Mammon, but the name of that old and melancholy idol has fallen into disfavor. The American media regard it as their patriotic duty to transform pagan enthusiasms once thought insane into glorious proofs of American freedom and enterprise. The mergers and acquisitions that now account for most of the trading on the stock exchanges bespeak a style of financial speculation comparable to the cathedral architecture of the High Gothic.

Almost every preacher or reform politician who ever has considered the problem of corrupt republics has observed, maybe not as succinctly as Montesquieu but invariably to the same point, that whereas monarchies fall by poverty, republics are brought to their ends by luxury. We know what is wrong with the American enterprise. The question remains as to whether enough people can agree to imagine some other way of awarding the prizes.[3]

Value is determined not by anything extraneous to human beings but by their desires. If we could let go our faith in money, who knows what we might put in its place? In the fifteenth century mountain landscapes were thought to be as worthless as urban

---

3. Psychiatrists with a practice among Wall Street financiers describe the resident superstitions in the language of clinical pathology. Writing in *The New York Times* in May 1987, Jay B. Rohrlich, identified as a "partner" in a "psychological consulting firm," compared the effects of addiction to money with those resulting from addictions to drugs and alcohol. Apropos the euphoric states associated with "the big numbers," Rohrlich said: "An 'injection' of money can make people feel instantly secure, victorious, strong, loved, proud and sexually attractive. Money becomes the antidote to a perceived sense of insufficiency."

slums. Mountains in our own time seem infinitely precious, both as places of residence and images of spiritual well-being. Given the engines of destruction currently at work in the world, it is conceivable that in twenty years a glass of clear water might be worth more than an appearance on the Johnny Carson show.[4]

The task at hand is a task of the imagination. It has less to do with economics than it does with metaphor, less to do with the making of laws than with the making of words that allow men to see their immortality, not in monuments or weapons, but in their children.

Against the world's weight, mankind possesses the greater energy of spirit formed by the mass of small but numberless acts of ordinary human beings going about the extraordinary business of telling the truth. The negotiations at every dinner table thus become as central to the human story as the discussions at Geneva; every hospital room bears witness to battles as critical to the human destiny as the battle fought at Gettysburg or Waterloo; every bedroom door opens into a desert or a garden.

In societies willing to earn the future instead of bidding up its price on a foreign market, the desire for life precedes the desire for profit. This elementary law of survival is bound to be denied as long as profit is believed to be a sacrament. Although we loot the world

---

4. In February 1987 the Worldwatch Institute published a report stating that if the exploitation of the earth's natural resources continued at its current rate, we could look forward not only to mass exterminations of plant and animal species but also to a changed climate and a severely damaged atmosphere. The United Nations reiterated the lesson in late April of the same year, publishing an even more ominous report about the likelihood of a "radically altered planet." Both reports mentioned the stupidity of spending so much money on weapons and so little on the preservation of the seas and forests. The American government's 1986 appropriation of $100 billion for the Navy's Trident II submarine and F-18 jet fighter programs would pay the cost of cleaning up 10,000 toxic waste dumps that contaminate the nation's water and soil.

of its resources, we cannot think of anything to do with the spoils except to build the tombs of the national security state. Afraid of shadows, retreating further into the realm of increasingly gigantic symbols, we hope to keep ourselves safe from death by embracing, as if they were beloved toys, the images of death. By presuming the presence of nonexistent enemies, we adopt the hypochondriac's device of staging an endless round of preemptive cures in order to postpone, perhaps indefinitely, our dying of natural causes.

People do not necessarily like to buy or rent other human beings. To do so they must repress too much of their own humanity, with the result that they become cold, rigid and scared. But what other choice do they have in a society in which the glorious name of profit justifies squalor, famine, dishonesty and war? The substitution of money for all other systems of value facilitates the attack on self, on culture, on country, on time past and time future.

We squander our fortune in order to become a nation deprived of the cultural and spiritual means to escape our confinement in a gilded cage. No matter how many objects we acquire, or how much experience we consume as if it were chocolate or Kleenex, we become smaller. As has been said more than once (but probably needs to be said yet again), it isn't the money itself that causes the trouble, but rather the use of money as votive ritual and pagan ornament.

If the heat and light imprisoned in the brilliance of a diamond could be released and transformed into bread, roads or schools, the worth of the diamond would warm the lives of thousands of people. So also with the human possibility imprisoned in many other sterile monuments dedicated to the majesty of wealth—in cruise missiles and the frantic speculation on Wall Street; in the Trump Tower and Roone Arledge's dramaturgy. Our dumb-struck awe in the presence of money's glory reduces us to the stature of dwarfs. If we could perceive our veneration as an act of piety—as ritual rather than necessity—maybe we would not be so timid. Maybe we could laugh at our childishness and wean ourselves of our fear. If it were possible to define "wealth" as well-being, as a wealth of understanding or kindness or humor, and if it were possible to define "net worth" as human character, as the worth of what a man or woman does and thinks, then, together with the foolish king of Lydia, we might escape the prison of our golden wish.

INDEX

Auden, W. H., 225, 259
Auletta, Ken, 33
Authors
    rich as good maxim, 79–80
    writer as outcast, past view,
      80
Avedon, Richard, 221

Baker, Russell, 274n
Bakker, Jim (Reverend), 50–51
Banks,
    safety deposit box, 252–53
Barry, Dave, 274n
Belmont, Augustus, 27
Bendix Corporation, 218n
Biddle, Livingston, 43
Biddle, Nicholas, 155
Bierce, Ambrose, 24n, 160, 198
Big Boys, The (Nader), 185n
Bingham, Sallie, 34, 269
Black Monday, 246–48
Black and White Ball, 200–1
Bloom, Allan, 280
Bloomingdale, Alfred, 138
Blount, Roy, 274n
Boesky, Ivan, 72, 101, 106, 113,
    133, 157n, 244n, 261, 276
Bradlee, Ben, 182
Brandeis, Louis, xiv, xxxiii
Brown, Claude, 30
Browne, Ray, 101n
Buchwald, Art, 274n
Buckley, William F., 72, 200, 272
Bundy, McGeorge, 116, 230, 273
Burke, Edmund, 276, 292
Burroughs, William, 164

Bush, George H.W., xiv, 195, 249
Bush, George W., xiv, xxxiii
Business conventions, protocols
    of wealth, 55–56

Calhoun, John C., 44, 69n, 153,
    287
Calvin, John, 39, 68
Capone, Al, 114–15
Capote, Truman, 200
Carnegie, Andrew, 72, 261
Carter, Jimmy, 46, 63, 136,
    143–44, 153, 215, 224, 226, 234,
    236n
Casey, William, 176n
Censorship, 273
Challenger, 107, 151n, 215
Cheating at American universi-
    ties, 108
Chesterton, G.K., 151n
Chevalier, Michel, 93n
Christian reawakening, 109
CIA, 176n, 229–30, 235
Ci-devant rich, 68, 247
Cimino, Michael, 210n
Cities, American, 68, 96, 129
Civil War era, 43, 190
Clemenceau, Georges, 142
Cleveland, Grover, xxi, 41
Clinton, Bill, xiv, xxxiii
Clinton, Hillary, xxiii
*Closing of the American Mind,
    The,* (Bloom), 280
Clubs, 196–99
    Bohemian, 196–97, 199
    legitimacy established by, 198

Collaboration, American way, 280
Collins, Admiral Frank C., 103–04
Coltrane, John, 53n
Competition, American business, 265n
Constitution of United States
    interests of framers, xviii, xix, xxi, 40–42, 155–56
Consumer debt of U.S., xxxiv, 30n, 191, 286
Consumption
    acquisitions of financial heroes, 72–73
    and economy, 70–71
    extremes of, 72–77
    foreign view of, 69
    of the golden horde, 74
    specialty foods, 74
    of 20th century rich, 68–73
    types of spenders, 68
Cooney, Joan Ganz, 34
Coover, Robert, 97
Corporate executives
    airplanes of, 185–86
    as celebrities, 218–19
    "finishing school" for, 220
    knowledge/expertise and, 216–17
    major accomplishments of, 277–78
    noble executives, examples of, 212
    privileges of, 183–84
    retirement, loss of institution-
al identity, 282
    ways/manners of, 184–85
Corporations
    corporate success, key to, 279
    as feudal system, 168
    galas of, 218–19
    government subsidies and, 217
    institutional identity of workers, 281–82
    mergers of in 1980s, 217–18
    profit maximization, 278
Cosell, Howard, 66
Counterculture, 21
Cravath, Paul D., 277
Credit, 240
    Americans and borrowing, 286–87
Crime/criminals, protocols of wealth, 56–57
Crime, romance of, 99–130
    Capone, Al, 114–15
    criminal enterprise behavior, normal types of, 102–8
    criminal as hero, 114–15
    Gallo, Joey, 122
    government and, 115–16
    lawyers, ABA *omerta* rule, 119
    multinational corporation, cautionary tales, 115–18
    New York City, corruption in, 105–8
    self-annihilation of rich, 124–30
    von Bulow, Claus, 99–100
Culture, of rich, 77–80

pathologies of wealth, xi, 9,
15, 25, 290
of heirs, 27
richest Americans, areas of
expertise, 52n
self as money, 268–69
services related to, 189–90
size in 1980s, 27
small preoccupations of, 35
unpleasantness, reactions to,
191–92
wealth/intellect disparity, 181
Essays, nineteenth century, 152
Europeans
attitude toward money,
compared to Americans,
258–59
profile of, 258

Fairlie, Henry, 266
Fennimore Cooper, James, xxxii,
114n
Fisk, James, 156
Flaubert, Gustave, 267
Food fights, 183
Ford, Gerald, 55, 195, 251
Foreigners
American rich compared to
foreign rich, 69
attitude toward money,
compared to Americans,
258–59
perception of Americans, 67
Frankfurter, Felix, 117
Franklin, Benjamin, xxii, 163,
276n, 289, 290

Fundraising dinners, protocols
of wealth, 54

Galbraith, John Kenneth, 159
Gallo, Joey, 100, 122
Garraty, John A., 34
Geography, literacy in, 234–35
George, Henry, 44
Getty, Ann, xvi, xvii
Giamatti, A. Bartlett, 23n, 271
Gibson, William, 144, 236
Gilbert, Eddie, 81
Gilbert, Rhoda, 82n
Gilder, George, 159, 178, 274n
Goldberg, Whoopi, 182n
Goldstock, Ronald, 105
Gorbachev, Mikhail, 273
Gossip of rich, 121–22, 149–50
Gould, Jay, 156
Government spending, 31–32
Graham, Katherine, 90, 200, 274
Grant, Ulysses S., 41, 114n
Great Depression, xxiv, 26, 36,
46
Greed, 5, 49, 68
*Greed and Glory on Wall Street:
The Fall of the House of Leh-
man*, (Auletta), 33–34
Greider, William, 62
Griswold, Whitney, 21–22
Groups, cooperative collabora-
tion, historical view, 280–81
Guest, Cornelia, 187n
Guevara, Che, xvi, 47, 204
Gutfreund, Mrs. John, 82n

115–16, 126, 271, 273, 275–76
Volcker, Paul, 245n
von Bülow, Claus, 36n, 99–100

Wall Street
  Black Monday, 246–47
  brokers, new breed, 253n
  corruption, 106–7
Wall Street (film), xvi, ix
War, production model of,
  144–45
Warhol, Andy, 80–81, 84, 180,
  243
Wealth of Nations (Smith), 154n
Wealthy. *See* Equestrian class
Webster, Daniel, 44, 153
Wedtech Corporation, 104
Weinberger, Casper, 31, 63, 116,
  269n
Welch, John, 185n
Westmoreland, William, 138n,
  236
Wharton, Edith, xiii, 26–27, 29,
  36–37, 126, 160, 205
Who Killed Society? (Amory), 84
Wicker, Tom, 51, 97, 274
Wilson, Woodrow, xxii, 41, 45,
  142, 153
Wolfe, Tom, xvi, 204

Woodstock Nation, 178
World War II, new rich, post-
  World War II, 8, 25–26
Wriston, Walter, 212
Writing/writers, 160–65, 263–64
  autobiographical writers, 164
  better writers, listing of, 160,
    162n
  books about rich/making
    money, 158
  money discussed in fiction,
    160–62
  risk factors, 272
  self-conscious variety, 162

Yale University, 21–24, 266–67
  "best people," expectations of,
    23–24
  humanities debate, 23–24
  informed gratitude, meaning
    of, 21
  in 1950s, 21–24
  purpose of education at, 22
  student uniform at, 206
  teaching style at, 21–42

Zorn, Richard, 30
Zuckerberg, Mark, xxxiv
Zuckerman, Mortimer, 209

Joshua Simpson

Lewis H. Lapham is the founding editor of *Lapham's Quarterly* and the Editor Emeritus of *Harper's Magazine*. His columns received the National Magazine Award in 1995 for exhibiting "an exhilarating point of view in an age of conformity," and, in 2002, the Thomas Paine Journalism Award. He was inducted into the American Society of Magazine Editors' Hall of Fame in 2007. His other books include *Fortune's Child, Imperial Masquerade, The Wish for Kings, Hotel America, Waiting for the Barbarians, Theater of War, The Agony of Mammon, Gag Rule, Pretensions to Empire,* and *Age of Folly*.

Thomas Frank (Foreword) is the author of *Listen, Liberal* and *What's the Matter with Kansas?* Frank is the founding editor of *The Baffler* and writes regularly for *The Guardian*.

CPSIA information can be obtained
at www.ICGtesting.com
Printed in the USA
JSHW041144160522
25957JS00002BA/2